English for Information Systems

STEVE HICK

PRENTICE HALL INTERNATIONAL ENGLISH LANGUAGE TEACHING
New York London Toronto Sydney Tokyo Singapore

First published 1991 by
Prentice Hall International (UK) Ltd
Campus 400, Maylands Avenue
Hemel Hempstead, Herts HP2 4EZ
A division of
Simon & Schuster International Group

© Prentice Hall International (UK) Ltd, 1991

All rights reserved. No part of this publication may be reproduced, stored in a retreival system, or transmitted, in any form, or by any means, electronic, mechanical, photocopying, recording or otherwise, without prior permission, in writing, from the publisher.
For permission within the United States of America contact Prentice Hall Inc., Englewood Cliffs, NJ 07632.

Typeset in 10½/12 pt Palacio
by MHL Typesetting Ltd, Coventry

Printed in Great Britain at The Bath Press, Avon

Library of Congress Cataloging-in-Publication Data

Hick, Steve.
   English for information systems / Steve Hick.
     p. cm. — (Prentice Hall International English language teaching)
   ISBN 0-13-279795-X
   1. Readers — Electronic data processing.   2. Readers — Information storage and retrieval systems.   3. English language — Textbooks for foreign speakers.   4. Information storage and retrieval systems.
5. English language — Technical English.   6. Electronic data processing.
I. Title.   II. Series: English language teaching.
PE1127.E44H53   1991
428.6'4'024658—dc20
                                               90-49093
                                                  CIP

British Library Cataloging in Publication Data

Hick, Steve
   English for information systems.
   1. Business firms. Information systems.
   I. Title
   658.4038

ISBN 0-13-279795-X

2 3 4 5   96 95 94 93

English for Information Systems

Other ESP titles of interest include:

BLAKEY, T.
*English for Maritime Studies (second edition)**

BRIEGER, N. and J. Comfort
*Business Contacts**

BRIEGER, N. and J. Comfort
*Early Business Contacts**

BRIEGER, N. and A. Cornish
*Secretarial Contacts**

BRIEGER, N. and J. Comfort
Social Contacts

BRIEGER, N. and J. Comfort
*Technical Contacts**

BRIEGER, N. and J. Comfort
Business Issues

DAVIES, S. *et al.*
Bilingual Handbooks of Business Correspondence and Communication

McGOVERN, J. and J. McGovern
*Bank on Your English**

PALSTRA, R.
*Telephone English**

PALSTRA, R.
Telex English

POTE, M. *et al.*
*A Case for Business English**

* includes audio cassette(s)

Contents

Acknowledgements vii
Summary of units viii
Introduction xvii

PART 1: People, products and facilities in business information systems

Unit 1: Companies, jobs, products and services — 3

Unit 2: Small systems and software — 12

Unit 3: Large systems and software (1) — 24

Unit 4: Large systems and software (2) — 34

Unit 5: Historical developments in information services — 44

Unit 6: Training and recruitment — 56

PART 2: Developing, producing, implementing and maintaining systems

Unit 7: Preliminary investigations — 71

Unit 8: Preliminary design — 79

Unit 9: System development — 89

Unit 10: System production planning	99
Unit 11: System production and testing	110
Unit 12: System implementation	125
Appendix A: Simulation and role play information for participant A	137
Appendix B: Simulation and role play information for participant B	143
Appendic C: Key to activities	148
Appendix D: Tapescripts	183
Appendix E: Unit by unit vocabulary	201
Appendix F: Vocabulary index	217

Acknowledgements

The author and publisher would like to thank the following for permission to use copyright and other material:

Association for Computing Machinery, Massachussetts, USA.
Apple Computer Inc., California (MacPaint and MacWrite are registered trademarks of Claris Corporation).
General Accident Life Assurance Co. Ltd, York, UK.
IBM World Trade Corporation, New York, USA.
Kodak Limited, Hemel Hempstead, UK.
Oxford University Press, Oxford, UK.
Sagesoft Limited, Newcastle upon Tyne, UK.
Videologic Limited.
VNU Business Publications, London, UK.

They would also like to extend their thanks to the following:

Mr C.W. Wood of General Accident Life Assurance, York, for his help and hospitality in providing access to written materials and in arranging observation of meetings and work procedures.
The directors of York Associates for providing opportunities for piloting materials, for their constructive criticism and for their generosity in allowing the author to use their computing facilities.
Mr Bob Impey of the Information Services Division at Oxford University Press.
Dr Alan Brown of the Department of Computer Science, York University.
Ms Hilary Hocking of the Swedish Telecommunications Administration training centre in Kalmar.
Mr Alistair Thomas of Videologic.
Mr Fred Peel.

Summary of units

PART 1   People, products and facilities in business information systems

UNIT 1   Companies, jobs, products and services

Input 1 ⟶ **Input 2** ⟶ **Language practice**

Listening

Introducing a new member of staff

Introductions and greetings

Describing jobs and responsibilities

Reading

Company brochure

Describing company, products and services

- Present Simple and Present Progressive (active)
- Greetings and introductions

Development 1 ⟶ **Development 2** ⟶ **Language summary**

Listening

Presenting a company

Describing hierarchical organisations and department functions

Informal presentation

Presentation of own company or organisation

- Sentence types
  Present tense statement and question forms
- Useful expressions
  Stating intentions
  Offering

Summary of units ix

UNIT 2 Small systems and software

Input 1 → **Input 2** → **Language practice**

Reading

Using a WYSIWYG word processor

Understanding instructions

Actions in sequence

Expressing capability and purpose

Listening

Using a micro database package

Asking for instruction

Giving instructions

Describing cursor and screen movements

Discourse features (1)

- Asking questions —
  Present Simple (active)
- Expressing ability and capability
- Gerund and infinitive
- Conditional instructions

Development 1 → **Development 2** → **Language summary**

Reading

Using an accounting package on a micro

Understanding and expressing sequences

Understanding and expressing simple conditions

Role play

Understanding instructions

Giving instructions

- Sentence types
  Conditional instructions
  'wh-' questions
  Yes/no questions
- Useful expressions
  Checking
  Moving between points

UNIT 3 Large systems and software (1)

Input 1 → **Input 2** → **Language practice**

Reading

Batch systems (1)

Describing functions

Describing processes

Actions in sequence

Reading

Large installation hardware

Static description:
- location
- structure

- Present Simple
  Active and passive,
  positive and negative

Development 1 → **Development 2** → **Language summary**

Listening

Batch systems (2)

Asking for information

Describing procedures

Describing functions

Role play

Using flow diagrams

Understanding processes

Describing processes

- Sentence types
  Active and passive:
  — statement forms
  — question forms
- Useful expressions

UNIT 4 Large systems and software (2)

Input 1 → **Input 2** → **Language practice**

Reading

On-line systems (1)
Order-processing

Actions in sequence

Expressing conditions

Expressing purpose and reason

Reading

On-line systems (2)
EFTPOS

Describing characteristics, properties and qualities

Making comparisons

- Present Simple active and passive
- Time sequence adverbials

Development 1 → **Development 2** → **Language summary**

Listening

Microfilm archiving

Presenting equipment features:

- size, speed, capacity
- capabilities

Making comparisons

Discourse features (2)

Informal presentation

Learner to present characteristics and strong points of a piece of equipment

- Sentence types
  Active and passive with time sequence adverbials
- Useful expressions

UNIT 5 Historical developments in information services

Input 1 → **Input 2** → **Language practice**

Reading

Programming languages

Describing past events

Actions in sequence

Listening

Database systems

Describing past events

Describing features and prices

- Past simple active and passive
- Past Progressive active and passive
- Past time adverbials

Development 1 → **Development 2** → **Language summary**

Reading

The changing faces of staff and software

Describing past in relation to present

Describing products and people

Comparing — expressing advantages and disadvantages

Informal presentation

Presentation of either:

- career history
- historical development of a current project

- Sentence types
  Past Simple and Progressive negative forms
  Present Perfect
- Useful expressions

Summary of units   xi

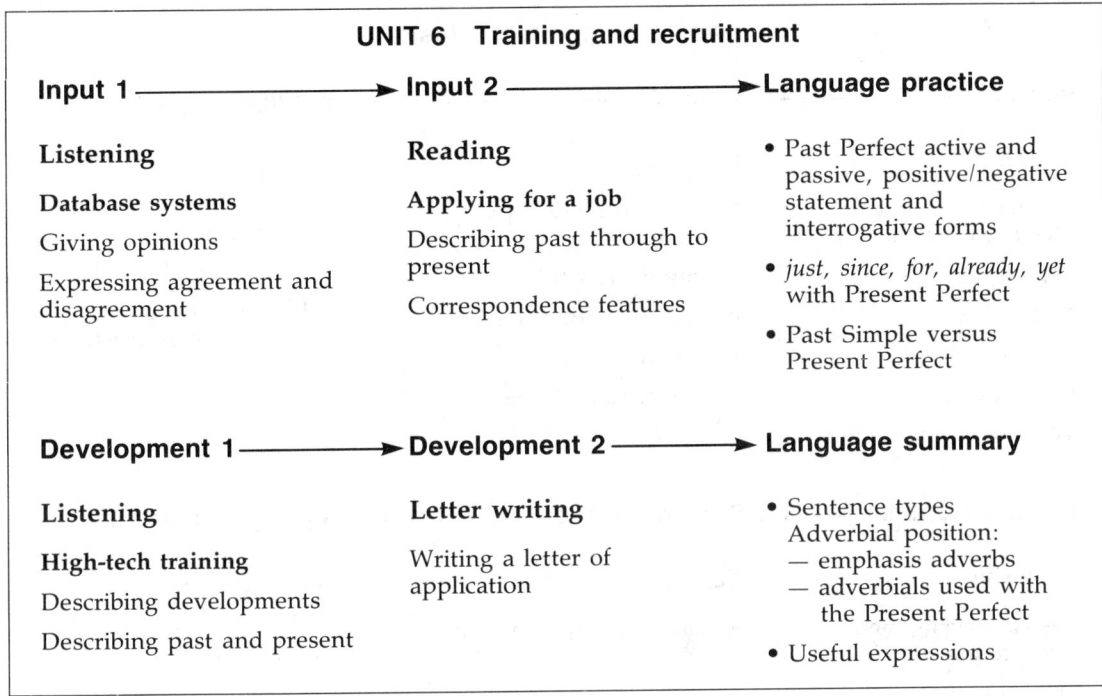

PART 2   Developing, producing, implementing and maintaining systems

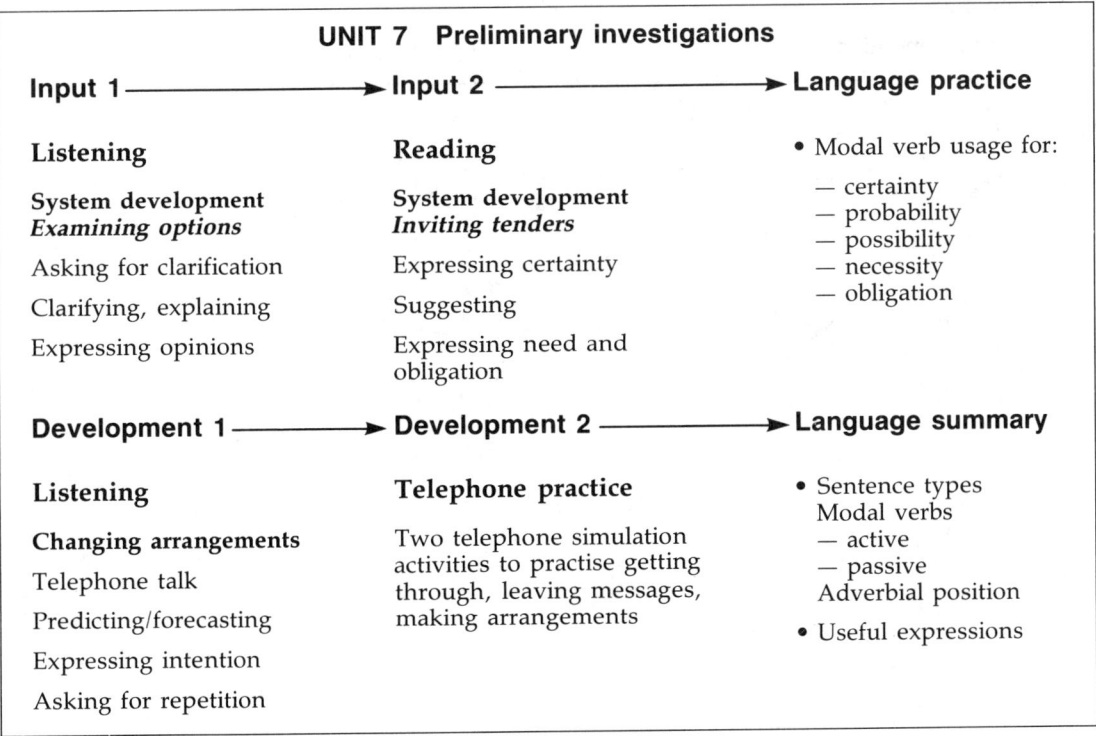

UNIT 8 Preliminary design

Input 1 → Input 2 → Language practice

Reading

System development
Meeting minutes

Reported speech:
- decisions
- intentions
- queries

Verbs of saying/asking

Listening

Maintenance and support
User support

Asking for repetition

Asking for clarification

Telephone talk

Phone, code and reference numbers

- Asking for repetition and clarification
- 'wh-' questions
- Reported speech
- Indirect speech for messages and instructions

Development 1 → Development 2 → Language summary

Listening

System development
Arranging a meeting

Telephone talk

Making arrangements:
- suggesting times
- declining
- accepting

Asking for repetition

Telephone practice

Arranging an appointment

- Sentence types
  Reported speech
- Useful expressions

UNIT 9 System development

Input 1 → Input 2 → Language practice

Reading

System development
Making recommendations

Written discourse links:
- cause/effect
- comparison/contrast
- additional points

Expressing hypothesis

Listening

System development
Design review

Expressing opinions

Agreeing and disagreeing

Comparing

Clarifying, correcting

- Connecting written ideas to express
  — contrast
  — cause/effect
  — additional points

Development 1 → Development 2 → Language summary

Listening

System maintenance and support

Explaining procedures and actions

Giving examples

Expressing result and consequence

Expressing purpose

Informal discussion

Choice of topics for informal discussion to provide practice for opinions, agreement and disagreement, exemplification, etc.

- Sentence types
  Subordinate clauses *with if, when, because* and *so that*
- Useful expressions
  Checking
  Asking for and giving help

UNIT 10   System production planning

Input 1 → Input 2 → Language practice

Listening

System production
Project planning

Suggesting
Hypothesising
Giving opinions

Reading

Maintenance and support
Response times

Expressing degrees of obligation
Expressing conditions
Predicting

- First conditional
- Second conditional

Development 1 → Development 2 → Language summary

Listening

System production
Manpower planning

Future time reference
- plans
- arrangements
- intentions
- predictions

Informal discussion

Giving opinions, asking for opinions
Making suggestions, asking for suggestions

- Sentence types
  First and second conditionals, positive and negative
- Useful expressions
  Future time expressions

UNIT 11 System production and testing

Input 1 → **Input 2** → **Language practice**

Reading

Maintenance and support
Error handling

Describing data

Reporting

Giving instructions

Listening

System production and testing
Screen specification

Describing location

Describing layout

Describing screen and field attributes

Diagnosing problems

- Active and passive with modals
- {*should, might, can't, must*} + verb stem
- {*should, might, can't, must*} + have + done, etc.

Development 1 → **Development 2** → **Language summary**

Reading

System production and testing
Field specification
Validity specification

Expressing obligatory requirements

Expressing optional requirements

Describing data

Role play

Designing a layout from a specification, followed by discussion and exchange of ideas with a partner

- Sentence types
  Reduced forms found in messages
- Useful expressions
  Numerical expressions

UNIT 12 System implementation

Input 1 → **Input 2** → **Language practice**

Input 1

Listening

Implementation
Training

Discourse features for presentations:

- introducing a talk
- describing intentions
- introducing a point
- closing a point
- classifying

Input 2

Reading

Implementation
Installation review

Diagnosing reasons for problems

Giving opinions

Recommending

Language practice

- *should* vs *would*
- *should have done*
  would have done
- Third conditional

Development 1 → **Development 2** → **Language summary**

Development 1

Listening

Implementation
Progress report

Discourse features for structuring a presentation:

- enumerating
- sequencing

Expressing past, present and future time

Development 2

Formal presentation

Formal presentation of information provided which complements that given in the meeting

Language summary

- Sentence types
  might have
  should have
  would have
  third conditional
- Useful expressions

Introduction

1 OVERALL AIMS

1.1 Target users

This book is aimed at people with an intermediate to advanced knowledge of the English language who need to use English to communicate on matters relating to computerised business information systems.

It is **not** just a book for computer specialists: it aims to provide language and communication skills for the many areas and situations in which **computer users** and **computer specialists** need to communicate with each other.

1.2 Methods of use

The course consists of this textbook and an audio cassette. Clear instructions are given at the start of each Activity about what to do; they offer guidance to both trainer and learner. Each Activity relates either to a cassette recording or a text.

Appendix C contains the answer keys for each Activity and Appendix D contains the tapescripts for the cassette recordings. The course can therefore be used as private study material as well as for group training.

The material is designed to be used either as a sequential course or as a resource from which to extract material for particular needs. Both language material and communication tasks become more difficult in later units.

1.3 Training approach and materials

Topics and skills have been included on the basis of maximum transferability and relevance to a wide variety of learners in terms of both linguistic and vocational needs. Materials are based on recordings and texts originating from discussions, meetings, presentations, phone conversations, reports, manuals and correspondence. They cover a wide range of high-frequency topics and issues.

Activities are structured so that learners can discover and learn new language and skills for themselves using their existing experience and knowledge. Development activities challenge them to apply language and skills from one activity to problem-solving in another area. Successful completion of activities depends on arriving at an understanding of, and acquiring the ability to use, certain key features. Learners are not asked to understand every single word from a text or recording. **Very few learners will ever be able to produce language at the level of difficulty of some of the input texts and recordings, but most will be faced with it and have to respond to it** by using less complex language with confidence. It is most important, therefore, to concentrate on the following:

- extracting important information
- understanding new vocabulary from the context in which it occurs
- deciding which words and expressions they need to be able to learn and use themselves
- understanding the function of, and copying the use of, important grammatical structures
- understanding and learning to use features which speakers use to communicate factual information when describing processes and features or when giving instructions
- understanding and learning to use language features which speakers commonly employ to organise, relate and sequence items of information effectively
- understanding and learning to use key features which speakers use to express opinions, attitudes and intentions

Grammatical features are presented in a way which emphasises their function. Learners at an intermediate or advanced level will have encountered most of those structural items which the book looks at in detail, but have often not understood how or why they are used, or how they are related to communicative needs within their own jobs. The material aims to remedy these problems while refreshing the learner's memory on details of form, as learners at these levels also frequently need reminding of sentence patterns and verb phrase construction. Many trainers dealing with such learners are asked to provide summaries of this type of feature; such summaries are therefore provided at the end of each unit.

The question of vocabulary poses problems. A wide variety of commercial and technical terms are used across the various topic areas. Many will be useful to all learners, but in some texts or recordings, words are used which are of more interest to those working in a particular field. Learners will therefore have to decide for themselves which items they need to learn actively. To explain every specialised term would take an enormous amount of time and space: Appendices E and F are therefore designed to be used together to help learners to make vocabulary-building an individual — and active — process.

Appendix E provides a summary of the important vocabulary in each reading text or tapescript on a unit and section basis. For each unit, three vocabulary lists are given containing key words from *Input 1, Input 2* and *Development 1*. Learners can therefore use these lists as the basis for constructing their own vocabulary lists of items which are important to them. *Appendix F* lists vocabulary for the whole book in alphabetical order with references to those units and sections where a particular word occurs. Learners can therefore use this Appendix to find a word and study its use in one or more situations.

2 BOOK STRUCTURE

2.1 The twelve training units

The training units fall into two main parts:

2.1.1 Part 1: People, products and facilities in business information systems

Units 1 to 6 focus on language and skill development for giving and understanding both information and instructions when:

- choosing and using hardware
- choosing and using software
- dealing with work flow and procedures within computerised business systems.

2.1.2 Part 2: Developing, producing, implementing and maintaining systems

Units 6 to 12 concentrate on language and communication skills required by both computer specialists and staff in user departments in developing and using computerised systems. Communication activities are examined and practised in realistic contexts covering all the stages in system development from feasibility study through to system implementation.

Each of the units in this second part also presents either a maintenance problem or a sales/purchase situation.

2.2 Unit structure

Each unit consists of six sections as follows:

- Input 1
- Input 2
- Language practice
- Development 1
- Development 2
- Language summary

Input 1 and Input 2

Cassette recordings and written texts provide the main input. Associated activities focus the student's attention on key language and communicatioin features.

Language practice

This section highlights the main language points from the two input stages and gives further practice opportunities for handling functions, structures and vocabulary.

Development 1

This section uses cassette recordings and written texts to extend the language features presented in the input stages to other issues and topics, and reinforces or extends features found in previous units. Associated activities again focus attention on key features.

Development 2

This section sets a task for individual, pair or group work. Tasks involve discussion, simulation, role play, presentation and writing activities. Certain units use material from Appendices A and B to provide role information for two individuals.

Language summary

Key sentence types and useful expressions are summarised for ease of reference.

2.3 Recordings and texts

Recordings are of:

- formal and informal presentations
- spoken dialogue (face-to-face or on the phone)
- discussions at meetings

Written texts are of the following types:

- software and hardware manuals
- company manuals detailing procedures and standards
- circulars, memos and letters
- sales literature
- reports
- system documentation (proposals, specifications)

2.4 The Appendices

Appendix A and *Appendix B* hold information for role plays involving two students. The 'information gap' between the two participants allows realistic communication exercises.

Appendix C contains the answer keys for each *Activity*.

Appendix D contains the tapescripts for all the tape recordings.

Appendix E provides a summary of important vocabulary on a unit by unit basis. For each unit, three vocabulary lists are given containing key words from *Input 1, Input 2* and *Development 1*.

Appendix F lists vocabulary for the whole book in alphabetical order with unit and section references. This is done so that learners can find a required item and study it in its context. To a certain extent it can also be used as an index to find topics of interest, although it is not its primary function.

PART 1
People, products and facilities in business information systems

UNIT 1 Companies, jobs, products and services

INPUT 1 Listening

Listen to the cassette recording for Unit 1, Input 1.

Activity 1

As you listen, look at Figure 1.1 below and draw lines to connect the different people to their jobs and responsibilities.

Job title	Name	Responsibilities
	Jenny Long	
Documentation co-ordinator	Peter Holmes	end user procedure manuals
Technical author	Mr Blakely	technical manuals
	Les Barton	database documentation
Information Services Manager	Sandra	training materials
	Brian	

Figure 1.1

English for Information Systems

Activity 2

Listen again and try to complete the following extracts from the conversation.

Receptionist: Good morning.

Peter: _____ _____. _____ _____ Peter Holmes. I'm starting today as a technical author.

Jenny: Good morning. You _____ _____ Peter Holmes.

Peter: That's right.

Jenny: _____ Jenny Long. _____ _____ _____ _____.

Peter: _____ _____ _____ _____.

Jenny: Good morning, Mr Blakely.

Mr Blakely: _____ Jenny.

Jenny: _____ _____ _____ _____ _____ Peter Holmes, the new technical author. Peter, Mr Blakely.

Peter: _____ _____ _____ _____.

Mr Blakley: _____ _____ _____ _____, Peter.

Jenny: Can I introduce you all to Peter Holmes, our new technical author.

Les: _____. Les Barton.

Peter: _____

Jenny: And _____ _____ Sandra.

Peter: _____ to meet you.

Sandra: _____ to meet you.

Jenny: And last but not least, Brian.

Brian: _____ _____.

Peter: _____. Do you all do the same sort of thing?

INPUT 2 Reading

The text below describes some of the services of a large company which produces business and financial software.

Activity 1

Read the text and try to put the five headings in the box back in the correct place in the text

> Only the best   Compatible environments
> Training courses   User groups   Customer support

The company

Established in 1965, we have gained a world-wide reputation for high-quality financial applications software. With the backing of an extensive Research and Development programme we are able to maintain our reputation for providing some of the best software available today.

Our systems are installed all over the world in mainframe and minicomputer environments. We back our integrated product line with first-class training and support while the continuous enhancement of our systems ensures up-to-date facilities.

__1__

These last from one to five days and offer hands-on training. They help users to optimise systems and to implement the systems successfully in their own environment.

__2__

Through our world-wide network of customer support groups, our teams can visit client sites anywhere. Our telephone hotlines provide a fast and efficient response to customer requirements.

__3__

These provide a vital channel for you to communicate feedback on product developments and system improvements. They also offer an extremely useful forum for different customers to discuss ideas and compare experience.

__4__

Our systems can be installed on a wide range of mainframes.

__5__

When you decide to buy from us you are buying from a company which aims to provide excellent services to match its top-quality products.

English for Information Systems

Activity 2

Find words from the passage to complete the following table of related words.

Verb		Noun	
to back	9	1	implementation
2	to require	maintenance	10
3	11	provision	communication
4	to develop	installation	12
to train	to improve	5	13
to support	14	6	discussion
to enhance	15	7	comparison
8	16	optimisation	decision

Activity 3

Now use words from the table to complete the following text.

Before a company ___(a)___ to buy an expensive software package it is necessary for the people who need the software to ___(b)___ their ___(c)___. Then they need to ___(d)___ the different packages on the market which can meet these ___(e)___.

However, the ___(f)___ of the different products is not enough on its own; the buyer also needs to look at the services which different companies ___(g)___ following the purchase of a piece of software.

Talk to other companies which use the software that you are interested in. Does the supplier provide initial user ___(h)___ when they first ___(i)___ the software? How good is their post-implementation ___(j)___? What is ___(k)___ like between the supplier and client companies? Does the supplier listen to constructive comments from customers in order to ___(l)___ and ___(m)___ their products?

LANGUAGE PRACTICE

Section 1

Look at these two sentences:

(a) Les **handles** end user procedure manuals and training materials.
    (his normal job)

(b) Les **is working** with Sandra on a technical manual.
(current activity, but it's not his normal job and it's only temporary)

Now choose the correct form of a suitable verb to complete the following sentences. All the necessary information and language are in Input 1 or Input 2.

1 The cassette recording for Input 1 is about Peter Holmes. He ..... his new job today, so Jenny ..... him round the building and ..... him to the other members of staff.
2 Mr Blakely can't stop to talk because he ..... to a meeting.
3 Brian ..... database documentation and Sandra ..... technical manuals.
4 Sandra and Les ..... together on a new technical manual.
5 Technical support teams from the software company ..... client sites throughout the UK.
6 Telephone hotlines ..... a fast and efficient response to customer requirements.
7 User groups ..... a vital channel for customers to communicate feedback and ideas.

Section 2

Look at the following expressions and put a tick (✓) in the 'formal' or 'natural' column on the right. If you think the expression is suitable for both formal and informal situations, put a tick in both columns.

	Formal	Natural
1 Good morning / Good afternoon / Good evening	☐	☐
2 'Morning / 'Afternoon / ' Evening	☐	☐
3 Hello	☐	☐
4 Hi	☐	☐
5 Hello there	☐	☐
6 How do you do?	☐	☐
7 Pleased to meet you	☐	☐
8 Nice to meet you	☐	☐
9 Wood. George Wood.	☐	☐
10 I'm Elizabeth.	☐	☐
11 My name's Tarik Patel.	☐	☐
12 Can I introduce you to (Ms Williams)?	☐	☐
13 (Mrs McGregor), this is (Miss Pankowski).	☐	☐
14 Have you met (Nasreen)?	☐	☐
15 Do you know (Gerry Mancini)?	☐	☐

DEVELOPMENT 1   Listening

Listen to the cassette recording for Unit 1, Development 1. Keith Davies is the Computer Processing Manager in a large installation within a multinational company. He is explaining the structure of the UK Information Services (IS) Division to a new member of staff, Paul Hines. Paul is the new Assistant Manager for the Computer Production Section.

Activity 1

Before you listen, find Keith Davies and Paul Hines on Figure 1.2 below and write in their job titles. Then, as you listen, complete the diagram (Fig. 1.2) with:

- job titles,
- names of people or
- names of departments or sections.

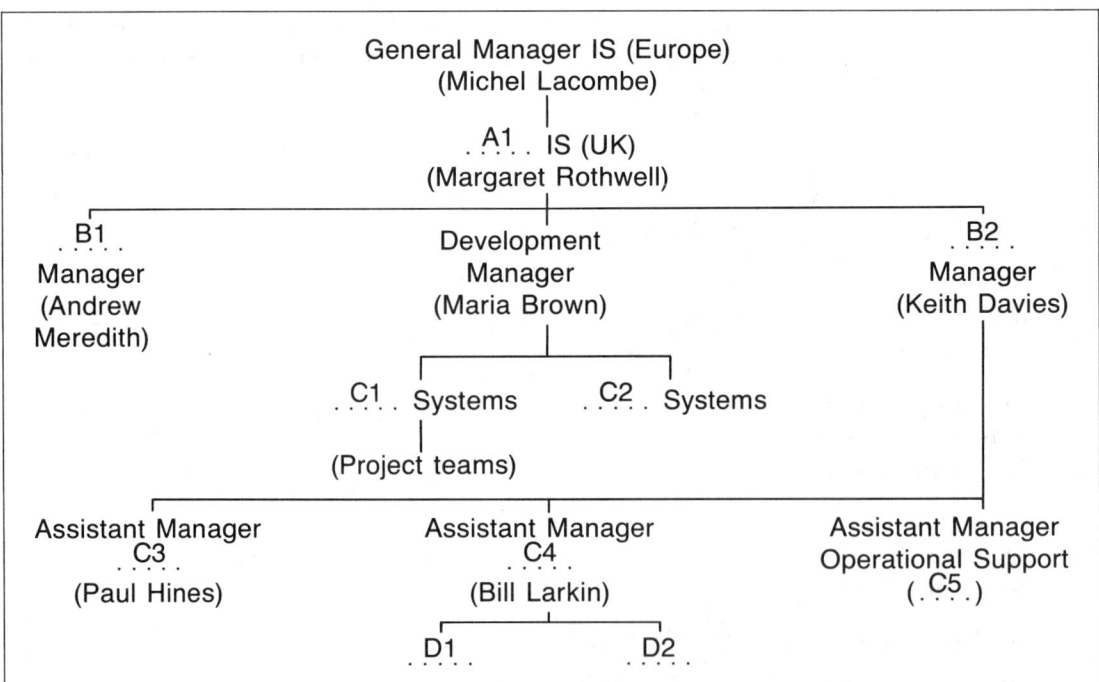

Figure 1.2

Activity 2

Look at the following sentences:

European HQ *is based in* Brussels.

Michel Lacombe *is based at* HQ.

The Development Department   *is broken down into* / *is divided up into* / *is split into*   two sections.

Maria Brown   *is in charge of* / *is the head of*   the Development Department.

The Development Department   *is headed by*   Maria Brown.

Paul Hines   *reports to* / *is accountable to* / *comes under*   Keith Davies.

The Planning Department   *is responsible for* / *looks after*   strategic planning.

Now use the language that you have heard and seen to describe the organisation of the Computer Production Section in Figure 1.3.

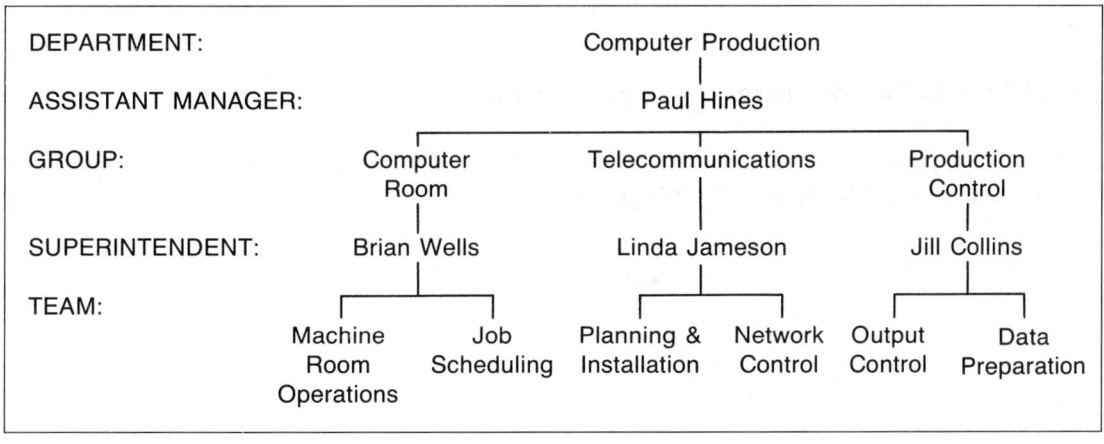

Figure 1.3

Activity 3

Listen again and complete the following list which gives details of the activities in some of the departments.

1 Planning Department: Long-term planning

   Concerned with:
   - security arrangements
   - .(a).
   - .(b).
   - compatibility between sites

2 Development Department

   Strategic Systems Section: Develop new systems
   - involved in use of Fourth generation languages
   - produce .(a).
   - look into .(b).
   - look at security software

3 Processing Department

   Operations Support Section: Change management
   - co-ordinate interfaces between different systems
   - review .(a).
   - check security arrangements conform to standards
   - monitor .(b).
   - look after handover arrangements
   - liaise on .(c). and .(d). planning

DEVELOPMENT 2   Informal Presentation

Use language from Unit 1 to give a short presentation of the activities and organisation of your own company, university, school, college, etc.

LANGUAGE SUMMARY

Sentence types

Sandra **looks after** the technical manuals.
Our teams **visit** client sites.

Does the supplier **provide** initial user training?
Do you all **work** on the same sort of thing?
What **do** they **do** exactly?

I am working with Sandra.
Jenning **is showing** Peter round.
Les and Sandra **are working** together.

Is Jenny **showing** you round?
Are you **starting** today?

Useful expressions

to show someone round
I'll just let {her/him/them} know you're here.
I'll be down in a second.
I'll come and {talk to/see} you later.
Would you like to take a seat?
Would you like a coffee?
Would you like to come this way?
Let's see if {he's/she's/they're} in.
Please call me (Jenny).
Last but not least ...
... the same sort of thing.

UNIT 2 Small systems and software

INPUT 1 Reading

The following text describes some of the basic techniques and operations for using a WYSIWYG ('What You See Is What You Get') word-processing package. It is a WIMP ('Window Icon Menu Pointer') package. The text explains five new words that the software manual uses. The manual also gives five symbols for the five techniques.

Activity 1

Read the text. As you read, try to complete the key in Figure 2.2 on page 14 with the meaning of the five symbols.

There are five basic mouse operation techniques:

Clicking the mouse selects or activates an application or a document.

Pressing the button on the mouse starts a continuous action.

Dragging the mouse lets the user choose from a menu or move something.

Double-clicking the button allows the user to select or activate something quickly.

Shift-clicking (holding down the SHIFT key and clicking the mouse button) enables the user to extend or shorten a selection.

To click

- Position the pointer (by moving the mouse) on the item that you want to activate.
- Press the mouse button and release it immediately.

To press

- Position the pointer on something.

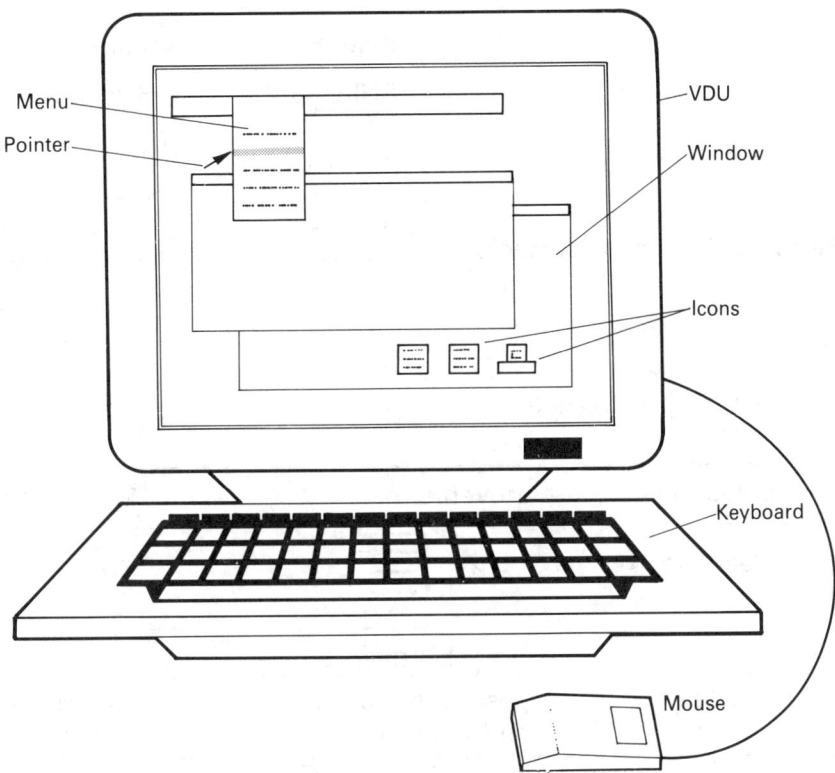

Figure 2.1 WIMP features.

- Without moving the mouse, press and hold the mouse button. The selected action continues until you release the mouse button.

To drag

- Position the pointer on something.
- Press the mouse button and hold it down while moving the mouse to a new position.
- Release the button.

To double-click

- Position the pointer on what you want to select or activate.
- Press and release the mouse button twice in quick succession.

To shift-click

- Select a feature (e.g. by clicking).
- Position the pointer where you want the selection to end (e.g. at the end of a section of text).
- Hold down the SHIFT key and click.

14 English for Information Systems

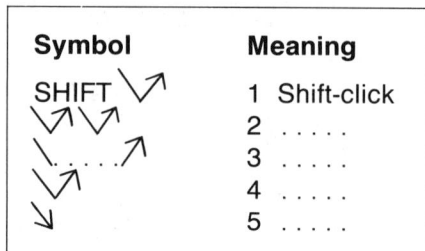

Figure 2.2 Key to symbols.

Activity 2

Look at the diagrams and sentences below:

Action	Selection	Movement	Mouse technique
SELECT	MacWrite	→ [MacWrite icon]	↗
To select	MacWrite,	position the pointer on the MacWrite icon	and click the mouse.
CHOOSE	'Open'	→ [File menu]	\..... Open ..↗
To choose	'Open',	position the pointer on 'File'	drag to the 'Open' command and release the mouse button.

Figure 2.3

The next two sentences express the same idea:

1 You can select the MacWrite program *by positioning* the pointer on the MacWrite icon and *clicking* the mouse.

2 You can choose 'Open' from the file menu *by positioning* the pointer on 'File', *dragging* to the 'Open' command and *releasing* the mouse button.

2 Small systems and software

Now write instructions for the diagram below:

Action	Selection	Movement		Mouse technique
SELECT	MacPaint	↦	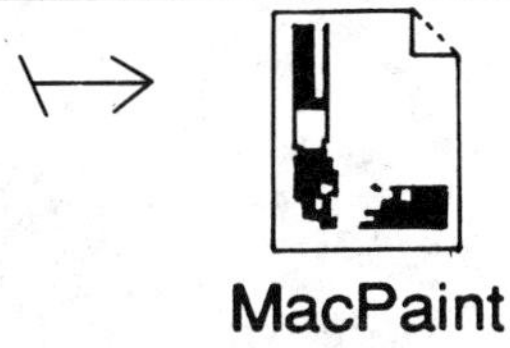 MacPaint	 ↘↗
CHOOSE	'Close'	↦	[File menu with Close highlighted]	 \...Close..↗
CLOSE	MEMO1	↦	[MEMO1 icon]	↘↗
		↦	[File menu with Close highlighted]	\...Close..↗
OPEN	MEMO2	↦	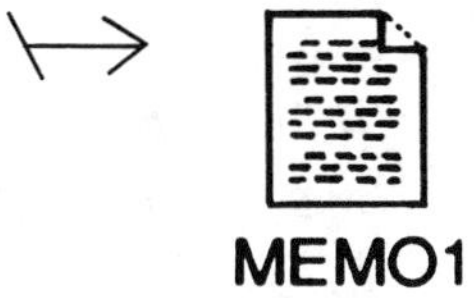 MEMO1	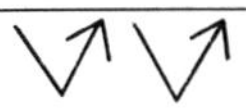 ↘↗ ↘↗

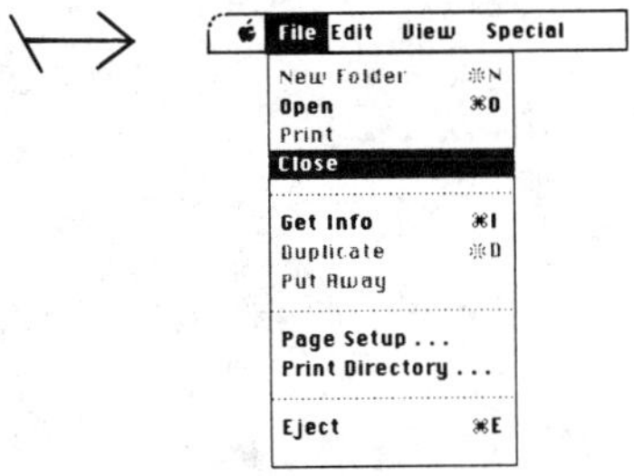

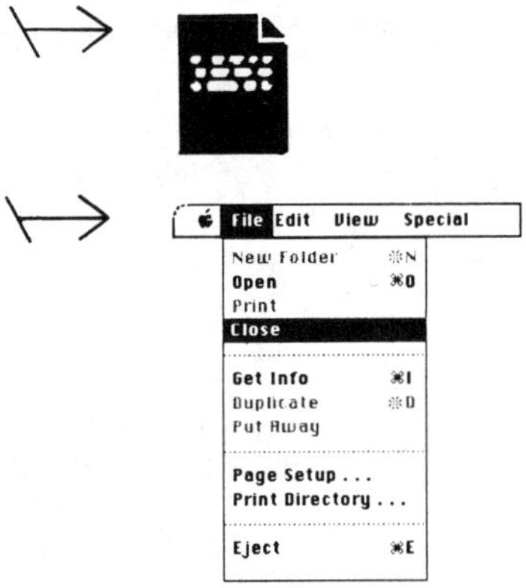

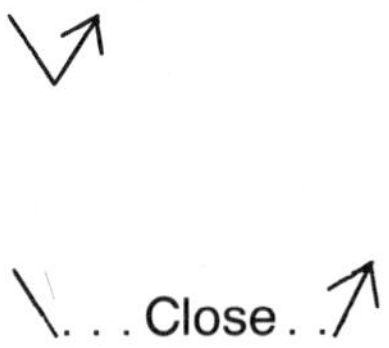

Figure 2.4

1 To select .....

2 You can .....

3 To close MEMO1 .....

4 You can .....

16   English for Information Systems

INPUT 2   Listening

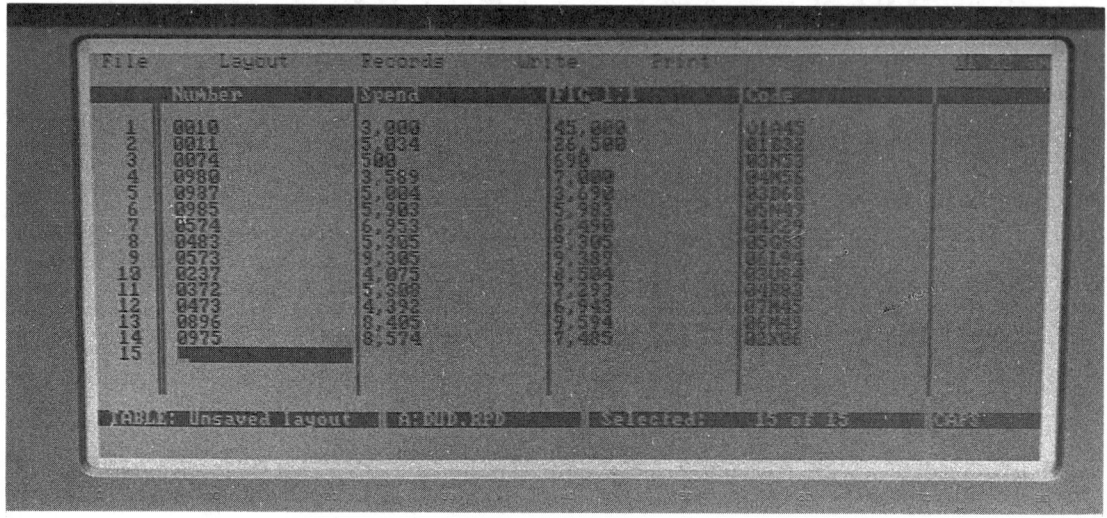

Figure 2.5   Spreadsheet display format.

Find the cassette recording for Unit 2, Input 2. The conversation you will hear is about how to use the cursor control keys in a database package for a low-cost micro.

Activity 1

Listen to the cassette. As you listen make a note of the functions of the different keys in the diagram. Answer questions 5 and 6 at the top of the next page.

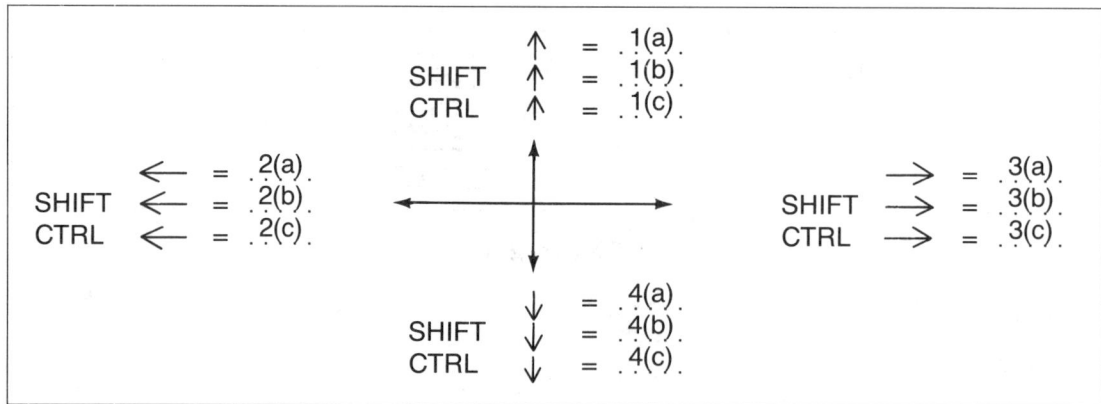

Figure 2.6

5 How do you roll upwards one record at a time if you are on the bottom line of the display?
6 How do you make the screen scroll downwards when you are on the top line of the display?

Activity 2

Look at the following questions and the answer:

Question:

How do I/you
Which key do I/you use to   } display the next screenfull of data?
What do I/you do if I/you want to

Answer:

Hold down the SHIFT key and press the 'cursor down' key.

Use similar sentences and the information in the diagram to ask and answer questions about the following.

1 Get to the next record.
2 Move to the start of the last field in the record.
3 Go to the last record in the display sequence.
4 Display the previous record when you're on the top line.
5 Move the cursor to the next character in the field.
6 Go back to the first field in the record.
7 Get to the first record in the display sequence.

Activity 3

Look at the tapescript of the cassette recording and find the following.
1 An expression which Rachel uses in the first paragraph to introduce her subject.
2 An expression she uses near the end to avoid answering a question immediately.
3 An expression she uses to add one more piece of information.
4 An expression she uses to finish a topic.
5 An expression she uses to introduce the next topic.

LANGUAGE PRACTICE

Section 1

Look at the following sentences which describe the function of an action or thing.

Action/thing	Function
Pressing the mouse button	starts a continuous action.
The 'cursor down' key	takes you to the next line.

To ask about the function of an action, a person or a thing, you can say:

What does	pressing the mouse button a systems analyst the 'cursor down' key	do?

And to answer:

It	starts a continuous action.
He/she	analyses business systems.
It	takes you down to the next line.

You can use similar sentences to ask about the meaning of a word:

What does	'clicking' 'icon' 'WYSIWYG'	mean?

And to answer:

(It means)	positioning the mouse and then pressing and releasing the mouse button.
(It means)	a small picture or symbol.
(It means)	'What you see is what you get'.

Now use the information in Input 1 and Input 2 to ask and answer the following questions:

1 What ..... do?   It selects or activates .....
2 ..... 'dragging' mean?   It means .....
3 .....?   It ..... the user choose from a menu or move something.
4 ..... 'WIMP' .....?   ..... Window, Icon, Menu, Pointer.
5 .....?   It takes you to the start of the next field in the same record.
6 ..... 'cursor up' do?   .....

Section 2

Look at the following sentences which describe what it is possible to do:

| Dragging the mouse | enables you to
allows you to
lets you | choose from a menu easily. |

Complete the following:

1 Pressing CTRL and the 'cursor up' key together .....
2 Using the cursor control keys .....
3 A WYSIWYG wordprocessor ..... the layout on the VDU.
4 Pull-down menus ..... easily.
5 Double-clicking on the MEMO2 icon .....

Section 3

Input 1 and Input 2 show you different ways to give instructions:

Simple instruction:

Move the mouse.

Press SHIFT and 'cursor right'.

Aim + instruction:

To open MEMO1 double-click on the MEMO1 icon.

To get to the start of the next field press the 'cursor right' key.

Possible action or aim + method:

You can open MEMO1 by double-clicking on the MEMO1 icon.

You can display the next screenfull of data by pressing the SHIFT and 'cursor down' keys at the same time.

If you want to open MEMO1, double-click on the MEMO1 icon.

If you want to display the next screenfull of data, press SHIFT and 'cursor down'.

Use the examples above to complete the following instructions:

1 display / previous screenfull of data / SHIFT and ↑
2 go back / first field in a record / SHIFT and ←
3 get to / last record in a display sequence / CTRL and →
4 select / MacWrite / position pointer / click mouse
5 choose application / drag

20   English for Information Systems

DEVELOPMENT 1   Reading

The text below explains how to load and sign onto an accounting package for a business micro.

Activity 1

Read the text. As you read, enter details of the procedure in the flowchart (Figure 2.7).

To run the accounts program, follow these simple instructions:

Step one: Place a copy of your Accounts program disk into drive A of your computer.

Step two: Put your Ledgers diskette into drive B.

Step three: Press the [RESET] button on the computer.

If the machine has an automatic loading facility, it loads the program. If your machine does not have this feature, wait for the system prompt A> to appear and then type:

   ACCOUNTS [RETURN]

Wait a few seconds until the following message appears on the screen:

   Please insert your ledger diskette into drive B and then press the [RETURN] key.

If the Ledgers diskette is not already in drive B, place your ledgers diskette into drive B.

Press [RETURN].

The system now asks you for the password. If you do not input the correct password after three attempts it locks you out of the program and returns you to the system prompt.

If your password is correct the system asks you to input today's date. Enter the date in the format [DDMMYY].

Wait a few seconds until the Accounts menu appears on the screen.

To make your selection from the menu, simply key in the option number (e.g. 16) and press [RETURN].

If you choose options 11, 12, 13 or 14 the system displays an additional menu. Select an option from these secondary menus by entering the option number and pressing [RETURN] as with the main menu.

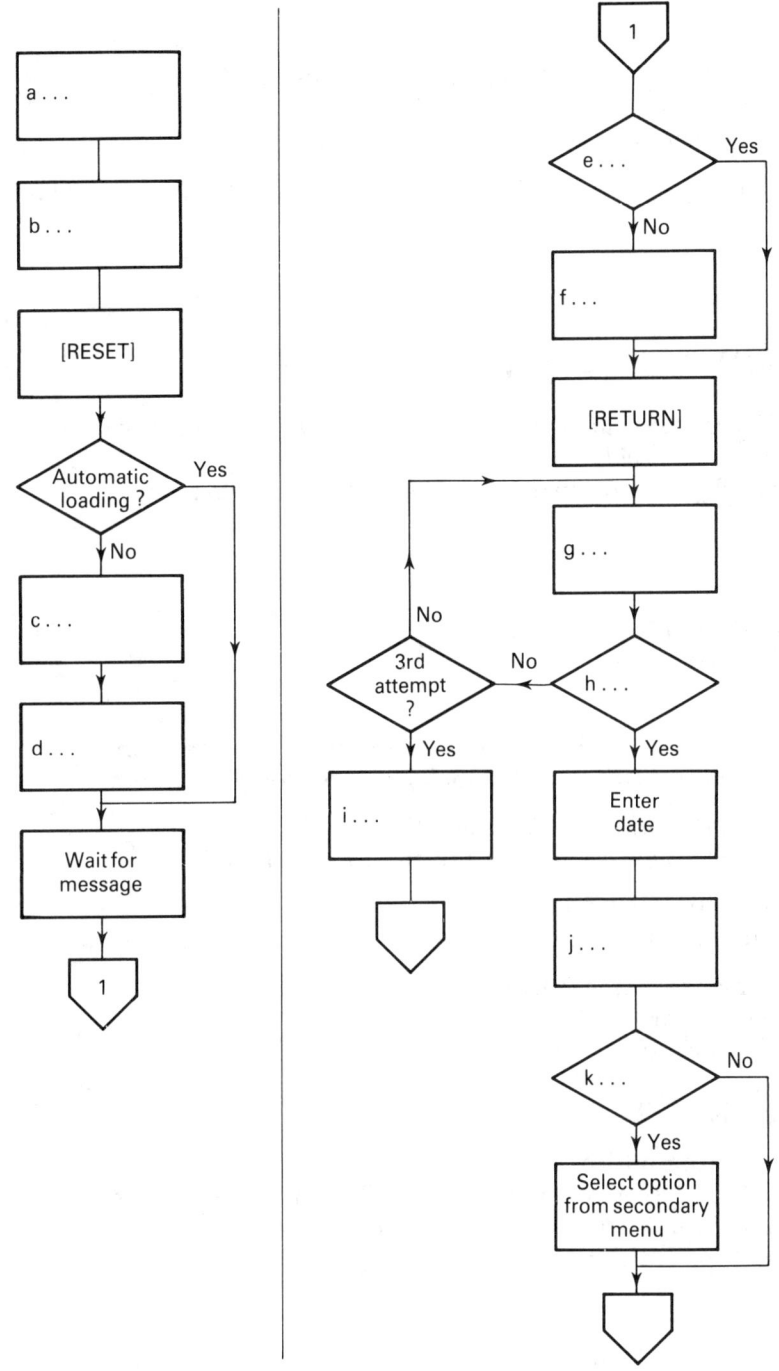

Figure 2.7

Activity 2

The flowchart opposite (Figure 2.8) illustrates how to use a LABEL utility which is one of the programs in a database package. Use the flow diagram and language from Activity 1 to complete the instructions for someone who wants to use the package.

If you are not already in the database handling program key in *DATBAS and press [RETURN] .....

DEVELOPMENT 2   Role Play

Work with a colleague. Appendix A and Appendix B in the back of the book contain information for two people, A and B. Decide with your partner who is who. Look at the information for your role only in the appropriate Appendix and follow the instructions there.

LANGUAGE SUMMARY

Sentence types

If you press the 'down cursor' key the cursor **moves** to the next line.
If you don't use the correct password it **locks** you out of the system.

When you create a new format file you **use** the SF command.
When you use the SF command it **puts** the file in directory F.

How **do** I **display** the next one?
How **do** you **change** the order?

Does the left cursor **take** me back?
Does it **scroll** downwards?
Do you **mean** the end of the file?

Useful expressions

Do you mean ... (the end of the file)?
Alright? Right? O.K.? Are you with me? = Do you understand?
Let's look at how you ... (use the cursor keys).
What about ... (up and down?)
That's right.
I see.
There's just one more thing.
I'd like to show you ...

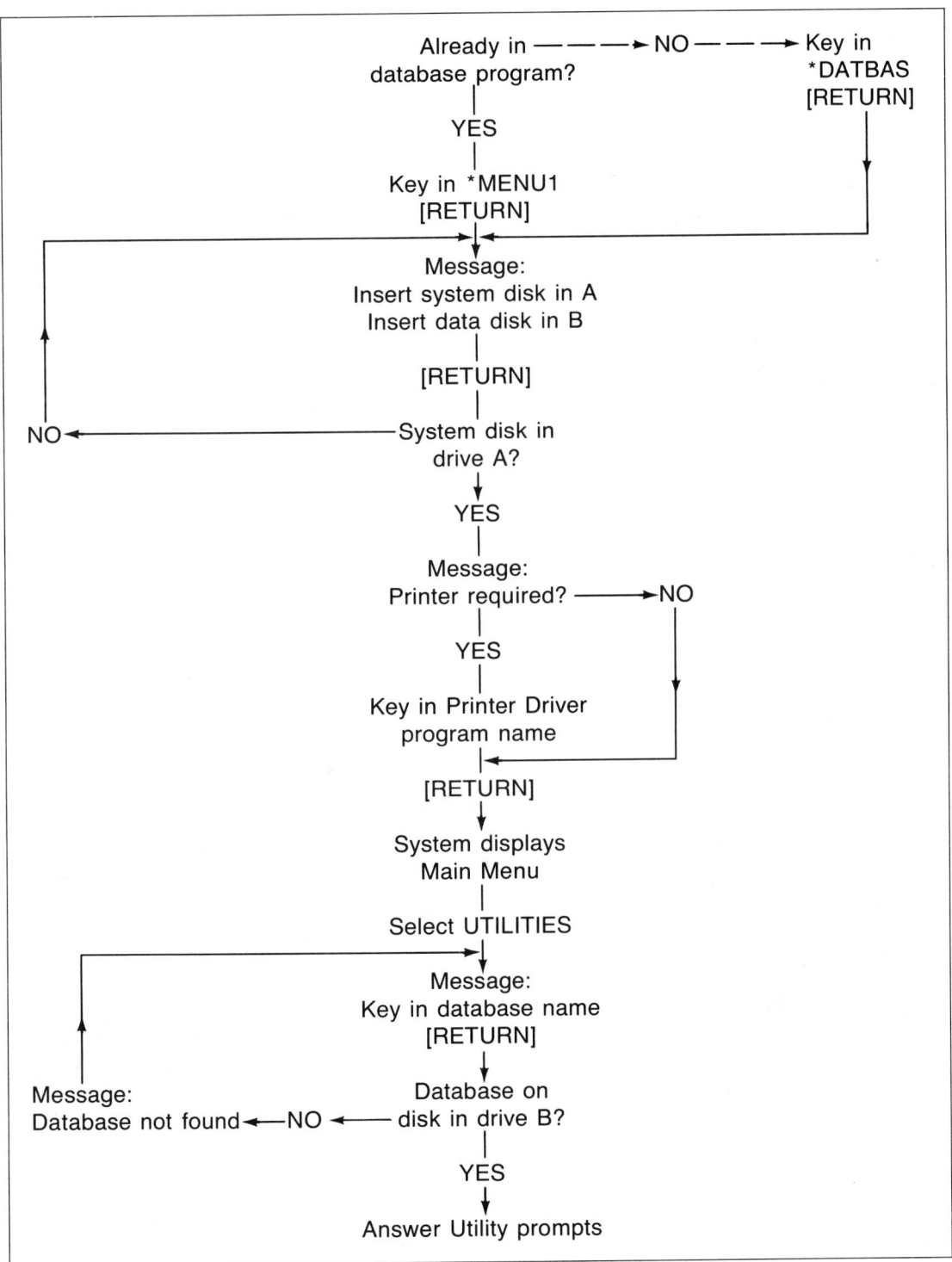

Figure 2.8

UNIT 3 Large systems and software (1)

INPUT 1 Reading

The texts below describe the batch part of the daily processing activities within the central office of a bank.

Activity 1

Read the texts in the left- and right-hand columns and use the words in the boxes to complete them. The first two in each column are done for you.

The functions of personnel

A1:

collect	check
pass	fill in
need	**enter**
initial	

The clerks in the various departments **enter** transaction details on the input advices that they **need** for the type of work within their section.

The clerks ___1___ the completed documents to the supervisors who ___2___ the contents, ___3___ the documents and ___4___ them into batches. They then ___5___ a batch control document for each batch.

The clerical processes

B1:

are passed	(are) initialled
are needed	**are entered**
is completed	(are) checked
are grouped	

Within the various departments, transaction details **are entered** on whichever input advices **are needed**.

The completed documents ___1___ to the section supervisors, ___2___ and ___3___. They ___4___ into batches and a batch document ___(5)___ also ___5___ for each batch.

A2:

includes	key in
use	take
distributes	hand
identifies	

The batch document ___1___ details of how many documents there are in the batch, the batch type, batch number, submission date and a source code which ___2___ the section that the documents are from.

Messengers ___3___ the batched documents to the data preparation section at frequent intervals during the working day and ___4___ them to the data preparation supervisor. The supervisor ___5___ the work among the keyboard operators who ___6___ the details from the advices. They ___7___ preformatted screens to make the data entry process quicker.

B2:

is entered	are keyed in
is identified	(are) stored
are processed	are taken
are used	

The batch document includes details of batch type, batch number, time and date, the number of documents in the batch, etc. Each departmental section ___1___ by a special source code; this (2) also ___2___ to show the originating section.

The documents (3) then ___3___ to the data preparation section at regular intervals throughout the day. The details from the advices (4) then ___4___ and ___5___ on disk until they ___6___ at the end of the day. Preformatted screens ___7___ to speed up entry.

Activity 2

Now use text A3 to complete B3 and vice versa.

The functions of program components

A3:

The computerised system ___1___ of four main programs.

The Input Transaction Control program checks the control items for valid source codes, batch numbers, etc. It also ___2___ sure that the number of documents in a batch ___3___ the number on the batch advice.

The computer processes

B3:

The computerised system consists of four main steps: Input Transaction Control, Input Validity Control, Main Processing and Print Edit.

In the first stage, the validity of control data items ___1___ . This also includes making sure that the number of documents within a batch and the total on a batch advice match each other.

26 English for Information Systems

Input Validity Control carries out checks on the actual data on the input advices. It validates items such as post codes, account numbers and bank sort codes. In addition, it __4__ cross-checks between related items.

The Main Processing program __5__ the data base. It adds new records, __6__ obsolete ones and amends or __7__ other records as appropriate. In preparation for the final program it extracts data for subsequent printing and __8__ them into line-length print records which it outputs to a dump file.

The Print Edit program handles the processing of the dump file. It sorts the records by type and destination and __9__ all the various kinds of output for the different departments.

In the second step, checks __2__ out on the actual data items on the input advices. Items such as post codes, account numbers and bank sort codes __3__. Cross-checks are also performed between related items.

In the Main Processing stage the data base is updated. New records __4__, obsolete ones are deleted, others __5__ or changed. Information for print records __6__ and assembled into line-length print records which __7__ to a dump file.

The processing of the dump file __8__ by the final stage: Print Edit. Print records __9__ according to type and destination. The outputs for the different departments are then printed.

INPUT 2   Reading

Read the following text which describes some of the computer facilities that a Finnish company uses at an installation in France.

Activity 1

Label the different types of equipment in Figure 3.1.

The new installation in Lyons provides computing facilities both for the production plant there and for the French sales offices in the area.

The main processor is a Hewlett Packard HP3000XE. Other equipment in the computer room includes the main system printer and the console terminal, which is connected to its own log printer.

The equipment in the production plant consists of Panasonic microstations. Each of these incorporates a VDU screen, keyboard, bar code reader and local printer.

These microstations are linked to the main computer via a channel controller, which connects them to the ATP ports on the HP3000XE. The microstations handle the labelling operations within the plant and relay production and packaging data to the central processor.

3 Large systems and software (1)

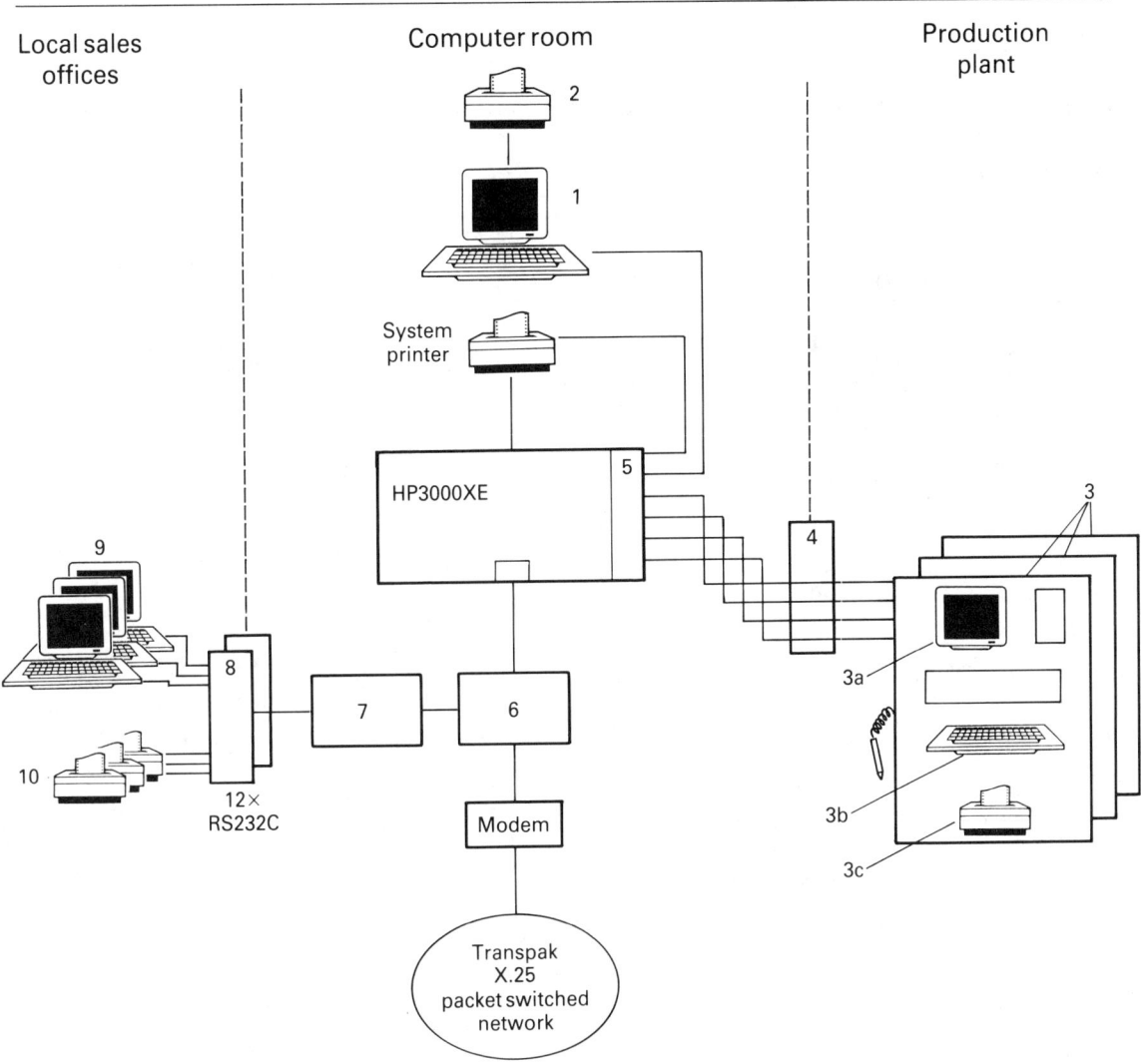

Figure 3.1

An X.25 switch connects the central processor to both the local area network and the packet switched data network. An HP Multimux controls the traffic on the LAN side. The link between this multiplexor and the terminals and local printers in the local sales offices is provided by cross-connection cabinets, each of which contains twelve RS232C interfaces.

The packet switched network handles the long distance traffic between Lyons and other installations in France. It also provides the link with Finnish HQ and the installations in West Germany, Holland, Switzerland and the UK.

Activity 2

Look at Figure 3.2. It shows part of the computing facilities which are used by the Costa Nueva Telecommunications Administration. Use the information in the diagram and the language from Activity 1 to complete the text.

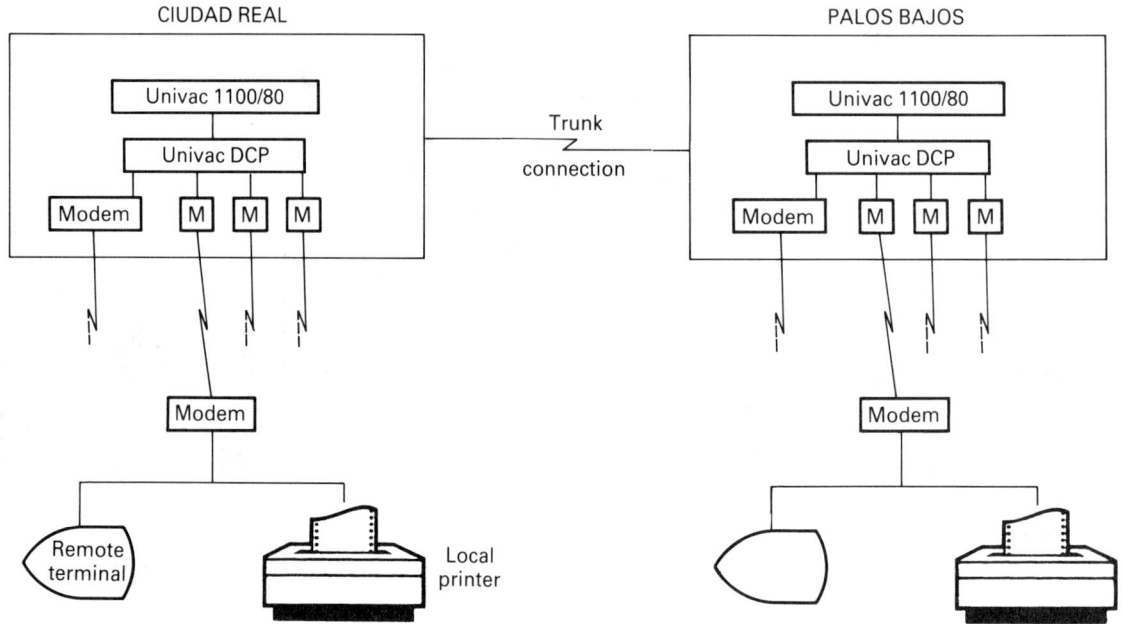

Figure 3.2

Two installations ..1.. the main processing power: one in Ciudad Real, just outside the capital, and one in Palos Bajos in the south-east. Each of these centres ..2.. two computers: a Univac 1100/80 main computer and a Univac DCP. The latter are communications computers which ..3.. the traffic between the two computer centres and with other facilities in the network. The two computer centres ..4.. to each other via a 48 kb/s trunk connection.

The system ..5.. large central database files in both Ciudad Real and Palos Bajos. Peripheral equipment in each centre ..6.. disc and tape storage units and high volume printing equipment.

User equipment in the sales offices and field units such as field depots and manned telephone exchanges ..7.. VDU terminals and keyboards, local printers and telex terminals. Modems in the outstations ..8.. the remote users to the data network.

LANGUAGE PRACTICE

Look at the following summary of Present Simple third person verb forms for active/passive, singular/plural and positive/negative.

1 Positive

Active singular	The supervisor **checks** the document. He/she **checks** the document.
Active plural	Messengers **collect** the documents. They **collect** the documents.
Passive singular	For each batch, a batch advice **is completed**. It **is completed** for each batch.
Passive plural	The documents are **batched**. They **are batched**.

2 Negative

Active singular	Print Edit **does not update** the main files. It/he/she **does not check** the data.
Active plural	The messengers **do not check** the documents. They **do not check** the documents.
Passive singular	The database **is not updated** during ITC or IVC. It/he/she **is not linked** to head office.
Passive plural	The main files **are not updated** in ITC or IVC. They are **not linked** to head office.

Activity

The following text describes some interactive video (IV) control software. Try to complete the description with the correct form of the verb in brackets; e.g. (= for example):

(1: accept) = *accepts*
  or *accept*
  or *is accepted*
  or *are accepted*

(2: not/accept) = *does not accept*
  or *do not accept*
  or *is not accepted*
  or *are not accepted*

VideoLogic's Multi-media Interactive Control (MIC) system software, version 2, is hardware independent. It (1: work) as an extension to PC DOS. The MIC components (2: enable) the PC to handle interactive video. With this software, users (3: not/limit) to specific hardware. VideoLogic now (4: license) its software to courseware manufacturers. The licences (5: allow) manufacturers to concentrate on course content: less time (6: need) for making the courseware portable.

The MIC system software currently (7: consist) of three main modules: videodisc player control, display control and input control.

The videodisc player control module (8: design) so that the user (9: not/depend) on a particular manufacturer's videodisc player.

The input control module (10: provide) users with a great deal of flexibility for communicating with the system: they (11: not/force) to use a particular input device but can choose between keyboard, mouse or touch-screen.

DEVELOPMENT 1 Listening

Find the recording for Unit 3, Development 1. The conversation takes place in an insurance company and is related to the procedures for handling rejected payments.

Activity 1

The left-hand list below contains the first half of six sentences. Listen to the conversation and try to match these with a suitable second half from the right-hand list.

1 Most of the rejections ...

2 The data preparation clerks ...

3 Sometimes the wrong information ...

4 When a payment transaction is rejected, Paul ...

5 If Paul can't find the reason for the rejection, the people in the DP Department ...

6 Most of the problems ...

(a) ... is entered in the Accounts Department.

(b) ... are caused by clerical errors.

(c) ... are sorted out by using the enquiries system.

(d) ... run a special search program.

(e) ... key in the data wrongly.

(f) ... uses the enquiry system to find out why.

Activity 2

Look at the question forms in the box below. Then use them to complete the questions in the pairs of sentences which follow.

> do you find out
> are most of the mistakes made
> is a rejected transaction resubmitted
> does Paul do
> do you get
> are transactions rejected

1 Q: How often ..... a printout of rejected transactions?
  A: We get one every day.

2 Q: Why .....?
  A: It's usually because of errors on the input advices.

3 Q: When .....?
  A: Most of them are from when clerks in the Accounts Department fill the input advices.

4 Q: How ..... why transactions are rejected?
  A: In most cases, by looking at the enquiries system to find the appropriate customer or policy details.

5 Q: What ..... if he can't find out what the problem is on the enquiries system?
  A: He puts in a special search request to the DP Department.

6 Q: How .....?
  A: When Paul knows what's wrong he fills in another payment advice but enters the function as a resubmission.

DEVELOPMENT 2   Role Play

Work with a colleague. Appendix A and Appendix B at the back of the book contain information for two people, A and B. Decide with your partner who is who. Look at the information for Unit 3 for your role only in the appropriate Appendix and follow the instructions there.

LANGUAGE SUMMARY

Sentence types (statements)

The supervisor **distributes** the work *among the operators*.
The clerks **pass** the documents *to the supervisors*.

Information for printing **is assembled** *into print records*.
The details **are stored** *on disk*.

Sentence types (questions)

The following tables summarise the verb *question* forms for the Present Simple third person for active/passive, singular/plural and positive/negative.

1 Positive

Active Singular

> **Does** the supervisor **check** the document?
> **Does** he/she **check** the document?

Active Plural

> **Do** messengers **collect** the documents?
> **Do** they **collect** the documents?

Passive Singular

> **Is** a batch advice **completed** for each batch?
> **Is** it **completed** for each batch?

Passive Plural

> **Are** the documents **batched**?
> **Are** they **batched**?

2 Negative

Active Singular

> **Does** Print Edit **not update** the main files?
> **Does** it/he/she **not check** the data?

Active Plural

> **Do** the messengers **not check** the documents?
> Do they **not check** the documents?

Passive Singular

> **Is** the data base **not updated** during ITC?
> **Is** it/he/she **not linked** to HQ?

Passive Plural

> **Are** the main files **not updated** in ITC?
> **Are** they **not linked** to HQ?

Useful expressions

At the end of the day
At frequent intervals
During the working day

It's mostly to do with ... (clerical errors).
It's not quite as simple as that.
What happens if ... (they don't match)?
What's wrong?

Special note

Data is a word which causes problems. Grammatically it is really a plural word (the singular is *datum*). For example:

> These data are valid

is a grammatically correct sentence. However, when speaking, most people say

> This data is valid

and use the word *data* as an abstract word like information. If you want to specify the singular, you can say *a piece of data* or *a data item*. *Datum* is used very little.

UNIT 4 Large systems and software (2)

INPUT 1 Reading

Read the following text which describes part of an order processing system within a manufacturing company.

Activity 1

Label the diagram in Figure 4.1 and draw lines to show the possible links between the subsystem displays.

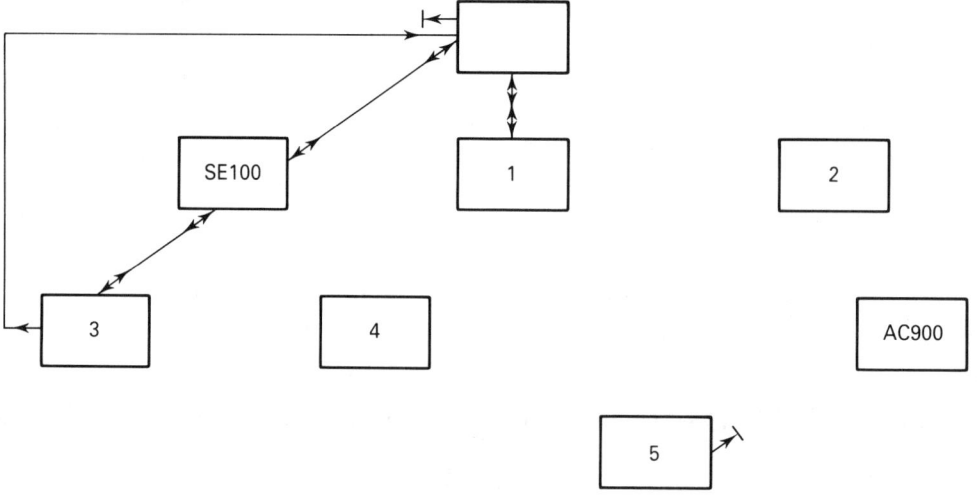

Figure 4.1 Sales Order Processing: Screen displays and access routes.

The Sales Order Processing system comprises an on-line Stock Enquiry subsystem (SE) and an on-line Order Entry subsystem (OE). These subsystems are accessed via DL100, the master menu display of the Direct Link (DL) system.

The following paragraphs summarise the parts of the system which Sales Department and Finance Department personnel use for:

1 Handling telephone enquiries about stock availability.

2 Processing orders placed by mail or over the phone.

1 Stock Enquiries (SE)

When a customer makes a telephoned enquiry about the availability of stock the sales assistant selects SE from the DL100 master menu. An SE menu is then displayed (SE100) on which the assistant can enter the part number(s) for which details are required.

The Part Number Status Details display (SE110) then provides details of quantities on hand, reorder levels, reorder quantity and the date when the next consignment is due if an item has already been reordered. Details of up to 12 part numbers at a time can be displayed on the screen. The sales assistant can therefore inform customers about the availability of the stocked items while they are on the phone.

If the customer then decides to place an order, the assistant can return directly to the DL100 menu to obtain the Order Entry system.

2 Order Entry (OE)

When a request for an order is received by mail or by phone, Sales Department staff select OE from the DL100 menu to obtain the Order Entry system menu (OE100).

First of all the Customer Details display (OE110) is requested. For established customers, only the name is entered; client information is then retrieved from the database and displayed. This can be checked and amended if necessary before details of the order are entered. For new customers, details such as the address and contact name are also keyed in. All input data are then validated.

Next — as soon as the customer details are accepted by the system — the Order Details screen (OE120) is displayed. Details of up to 12 different part numbers can be entered per screen. Once a screen is full, the details are saved and a new OE120 is displayed. After keying in all the details of the order the operator requests acceptance confirmation.

At this point, if any items are out of stock, or if the full number can not be supplied, an SE110 is displayed automatically (see 1 above). The operator can then return to OE120 and choose one of two alternatives: either the whole of the order can be held back until the customer can be contacted, or a part order can be submitted for the available items immediately while the remaining items are held for later confirmation or cancellation.

Provided the order is for an existing customer whose credit limit is not exceeded, the order is now processed fully. Stock details are updated, invoice, order preparation and despatch documents are produced and the customer's account details are adjusted.

Otherwise, however, the order is held until it is approved by the Finance Department who use an Orders Pending subsystem to look through orders awaiting approval. This subsystem is only available to Finance Department staff. By selecting OP from the

Accounting systems menu (AC100, obtained via DL100) they can obtain summaries of pending orders on AC900. A link is provided between this display and OE120 so that individual orders can be examined in more detail.

Activity 2

Use the completed diagram and the text above to say whether the following statements are true (T), false (F) or that you do not know (?):

1 *Once* the sales assistant knows the items are in stock OE100 *can be accessed* directly from SE100.

2 The sales assistant enters SE via the DL100 master menu; up to 12 part numbers *can then be entered* on SE100.

3 OE120 *can not be completed until* the customer details are valid.

4 The sales assistant *can check* credit references for new customers *while* they are on the phone by looking at AC900.

5 The operator *can go straight back* to DL100 *after* checking the availability of stock on SE110.

6 The system validates the client details *before* the Order Details screen can be filled in.

7 Provided the items are in stock, all orders *can be processed* fully *as soon as* the input data is entered.

8 Only Finance Department personnel *can access* the Orders Pending subsystem.

9 No orders *can be fully accepted until* they are approved by the Finance Department.

10 *When* stock is not available sales staff *can not submit part orders for new customers.*

Activity 3

In the sentences in Activity 2, various words are printed in italics. They tell you:

(a) the time sequence (*when, before,* etc.)

(b) what people **can do** (*can check, can not submit,* etc.)

(c) what **can be done** (*can be entered, can not be accepted,* etc.)

Study the order of words in the sentences to make sure you know where the 'time sequence' words come.

Make a list of all the 'time sequence' words used in these sentences and in the reading text from INPUT 1; study them so that you know how to use them yourself.

INPUT 2 Reading

Read the following text which describes some of the facilities of a supermarket check-out system.

Activity 1

Look at the statements which follow the text and say whether they are true (T), false (F) or not specifically stated (?) in the passage.

Figure 4.2 The IBM 3660 Supermarket System.

The Universal Product Code and Symbol are two developments that allow supermarkets and stores to improve their operations considerably.

The IBM 3660 Supermarket System is designed to be used with direct bagging check-stands which recognise the codes and symbols. Tests show that these check-stands and scanners can provide substantially improved customer throughput and higher checker productivity. The price of items that are symbol-marked do not need to be entered via a keyboard; the IBM scanning unit — the 3666 — automatically identifies the symbol-marked items that are pulled across it. The checker can use a fast two-handed motion, simultaneously bagging items.

The scanner is connected to the IBM 3663 Supermarket Terminal. As the scanner identifies each item, the terminal automatically retrieves the item's name and price. Checkers can enter items that are not symbol-marked either by keying the item number and letting the system supply the price, or by keying in the price of every item directly.

The Supermarket Controller is the heart of the system. It supervises up to 24 terminals and scanners and can provide price look-up and item movement data on up to 22 000 different items. At the end of the day, or at almost any other convenient time, summarised data can be transmitted to a System 370 at division or corporate headquarters.

The combined use of the Universal Product Code and the Supermarket System means that prices and price changes only need to go into the computer once. They do not have to go onto every item. For product-coded items, item price re-marking is eliminated. When you change a price, you only have to change the shelf labels.

The Supermarket System keeps track of item movement and transfers summarised data to the System 370. You can therefore use this data as input to programs which automatically reorder merchandise. This can mean significant savings as well as far greater control and accuracy over the store reordering procedure.

The typical supermarket stocks thousands of different items. With the Supermarket System you can determine exactly what is moving and get a clearer, much faster and far more accurate picture than you get from warehouse shipments. The automatic reordering capability which is made possible by point of sale data capture can also help to lower back-room inventory and provide better control of shelf allocation. All these things can help to increase profits.

The Supermarket System also supplies the data which is needed for improving the scheduling of store employees. It give dollar sales in 15-minute periods, customer counts, transaction data and other data on store labour activity. The Supermarket System can improve the results of existing labour-scheduling programs by providing more accurate and complete data as an automatic by-product of the check-out function. It is also an excellent tool for setting up newer and more advanced labour-scheduling programs. Either way, it can result in more effective use of personnel and substantial cost reductions.

Activity 1

Mark the following statements as true (T), false (F) or not specifically stated (?) in the passage that you have just read.

1 Introducing the 3660 means that the customer will benefit from much cheaper goods.

2 The Supermarket System makes the work of the check-out assistants far easier.

3 The new check-stands and scanners reduce the amount of time that customers have to spend in check-out queues.

4 The system eliminates the use of keyboards at the check-out, so assistants do not need to be trained in how to use keyboards to enter price information.

5 One of the major benefits is that it also enables a store or supermarket to hold greater quantities of stocks.

6 Profit margins are higher because the number of staff can be reduced.

7 The use of the system gives management a better idea of which items sell faster and can improve reordering procedures.

8 The system increases the job satisfaction of check-out assistants and other store employees.

Activity 2

The second paragraph describes some of the benefits that the Supermarket System can offer. For example:

- substantially improved customer throughput
- higher checker productivity

Now give yourself a time limit of 3 minutes to look through the last 3 paragraphs only and make a list of all the benefits that you can find.

LANGUAGE PRACTICE

Look at Figure 4.3 which summarises the manual processes which follow the computerised order processing system described in Input 1.

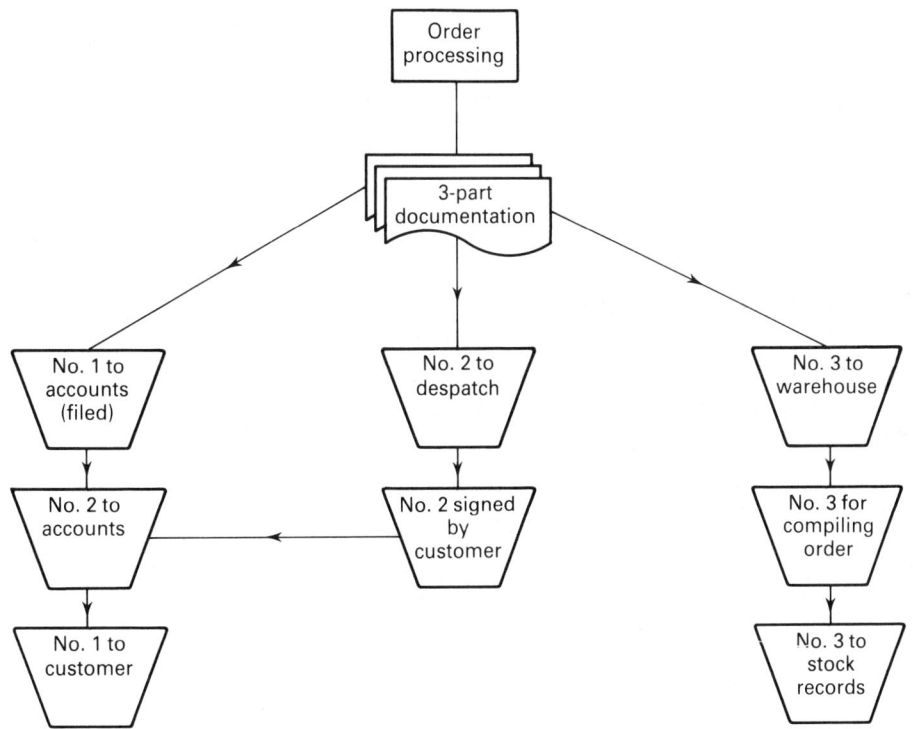

Figure 4.3 Order processing system.

English for Information Systems

Activity

Complete the text which describes what the diagram shows. Use words from the two boxes below. Use each word or expression once only. Make sure that you change the verbs to the correct form.

until		once
	at this point	
after	first of all	then
	as soon as	
while		when

to comprise	to use
to produce	to deliver
to file	to prepare
to separate	to send
to pass	to invoice

..1.. the order processing system ..2.. three-part documentation for each accepted order. The documentation ..3.. an invoice, a goods received note and an order note.
..4.. the documents are printed they ..5.. and sent to the different departments involved. The invoice ..6.. to the Accounts Department where it is filed ..7.. the goods are delivered. The goods received note is sent to the despatch section where it ..8.. to plan delivery schedules while the warehouse staff ..9.. the order. The order note is sent to the warehouse so that the order can be prepared.
..10.. the goods are ready they are moved to the despatch section.
..11.. the goods leave the warehouse the order note ..12...
The order is ..13.. sent to the customer along with the goods received note. This is signed by the customer ..14.. the goods ..15.. and returned to the despatch section by the driver. Batches of goods received notes .(16). then ..16.. to the Accounts Department. ..17.. the Accounts Department ..18.. the customer.

DEVELOPMENT 1 Listening

Find the cassette for Unit 4, Development 1. Someone from the Sales Department in the British part of a large multinational is introducing a French colleague to a range of microfilmers which will shortly appear on the French market.

Activity 1

Before you listen, look at the questions and diagrams opposite. ('Blips' are explained on the cassette.) Then try to answer the questions while you are listening.

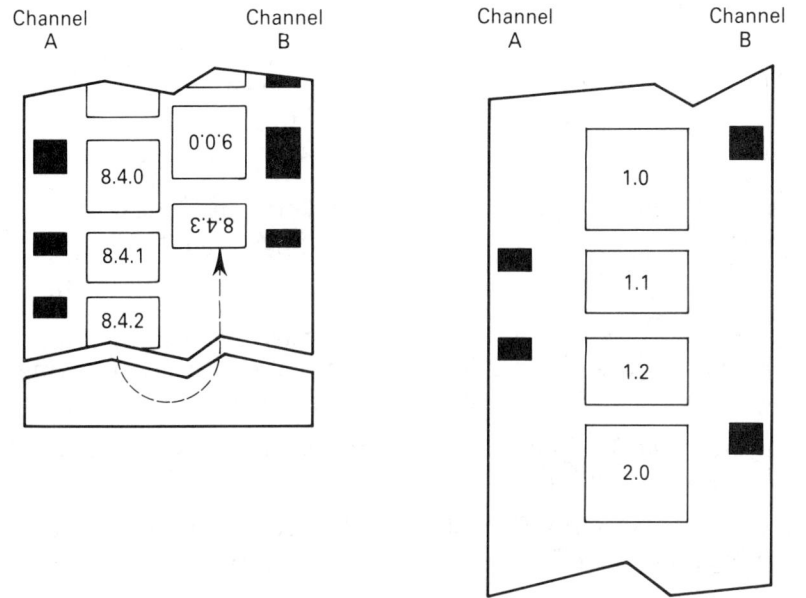

Figure 4.4 Examples of indexing.

1 What is the maximum speed of the film transport?
2 How many cheque-size documents will it film per minute?
3 What is the maximum number of A4 documents per minute?
4 How good do the documents need to be?
5 How flexible is the machine?
6 How high is the cassette capacity?
7 How expensive are the cassettes?
8 How big can input documents be?
9 What is the normal maximum size that people use?
10 What is the maximum thickness that it will accept?
11 How thin can documents be?
12 How big are the batch blips?
13 What size are the item blips?
14 How many people use three levels of indexing?
15 How often are two levels used?

Activity 2

When you want to introduce an important idea or emphasise something, you can sometimes change the word order.

	A	=	Item A
What we've got here		is	a very sophisticated machine.
What we need		is	a bigger machine.
	B	=	Action B
All you do		is	adjust a lever.
What the machine does		is	put the marks on during filming.
What you can do		is	use three levels of indexing.

Look at the following examples. The sentences on the left are from the cassette recording. The ones on the right mean roughly the same but they are much weaker.

A   What we've got here is the first of a range of intelligent microfilmers.   We've got the first of a range of intelligent microfilmers here.

B1   All (that) you do is adjust a lever.   You just adjust a lever.

B2   What the microfilmer does is put the marks on while it's filming.   The microfilmer puts the marks on while it's filming.

B3   What you can do is put different sizes of blips on.   You can put different sizes of blips on.

Now try to make the following sentences stronger.

1 We've got a very serious problem here.

2 You just need two levels for most applications.

3 You can use different cassettes for different departments.

4 It gives you a lot of flexibility.

5 It puts the two images side by side.

DEVELOPMENT 2 Informal Presentation

Choose a system or a piece of equipment that you are familiar with. Describe its main characteristics and strong points.

Describe the sort of people who find it useful and the extra facilities it gives which similar systems or equipment do not have.

LANGUAGE SUMMARY

Sentence types

The Sales Department **does not invoice** the customer *at this point* (= 1 department).

The Sales Department **do not invoice** the customer *at this point* (= the people in the department).

A customer **is not invoiced** *until the goods are delivered.*

Customers **are not invoiced** *until the goods are delivered.*

X	happens is done can happen can be done	*once as soon as when before after while*	Y	happens is done

X	**does not happen is not done** **can not happen can not be done**	*until*	Y	happens is done

Useful expressions

A3-sized documents
600 {a / per} minute / second / hour
about / around / approximately
extremely big > very big > big > {fairly / quite} big

The nice thing about X is ... (it's easy to operate).
All right?
If you look at ... (this next sample).
Another thing we can do is ... (film on both sides).
So that's the .... (1000 model).
(The controller is) ... the heart of the system.

UNIT 5 Historical developments in information services

INPUT 1 Reading

The following text describes the history of the development of the Ada programming language.

Activity 1

Read the text and complete Figure 5.1 to show the chronology of the main steps.

1975	DoD survey of costs
1975	Decision to develop a new language
1975	...1...
1975	...2...
1976	...3...
1977	...4...
1977	Invitation to bid for design contract
1977	...5...
1978	...6...
1979	...7...
1980	...8...
1983	...9...

Figure 5.1 The development of Ada.

Around 1975 the United States Department of Defense (DoD) did some studies to assess the reasons for the rapid increase in software development costs. At the time, they were spending over $3 billion a year on developing new software and maintaining old software.

The first major conclusion that they drew from these studies was that they needed to make a major investment in tools to increase productivity. The second was that they needed to improve the average programmer's level of programming methodology. They also discovered that they were using about 400 different computer languages and dialects — a very large number. The decision to develop a new computer language was a consequence of their findings.

As a result of their findings the requirements of a new computer language were developed by the DoD under the leadership of David Fisher. He consulted experts from the military, from industry and from the academic world. During this period — the mid-1970s — interest in developing new languages was growing generally as hardware costs were falling while software production costs were rising. A lot of research was therefore being done to develop better computer languages in other countries as well as in the US.

The development of the new language requirements took nearly three years and went through various stages of refinement. The 'Strawman' requirements appeared in 1975 and 'Woodenman' came shortly after in the same year. 'Tinman' followed in 1976 and 'Ironman', in 1977, was the final set of requirements. These documents did not attempt to design the language; they merely specified the required capabilities.

Each of them described the language requirements in progressively greater detail.
The DoD then invited bidders for the Ada language design project.

From the 20 bids which were made, the DoD selected four teams to develop prototypes of the new language. The teams were colour-coded Green, Red, Blue and Yellow. After 6 months their efforts were evaluated. In 1978 the Green and Red teams were selected to continue, and in May 1979 the final choice was announced: the Green language from a team based at Cii Honeywell Bull in Paris became preliminary Ada.

After 1979 the Green team continued alone during the testing and evaluation phases. During this period about 100 teams around the world tried to re-code existing applications in this preliminary Ada language. These teams reported the drawbacks they found and suggested improvements. On the basis of this experience, a proposed standard for the new language was produced in 1980. Finally, in February 1983, the Ada ANSI standard was agreed.

The requirements definition therefore took 3 years and the production of a standardised language took from 1977 to 1983. More than 1000 people from all over the world were involved.

Activity 2

Use the information in the text to put the following sentences in the correct order. Number 1 is marked for you.

  (a) They then selected four from the 20 interested parties who submitted bids.

  (b) As a result, a decision was taken to develop a new all-purpose language.

(c) They colour-coded the four teams and gave them 6 months to submit an outline version of the language.

(d) They then narrowed the choice down to two — the Red and Green teams.

1 = (e) In the early 1970s they *were spending* over $3 billion a year on software development and maintenance. An analysis *was carried out* and they *found* that a large number of languages *was being used*.

(f) A team was subsequently set up to specify requirements for the language; experts from many different fields were consulted.

(g) The final requirement specifications for the language were laid out in the 'Ironman' document of 1977.

(h) Finally, they chose the language from the Green team as the most suitable.

(i) At the end of this period they evaluated the results.

(j) Once the requirements were specified, the DoD asked people to submit bids for the design and production of the language.

Activity 3

Look at sentence (e) in Activity 2. There are four different verb forms in italics. The box below contains examples of these verb forms for one regular verb (report) and one irregular verb (take, took, taken).

		Active	Passive
Past Simple	(singular)	reported (took)	was reported (was taken)
	(plural)	reports (took)	were reported (were taken)

Past Continuous	(singular)	was reporting (was taking)	was being reported (was being taken)
	(plural)	were reporting (were taking)	were being reported (were being taken)

Now try to find further examples of these from the text in Activity 1 and put them in the appropriate box in the table below.

		Active	Passive
Past Simple	(singular)		
	(plural)		
Past Continuous	(singular)		
	(plural)		

INPUT 2 Listening

Find the cassette recording for Unit 5, Input 2. The recording is of a conversation which involves two people: Fred Peel and Alan Brown. Fred is talking to Alan and his colleagues at the University of York about a new database product. The date is June 1988.

Activity 1

Before you listen, look at the sentences below. Then, as you listen, choose the sentence from each group which is most accurate.

1. (a) Fred works for a US company called Ontologic.
   (b) Fred came across to the States about a year ago.
   (c) Ontologic are a Massachusetts-based company.
2. (a) VBASE is a relational database.
   (b) VBASE is an object-oriented programming language.
   (c) VBASE is an integrated database and programming language.
3. (a) Smalltalk Express asked Ontologic to market the product in the UK.
   (b) Smalltalk Express handle several products for Ontologic.
   (c) Ontologic chose Smalltalk Express to act as their UK distributor.

4 (a) Fred started to work for Ontologic full-time about a month ago.

(b) Fred joined Smalltalk Express as a full-time employee as soon as they started to handle VBASE.

(c) Fred started to handle VBASE as a representative of Smalltalk Express about a month ago.

5 (a) The commercial list price for a site licence costs about £90 000.

(b) The commercial list price for a single Sun is £2000 to £3000.

(c) The commercial list price for any number of users connected to a single file-server is £23 000.

6 (a) The price increases by 15% of the list price once the first five are sold.

(b) The price goes up by 50% of the list price as soon as the first five are sold.

(c) The price for educational users increases to 50% of the list price after the first five are sold.

7 (a) Maintenance is included in the basic price.

(b) Maintenance is optional.

(c) No maintenance contracts are currently available.

Activity 2

We saw in the Development section of Unit 4 that when you want to introduce an important idea or emphasise something, you can sometimes change the word order. Look at the tapescript of this recording and pick out the same sort of sentences from the conversation between Alan and Fred.

Activity 3

Something else that we saw in the Development section of Unit 4 was the use of words like very, quite, extremely *to increase or decrease the strength of an adjective. Look at the tapescript of this recording and pick out similar examples from Alan and Fred's conversation.*

LANGUAGE PRACTICE

In Input 1, Activity 3, we looked at the forms of the Past Simple and the Past Continuous. Look at these four sentences from Input 1:

1 (a) The 'Strawman' requirements *appeared* in 1975 and 'Woodenman' *came* shortly after in the same year.

1 (b) In 1978 the Green and Red teams *were selected* to continue, and in May 1979 the final choice *was announced*.

2 (a) During the mid-1970s, interest in developing new languages *was growing* generally as hardware costs *were falling* while software production costs *were rising*.

2 (b) (During the mid-1970s . . .) a lot of research *was being done* to develop better languages.

Each of the verb forms in the sentences above describe something that happened in the past that is completely finished and has no connection with the present:

1 (a) appeared; came

1 (b) were selected; was announced

2 (a) was growing; were falling; were rising

2 (b) was being done

Sentences 1(a) and 1(b) describe single completed events. They use the *Past Simple*. Sentence (a) is active while (b) is passive.

Sentences 2(a) and 2(b) also describe past actions, but the idea of continuity or gradual change is more important so the *Past Continuous* form is used. Sentence 2(a) is active while (b) is passive.

The *Simple* and *Continuous* forms are often used in the same sentence when one thing interrupts another. For example:

   I *was updating* the file when the machine *went* down.

The Continuous form is often used when two actions were continuing for quite a long time and at the same time. For example:

   She *was reading* the values from the screen while I *was checking* them on the printout.

Activity

Now try to complete the following dialogue with the correct form of a suitable verb from the box. If the verb is irregular, the three forms are given. With regular verbs you can make the second and third forms from the part in brackets. For example:

install (-ed) = > install, installed, installed

install (-ed)	intend (-ed)
sort (-ed)	disconnect (-ed)
go, went, gone	take, took, taken
reconnect (-ed)	try (tried)
do, did, did	spend, spent, spent
refit (-ted)	

A: Did you finish those alterations for Mick yesterday?

B: I'm afraid not Liz. I ..1.. to do it yesterday morning but the Data Capture system ..2.. down twice in our subsystem so Keith and I ..3.. most of yesterday morning on that.
   What a morning! You know the new cabling system ..4.. in our section all day yesterday, so we ..5.. to sort out what was wrong with Data Capture while all the electricians and people ..6.. bits of the ceiling down and parts of the floor up! Anyway, we ..7.. it all out.
   Then our part of the network ..8.. for most of the afternoon so I couldn't finish them then, either. They ..9.. a good job, though. The network ..10.. and everything else ..11.. by about 9 o'clock last night, so I can finish them this morning.

A: That's OK. Mick said they weren't all that urgent.

DEVELOPMENT 1 Reading

The following text describes some of the main changes which have occurred since the early days of commercial data processing.

Activity 1

As you read the text complete the information in Figures 5.2 and 5.3.

Over the past twenty to thirty years the jobs of people who work on commercial data processing applications and the tools which they use have changed substantially.
   In the early 1960s hardware costs were very high compared with software costs. Applications were written in assembly languages and the main priority was to write efficient code which maximised the use of the hardware.
   Languages were then developed which enabled programmers to code applications more quickly. These early high-level languages allowed programmers to write code which was more readable and which made its purpose clearer.
   These developments encouraged people to think about other issues that affected software costs. As hardware costs fell and software costs began to rise, writing

applications quickly was obviously still important. But a large application which took a team two or three years to write had to be maintained and adapted long after the people who wrote it moved to other projects or other companies. Program readability and maintainability were factors which influenced the design of later high-level computer languages such as Ada.

Ease of use and readability have been even more important in the development of fourth generation languages. Users of such languages are often either people who have no technical knowledge of computing or more computer-literate personnel who use prototyping methods to work very closely with user department staff.

Type of language	Main characteristics
1 Assembly languages	
2 Early high-level languages	
3 Later high-level languages	
4 Fourth generation languages (4GL)	

Figure 5.2

All these changes have had profound effects on the roles of user department representatives, programmers and systems analysts.

With increased use of distributed processing, authoring packages, fourth generation languages and prototyping, users have become much more involved in designing the applications which meet their requirements.

As modularity of program design has increased in importance, programmers have become more involved in the design process; with more modern computer languages, programmers have started to spend more time on program design than on coding and testing — the opposite of earlier high-level languages.

The development of information centres has created a demand for a new type of analyst who has to combine technical knowledge, business awareness, communicative ability and diplomacy.

Three main avenues are available for choosing such people. One traditional approach has been to promote people who have been programmers and train them as analysts. They have technical knowledge and are familiar with using program specifications. However, they often lack both business knowledge and communication skills.

A successful approach for some companies has been to take users with analytical minds who are good communicators and provide them with technical training. They are usually people who are more sensitive to commercial requirements and more sympathetic to the frustration that user departments feel. Nevertheless, they often fail to appreciate some of the technical problems that programming and operations staff face.

The third approach has been to take on graduate trainees who combine an ability to communicate with a higher and more general level of education. But even after training, such people still lack practical experience of both the commercial and the computing areas.

Type of background	Main characteristics	
	Advantages	Disadvantages
5 Programming		
6		
7		

Figure 5.3 Recruitment of systems analysts.

Activity 2

Study paragraphs 2, 3 and 4 from the reading text and make a list of all the verb forms.

Do the same with paragraphs 6, 7, 8 and 9.

How are the two groups of verbs different? Why are they different — what is the difference in the times they refer to?

Activity 3

Look at these four sentences which are very similar to sentences from the reading text.

1. (a) Early high-level languages allowed programmers to write code more quickly.
   (b) In the early 1960s, applications were written in assembly languages.
2. (a) Jobs have changed substantially.
   (b) Information centres have been introduced in many companies.

Sentences 1(a) and 1(b) are examples of the Past Simple. We use this when we specify the time of past events or give details of situations which are completely finished and completely separate from the present. Sentence (a) is active and sentence (b) is passive.

Sentences 2(a) and 2(b) are examples of the Present Perfect, which we use to describe experiences, developments or events, without specifying when they took place: they have been experienced *up to the present moment*. Sentence (a) is active and sentence (b) is passive.

Choose the most suitable option from the possible verb forms in the following sentences.

1 Systems analysts who ..... in business areas usually appreciate the difficulties that business people face.

| (a) worked | (b) were worked |
| (c) have worked | (d) have been worked |

2 Many different computer languages .....

| (a) invented | (b) were invented |
| (c) have invented | (d) have been invented |

3 The decision to buy a new mainframe ..... in Monday's meeting.

| (a) made | (b) was made |
| (c) has made | (d) has been made |

4 I ..... the report by fax before I went home.

| (a) received | (b) was received |
| (c) has received | (d) has been received |

5 when games for home computers ..... graphics were very simple.

| (a) introduced | (b) were introduced |
| (c) have introduced | (d) have been received |

6 Home computers ..... much more powerful, with faster processors and bigger memories.

| (a) became | (b) have become |

DEVELOPMENT 2 Informal Presentation

Prepare a short talk to answer one of the following questions.

(a) How has your job changed since you started?

(b) How has your profession or industry changed in the past 10 years?

LANGUAGE SUMMARY

Section 1

Sentence types

Around 1975, the DoD **did** some studies.

During this period hardware costs **were falling**.

Finally the Ada ANSI standard **was agreed**.

When they did the survey a large number of languages **was being used**.

In the four sentences above, the time expressions are very important, so they are put at the beginning of the sentence — a strong position. When the time is less important, the same expressions can go to the end of the sentence.

Section 2

The following tables summarise the negative forms for the past verb forms that we looked at in the Language Practice.

		Active	Passive
Past Simple	(singular)	did not report (did not take)	was not reported (was not taken)
	(plural)	did not report (did not take)	were not reported (were not taken)
Past Continuous	(singular)	was not reporting (was not taking)	was not being reported (was not being taken)
	(plural)	were not reporting (were not taking)	were not being reported (were not being taken)

Section 3

The formation of the Present Perfect is summarised for a regular verb (*finish*) and an irregular verb (*take, took, taken*):

I you we they the suppliers	have 've	finished taken	it.
he she it the boss	has 's	finished taken	it.

Negative forms

{I have not/I haven't/I've not} finished, etc.

{She has not/she hasn't/she's not} taken it, etc.

Question forms

Have {you/they/the suppliers} taken it? etc.

Has {she/he} finished? etc.

Useful expressions

At the time ... (they were using a lot of different languages).
As a result of ... (their findings).
(More than 1000 people from) ... all over the world ... (were involved).
I came across ... (a new company).
I'd rather not ... (call it a database).
It's more of ... (an environment than a database).
It's a sort of ... (C with operations).
(They deal with other products) ... in the same sort of area.
(I got involved) .... right from the start.
They're quite conversant with ... (this sort of product).
In other words ... (they know a lot about it).
What does that come to? = How much does it cost altogether?

UNIT 6 Training and recruitment

INPUT 1 Listening

Find the cassette recording for Unit 6, Input 1. You are about to hear more about the database product that we heard about in Unit 5, Input 2. Fred (the sales representative) is talking to Alan and Sonja of the University of York. The date is June 1988.

Activity 1

During the conversation, people are giving different opinions about the product. Look at the opinions below. As you listen, for each opinion choose the name of the person who gives it. Three of them (1, 2 and 5) have already been done for you.

1	Fred	Things are **really** moving.
2	Alan	I **certainly** think that we need some kind of experimentation vehicle.
3	Fred/Alan/Sonja	**Really** I think it's much better if we can actually *buy something in*.
4	Fred/Alan/Sonja	*I couldn't agree more.* I mean, why re-invent the wheel?
5	Sonja	Well, *it sounds very interesting*, but I think the basic problem is the money.
6	Fred/Alan/Sonja	I don't think that we can **really** go back and ask for another four-and-a-half straight away.
7	Fred/Alan/Sonja	Well, *you never know*. This is a **completely** different product.
8	Fred/Alan/Sonja	**Personally**, I don't think there's any doubt that university departments have to get into this.
9	Fred/Alan/Sonja	Yes, *I accept that*, but what we teach the students is our first priority.

10	Fred/Alan/Sonja	At a cost of £4000 for a Sun it's **probably** a worthwhile acquisition.
11	Fred/Alan/Sonja	*I take your point* that it's an interesting area to get into.
12	Fred/Alan/Sonja	I **certainly** think you're right and this is something we **definitely** have to move into one way or another.
13	Fred/Alan/Sonja	I think our best way forward is to have a much more thorough look at the documentation.
14	Fred/Alan/Sonja	I **certainly** agree that *it's worth looking into*.

Activity 2

Look at the two columns below. In the left-hand column there are some expressions which were in italics in the sentences above. Choose the phrase in the right-hand column which has the same meaning.

Look at the sentences to get the context and listen to the cassette again if you think a sentence does not give you enough information.

1	Really moving	(a)	actually moving
		(b)	moving quickly
3	Buy something in	(a)	buy something from inside our own organisation
		(b)	buy something from outside our own organisation
4	I couldn't agree more	(a)	I agree completely
		(b)	I disagree
5	It sounds interesting	(a)	It's not really interesting
		(b)	I think it may be interesting
7	You never know	(a)	It's always impossible to get this sort of information
		(b)	It may in fact be possible
9	I accept that	(a)	Thank you very much
		(b)	I realise that
11	I take your point	(a)	I understand your argument
		(b)	I don't agree
14	It's worth looking into	(a)	It's a good idea to find out more
		(b)	We must get it

Activity 3

Now find expressions from the sentences and the cassette which you can use yourself in discussion to give opinions. Put them into groups as follows.

Giving a personal opinion: . . . . .

Showing complete agreement: . . . . .

Showing that you understand, but that other arguments are important: . . . . .

INPUT 2 Reading

Activity 1

Read the letter of application opposite. As you read it, fill in the details on the input form. If the information required is not relevant for the applicant, put N/A (not applicable). If the information required is relevant but not mentioned in the letter, put ? for unknown.

Post reference number: Date of application:

Advertised in: on:

First name of applicant: Family name:

Address: Post code:

Experience: (tick the appropriate boxes)

Computing:

Applications programming	☐	Telecommunications	☐
Systems programming	☐	Supervisory	☐
Systems analysis	☐	Management	☐
Operations	☐	Training	☐

Other (specify):

Current employer name: Current employer address:

Present salary: Period of notice required:

Availability date: Foreign languages spoken:

                                        Ms Anne Blanshard
                                        Water Lane
                                        Flaxby
                                        York YO7 3DZ

                                        Tel: Whitwell (065 381) 713158

Mr G. Benton
Select International
FREEPOST
London W3 9BR
                                        23 September 1990

Dear Mr Benton

I would like to apply for the post which was advertised in 'Computing', 17th September of project leader in Oslo for the production of documentation and training materials for natural language interface products.

I currently work on a freelance basis as a software producer, training consultant and writer; you will see from the enclosed C.V. that my career to date combines considerable experience in these three areas of computing, training and writing.

Computing: I have worked as a programmer and analyst in a commercial data processing environment and am currently designing and producing microcomputer-based educational software.

Training: I have been involved in the fields of communication skills and commercial data processing as trainer, course designer and consultant.

Writing: My experience includes authorship of educational textbooks, commercial training packages, software documentation, software training manuals and programmer training materials.

I have also had a lot of professional contact with Scandinavia: I previously lived and worked in Norway and still travel to Sweden and Norway frequently to give courses in communication skills. I speak fluent Norwegian.

Finally, given my parallel interests in computing and linguistics (my original training was in modern languages) I am extremely interested in working in the field of natural language interfaces.

I hope that sending a C.V. is acceptable; I have to go to Norway for 2 weeks from this Saturday and may not receive an application form in time to complete and return it to you. The names and addresses of two referees are provided with the C.V. I can be available to start work any time after 1 November.

I look forward to hearing from you.

Yours sincerely

Anne Blanshard.

Activity 2

Find the groups of words from the text which mean the following:

1 Products for interfacing with natural language.
2 Software which has been written for educational purposes and which runs on microcomputers.
3 The processing of data in commerce.
4 Manuals for training people to use software.
5 Materials which train people to be programmers.

LANGUAGE PRACTICE

Look at these examples of language from the conversation about the database product.

The people in Leeds *have decided* to go with it now.

They*'ve had* about three months' experience of using it.

The people in Glasgow *have* **just** *come* back from the States.

I *haven't had* so much interest in a product **for** a long time.

I*'ve* only *been* in this office **since** yesterday.

The people who*'ve* **already** *used* it are looking at both areas.

He probably *hasn't heard* of me **yet**.

The verb forms in italic are examples of the Present Perfect tense, which we looked at in Unit 5, Development 1.
　　Because of the close connection with the present, the Present Perfect is often used with words such as *just, for, since, already, yet*.

Look at these examples from the conversation about the database:

just gives the idea of something very recent:

　　I've *just* finished.
　　They've *just* gone.

for is used with a period of time up to and including the present moment:

> I haven't seen her *for* a long time.
> She's been in Paris *for* 3 months now.

since is used with a point in time (date, day, time, etc.) to show a connection with the present moment:

> I haven't seen her *since* she went to Paris.
> She's been in Paris *since* July.

already is usually used with positive ideas about something which has happened 'before now':

> A: Are you going to finish that letter?
> B: I've *already* finished it.

yet is similar, but is used with a question, or a negative idea:

> A: Have you finished that letter *yet*?
> B: I'm afraid I haven't had time *yet*.

Activity 1

Complete the following extracts from the news section of a computer magazine from October 1988.

When you see '…(1-they/not/sell)…' etc., put the correct form of the verb (= they have not sold).
When you see '__(a)__' etc., choose one of the five words just, for, since, already, yet.

Tandy US has __(a)__ launched another complete range of PC-compatible computers. In addition …(1-they/launch)… a compact home facsimile machine. This has __(b)__ appeared on the US market at $1299 but …(2-they/not/decide)… whether to sell it in the UK __(c)__.

Hyundai's range of Korean built PC-compatibles …(3-arrive)… on the UK market at last. The machines …(4-be)… available in the US and the rest of Europe __(d)__ quite a while __(e)__, but …(5-only/be)… on sale in the UK __(f)__ the beginning of this month.

Personal Computer Peripherals …(6-extend)… its Macbottom range of external hard disks: …(7-they/introduce)… a new 70Mb drive.

Activity 2

Do the same with the following two conversations. The box below contains details of the irregular verbs you need.

When you see '___(a)___' etc., choose one of the five words just, for, since, already, yet.

> meet, met, met
> know, knew, known
> be, was/were, been
> have, had, had
> see, saw, seen
> leave, left, left

At the beginning of the conference:

A: Joan, ...(1-you/meet/?)... Zygmund Korczinski from the Polish telecommunications administration?

B: No, I haven't, actually. How do you do. Joan Hayes, British Telecom.

C: Pleased to meet you.

A: And this is Carina Asplund, from ....

B: ...(2-we/meet)... ___(a)___, actually. Hello again.

D: Hello.

A: And I think you know Azadeh Nassiri.

B: Oh, yes, ...(3-we/know)... each other ___(b)___ a long time.

At the end of the conference:

A: Well, ...(4-it/be)... very nice meeting you.

B: Nice to have met you too. I'm sorry ...(5-we/not/have)... very much time to talk but we'll see you again next month.

A: Yes, don't worry. Oh, ...(6-you/see/?)... Carina? ...(7-she/leave/?)... ___(c)___ ?

B: Yes, she's ___(d)___ gone, I'm afraid.

A: Oh, that's a pity. I wanted to say goodbye. Never mind. I'll see her in Brussels. Right. I really must go. Goodbye, Zygmund. Take care.

B: You too. 'Bye Joan.

DEVELOPMENT 1   Listening

Find the cassette recording for Unit 6, Development 1. Alistair Thomas of VideoLogic Ltd is telling Steve Hick of Linguacraft about the development of the Interactive Video (IV) market in the UK. The date is July 1988.

Activity 1

As you listen, complete the following notes:

First major field of use:	.1(a).
Two major users in this field:	.1(b). .1(c).
Examples of uses in this field:	.1(d). .1(e). .1(f). .1(g).
Second major field of use:	.2(a). .2(b).
Typical users:	.2(c). .2(d).
Typical uses:	.2(e). .2(f).

What other key reasons does Alistair give for development in this area where CAD/CAM (Computer aided design/manufacture) are involved?

..3..

Activity 2

In the first six units of this book we have seen the use of some important English verb 'tenses' in both the active and the passive.

The conversation that you have just listened to included various examples. Listen to the recording again; as you listen try to complete the following extracts with the exact words of the speakers.

Notice the pronunciation of auxiliary verbs (has/have, is/are), which are often difficult to hear (A = Alistair, S = Steve).

1 A: Lloyds Bank, back in 1985 .(a). themselves to 1500 systems, which .(b). an investment of some £4 million plus in the technology and since then they .(c). about another £12 million or so on applications.

2 S: Is it mostly the financial and high-tech sectors that .(a). it then?

    A: Not only, no. It .(b). for skills such as welding. British Nuclear Fuels .(c). it for safety training.

3 A: Most of the major banks .(a). these things called information kiosks, for example, because they .(b). to get into things like stocks and shares, mortgages, insurance, etc. — new areas for the bank. People .(c). up to a stand-alone terminal in the bank and they .(d). with it via a touch-screen.

4 A: ... produce them in half the time. So product life cycles .(a). shorter, the products .(b). more sophisticated and the potential users .(c). less and less about the equipment that they .(d). to use.

Activity 3

In the following exercise you need to find a suitable verb from the box and then put it in the correct form to complete the text. We have looked at the following tenses in both the active and passive in the first six units:

- Present Simple
- Present Continuous
- Past Simple
- Past Continuous
- Present Perfect

Look back at the Language Practice in this unit and in the Language Practices and Language Summaries of previous units if you are not sure about the use of the different verb forms. The first one has been done for you.

to supply	to place	to sell (sold, sold)
to include	to emerge	to grow (grew, grown)
to estimate	to become	to reach
to penetrate	to be (was, been)	**to found**
to enable	to be	to establish

(This text was written in 1988.)

VideoLogic ltd. *was founded* in 1984 to exploit the convergence of four main communications media: television and video, the computer, publishing and telecommunications.

Interactive Video (IV) . (a) . the first main discipline which . (b) . from the convergence of these technologies. Since 1984, VideoLogic . (c) . itself as Europe's largest Interactive Video development group and has an impressive client base which . (d) . such companies as IBM and Lloyds Bank.

VideoLogic . (e) . high technology printed circuit boards, software and consulting support for the provision of interactive video through the use of videodisc players with IBM PCs and compatibles.

VideoLogic's first key development following the founding of the company . (f) . the Multimedia Interactive Control system (MIC) together with associated hardware. MIC comprises an integrated hardware and software system which . (g) . an IBM PC or compatible to function as a multimedia interactive terminal.

Since 1985, when Lloyds Bank . (h) . an initial order for 1500 systems, MIC . (i) . the market leader in the UK, the de facto standard in Europe and . (j) . the US market. The company's products . (k) . currently in 20 countries through a network of 160 dealers.

Although the market is still only a few years old it . (l) . rapidly at the moment and . (m) . a current world-wide value of around £115 million already. It . (n) . that this will double by 1990.

DEVELOPMENT 2 Letter Writing

Look at the four job advertisements below and on the next page. Choose one of them (or another one of your own choice from another English language source) and use the example of the letter in Input 2 to write a letter of application. Be careful with your verb tenses!

COULD YOU RUN OFFICE SERVICES FOR US?

SALARY RANGE TO £18,000

We're looking for someone to assume full responsibility for the provision of efficient office services throughout our business, including high-calibre secretarial support for senior management. Supervising a team of four but very much part of the action yourself, you will prioritise work, guarantee things happen on time and generally ensure an accurate, quality response. As you'd expect of a brand-new, state-of-the-art manufacturing and office complex, the very latest equipment and systems are in place, including WPs, electronic mail and desk-top publishing — mainly using IBM PCVs or compatibles.

Your recent experience of office administration should include the broadest range of secretarial and support duties: rushing out copies of key documents, making international travel arrangements, organising cover for vital tasks — often at the same time! Ours is a friendly, professional environment where everyone participates on equal terms: you will play an important part in contributing to the overall efficiency of our business. You must have a recognised qualification and possess excellent interpersonal skills.

An excellent starting salary will be backed by a valuable package of non-contributory benefits including pension, life assurance and healthcare schemes. We also offer very good development prospects for anyone with the talent and ambition to progress.

Call Rodney Hardcastle for more details and an application form on 0300 62333. Or send him your full cv at Eurobuild (A Division of Cromwell Construction plc), Victoria Way, Coombe Hill, Cheltenham, Gloucestershire GL42 1QY.

Eurobuild

COMPUTER MANAGEMENT SERVICES LTD

PROGRAMMER / ANALYSTS

Salary — Negotiable Benefits

We are a dynamic successful Software House with an established range of clients in Local and Health Authorities.

Our incredible growth rate leads to continuous recruitment of ambitious Programmer Analysts who have the desire to make a significant contribution to an expanding Company.

Ideally, you should have 3–5 years experience, but recently qualified applicants are not excluded.

Experience of working in a 4GL environment would be an advantage, but not essential.

Interested? Then write with a full C.V. to:

**Avril Taylor
CMS Ltd
York House
15–19 Wood Lane
COVENTRY CV1 3LB**

INFORMATION SERVICES MANAGER

Tonbridge £25K + Car

You have at least one year's experience in Management Information Systems analysis and development. With your commercial understanding and man-management skills, you want a challenge that pushes your talents and experience to the fore. This is it.

We are Montrose Bakeries, market leader in our sector of the food industry. Now, at the centre of our national operation we are set to introduce a new 'Executive Information System'. As Information Services Manager you'll be responsible for developing and implementing this major project.

From the outset it will be down to you to determine and meet the needs of potential users ... and to ensure that adequate instruction and training is provided. You'll have the interpersonal skills to interview and influence the most senior management and the creative approach that suits our open culture.

In addition to a competitive salary you can look forward to the benefits you would expect from a large, successful company.

Please write enclosing CV to Mr Colin Young, Personnel Manager, Montrose Bakeries, Montrose House, Station Road, Tonbridge, Kent TN12 1TU.

Technical Computer Systems Operators

ATEX — SUN — Bespoke Systems

Additional computer operation and end user support staff required for our technical centre in London. Support must be provided for our 320 terminal ATEX editorial and classified text management systems, Information International graphics system and associated ethernet applications based around Sun Microsystems terminals, IBM PCs and Macintosh page composition.

Where required, training will be supplied for typographical composition, graphic arts and telecommunication applications and associated systems.

The successful applicant will work directly with our technical staff in support of the daily production of our news products and the editorial and advertising staffs which create them. Shift working is scheduled any five days out of seven. Compensation is very competitive and in line with the standards of a major London based newspaper.

He or she will have demonstrated exceptional ability in computer operations or an above average aptitude to learn technical operations. Our existing staff comes from a mixed background, ranging from highly technical computer applications, to graphics arts trades, or clerical positions with good technical aptitude.

Apply to:

Roger L. Greenaway
The Tribune
131 New Cross Road
London EC1N 2OE

LANGUAGE SUMMARY

Sentence types

I *really* **think** we need X.
We *definitely* **have** to move.
I *certainly* agree that **it's** worth looking into.

Things **are** *really* **moving.**
Things **are** *definitely* **changing.**
Product life cycles **are** *generally* **getting** shorter.

We've *just* **finished.**
She's *already* **gone.**
We've *never* **met** her.
They've *also* **launched** a fax (facsimile) machine.

We've **known** her *since 1985*.
I've **been** an analyst *for a long time*.
We **haven't bought** the new printer *yet*.

Useful expressions

Things are really moving.
We need some kind of ... (experimentation vehicle).
Why re-invent the wheel?
(Ingress is more widely available.) Apart from which ... (the textbooks are written).
Our best way forward is to ... (have a much more thorough look).
Sorry we're late.
You will see from ... (the enclosed C.V.) ... that ....
We've already met, actually.
It's been very nice meeting you.
Nice to have met you (too).
We'll see you again ... (next month).
Don't worry.
That's a pity.
Never mind.
I really must go.
A: Take care. B: You too.
That's quite a/an ... (sum of money/investment).
(The finance sector) ... is taking X to heart.
There's a kind of ... (training element).
Absolutely.
To a certain extent ... (the problems are the same).

Special note

The expressions for giving opinions from Input 1 are not included here, but they are very useful. Look back at your own list which you made from the tapescript.

PART 2
Developing, producing, implementing and maintaining systems

UNIT 7 Preliminary investigations

INPUT 1 Listening

Find the cassette recording for Unit 7, Input 1. You will hear a conversation between three people (Graham, Gerry and Shirley). They are discussing whether to do a large new project in-house or with outside help.

Activity 1

Look at the following questions and try to answer them as you listen.

1 (a) Does Gerry think they should do the project entirely in-house?
  (b) If so, why? If not, why not?
2 (a) Does Shirley think they should do the project entirely in-house?
  (b) If so, why? If not, why not?
3   What does she think they should discuss?
4   What possibilities does she mention?
5   What should they do first?
6   What should they be careful about?

Activity 2

Shirley says 'there'll be certain types of equipment that'll only be needed in the initial stages'. Discuss the following questions with a colleague or colleagues.

What sort of project might only need certain types of equipment in the early stages?

What sort of equipment might it be?

English for Information Systems

Activity 3

The last thing that you hear in the discussion is Graham saying 'Have you?' The way that he says it — the tone of his voice — may help you to guess his feelings when he says this. What do you think his feelings might be? Why do you think he might feel this way?

Activity 4

In the discussion, Graham uses certain expressions to ask people to be more precise — to clarify what they mean. Listen again and try to make a note of the questions he asks to try to make the following statements clearer.

Gerry:	(...) I think it'll be far too costly (...)
Graham:	..1..?
Gerry:	In terms of time and resources.
Graham:	..2..?
Gerry:	I don't think we've got the staff.
Graham:	..3..?
Shirley:	(...) it's what sort of relationship we want with an outside supplier (...)
Graham:	..4..?
Shirley:	If we invite people to tender (...) we might (...) or we might (...) or we may (...)
Graham:	..5..?

INPUT 2 Reading

In Input 1 speakers used language to express attitudes to future events or situations:

+++	Certain	It'll be too costly. We **definitely won't** be able to ...
++?	Probable	It'll **probably** be better to sub-contract ...
+??	Possible	We **might** produce certain parts ... We **may** be able to form a partnership.

Language was also used to express recommendations, requirements and obligations:

!	Recommending choosing the best option, describing requirements: That's what we **should** look at. The question is whether we **should** do it in-house. We've been **asked to** look at different ways of ...
!!	Expressing obligation, absolute necessity: We **must** be careful to get the right sort of agreements.

Activity 1

Read the following extract from an 'invitation to tender' document which was drawn up after the Input 1 meeting. What is the writer's attitude about the items in Figure 7.1 on page 74? Use the symbols from the tables above (+ + +, + +?, +??, !, !!) to complete the table in Figure 7.1. Some of it has been completed for you.

Suppliers are asked to submit proposals for the production of a system which must be able to capture data efficiently in an acceptable machine-readable form. Both the functions of the system and the method of operation must be described fully in the proposal.

Potential suppliers are asked to complete the questionnaire in Section 7 of this document. The proposal and completed questionnaire should be submitted no later than July 31.

Suppliers should state clearly the nature of the business relationship that they wish to establish with Inter-Tran. This statement must identify the contributions of both the supplier and Inter-Tran. It must also specify in detail the proposed ownership, copyright, selling rights and marketing rights of any hardware or software which is used in or produced by the system.

The select supplier(s) will then be asked to produce a 50-page sample of the output from the proposed system. This sample will be distributed to end users to obtain feedback on proposed layouts.

The initial phase of the project will probably take at least 3 years and the secondary phase may take as much as a further 5. Suppliers must therefore be able to provide written guarantees of their long-term commitment to the project.

To minimise the effect of problems which may occur following the implementation of any phase, support staff should be available on the telephone at any time during normal working hours.

. . . . .	1	Efficient capture of data in machine-readable form
!!	2	Full description of system functions and operational methods
. . . . .	3	Completion of questionnaire
. . . . .	4	Submission of proposal and questionnaire by July 31
!	5	Clear statement of proposed business relationship
. . . . .	6	Identification of contribution of supplier and Inter-Tran
. . . . .	7	Detailed specification of ownership, copyright, etc.
. . . . .	8	Production of 50-page output sample
. . . . .	9	Distribution of output sample to end users
. . . . .	10	3-year timescale for phase 1
. . . . .	11	5-year timescale for phase 2
. . . . .	12	Provision of written guarantees of commitment
. . . . .	13	Occurrence of post-implementation problems
. . . . .	14	Availability of support staff

Figure 7.1

Activity 2

Use verbs from the text and nouns from Figure 7.1 to complete the following table.

Verb	Noun
capture	1
describe	2
complete	3
submit	4
state	5
6	identification
7	specification
8	production
9	distribution
10	provision
11	occurrence

LANGUAGE PRACTICE

The following memo deals with response time problems in a large installation.

Activity 1

Use words from the box below to complete the text. Where you see a symbol in the text, choose an 'attitude verb'; where you see a number, choose the correct form of an 'action verb' (for example 'submit' or 'be submitted'). You can use the same verb more than once.

Attitude verbs	Action verbs	
will	submit	solve
will probably	be	monitor
should	continue	delay
are asked to	cause	decrease
might	note	apply
must	review	avoid

!	= requirement/strong recommendation
!!	= obligation/absolute necessity
+ + +	= certain future event/situation
+ +?	= probable future event/situation
+??	= possible future event/situation

The changeover to the new computer has not solved the problems of slow response times for the user department during peak business hours. Rebecca [+ + +] therefore ..1.. to work with the supplier's engineers and we hope that the problem [+ + +] soon ..2..

In the meantime, staff in the Data Processing Existing Systems and New Systems areas [!] ..3.. the following restrictions on job submission between the peak business periods of 9.30 to 12.30 and 14.00 to 15.30.

1 Class A batch production job [!!] not ..4.. in the morning period and [!] only ..5.. during the afternoon period with project leader approval.

2 Class H batch production jobs [!!] not ..6.. during either of these periods under any circumstances.

3 Test jobs [!!] not ..7.. during the morning period and staff [!] ..8.. the afternoon peak period wherever possible.

Point 3 above [+ + +] not ..9.. to staff who are working in project team T6 where restrictions [+??] ..10.. the high priority MX system.

Business enquiries are always high at this time of year and pressure on the system [+ + +] definitely not ..11.. before the Budget at the beginning of next week. The situation [+ + +] ..12.. two days after the Budget when we [+ +?] ..13.. able to lift the afternoon restrictions. Meanwhile, project leaders [!] ..14.. the effect of these restrictions and report any problems which they [+??] ..15...

DEVELOPMENT 1 Listening

Find the recording for Unit 7, Development 1. Maurice Damoiseau is phoning the Inter Accident Insurance Company.

Activity 1

As you listen try to make a note of the essential information. Use the prompts and table below to help you.

1 The extension number that he wants: .....
2 The person who answers: .....
3 The person that Maurice wants to speak to: .....
4 The department that he wants: .....
5 The person who answers in the department that he wants: .....
6 The reason why he's phoning: .....

	possible	probable	certain/impossible
7 Arrival in time for the meeting	☐	☐	☐
8 One hour longer to wait	☐	☐	☐
9 More than an hour longer to wait	☐	☐	☐
10 Arrival at about midday	☐	☐	☐

11 Maurice's suggestions: .....
12 Paula's offer: .....
13 The reason why her offer is not necessary: .....

Activity 2

Try to complete the following telephone conversation. If you want, listen to the recording again and use the expression you hear on the tape.

	S:	Future Solutions, good morning.
1	G:	_____, _____ _____ _____ _____ Leif Anderson in Information Services, please.
2	S:	_____ _____ line, please. Trying to connect you.
3	K:	Information Services, Kristina Korczinski _____.
4/5	G:	Hello, _____ _____ Gabriella Rossi. _____ _____ _____ _____ Leif Anderson please?
6 7/8 9	K:	I'm sorry, they've put you _____ _____ the wrong extension. _____ _____ just hold the _____ a second and I'll ask the switchboard to _____ _____ through.
	S:	Switchboard.
10	K:	Hello, could you transfer this call to _____ 548 please.
	L:	Information Services, Anderson speaking.
11	G:	Hello, _____ _____ you, Leif? It's Gabriella.
12	L:	_____. I wasn't expecting you to call. Problems?
	G:	Yes, I'm afraid I have to ......

Activity 3

What do you think Gabriella might have to do? What do you think the problem might be? Discuss with your colleague(s).

DEVELOPMENT 2   Telephone Practice

Work with a colleague. Appendix A and Appendix B in the back of the book contain information for two people, A and B. Decide with your partner who is who. Look at the informtion for Unit 7 for your role only in the appropriate Appendix and follow the instructions there.

LANGUAGE SUMMARY

Sentence types

We **should do** it ourselves.
We **must be** careful.
It**'ll be** too costly.
We **might produce** certain parts ourselves.
We **may form** some sort of partnership.

The sample **will be distributed** *to end users.*
The proposal **should be submitted** *not later than 31 July.*
The functions **must be described** *fully.*
Some equipment **will** *only* **be used** *in the first stages.*

It'll *probably* **be** better.
We *probably* **won't need** it.
It'll *definitely* **be** cheaper.
It *definitely* **won't be** cheaper.

Useful expressions

Is it feasible to ... (do it ourselves)?
I think it's out of the question.
In what way exactly?
There's no way we can ... (do the two things at the same time).
... a whole range of ... (possibilities).
(Gerry and I have) ... come up with a few ideas.
This is .... (Mr X) ... from ... (Kodak, Paris).
Hello / Good morning / Good afternoon, ... (Diane Bateson) .... speaking.
{Hold the line, please / One moment please}
A: Is that .... (Patricia Ross)? B: Speaking.
Would you like to leave a message?
I wonder if it might be better to ... (postpone the meeting)?
Thank you very much, but that won't be necessary.
Oh, I see.
I'll make sure ... (Ms Daniels gets the message).
Thank you for ringing.

Could I speak to ... (Customer services / Alan / someone who deals with X) ..., please?

Could you {put me through to / give me} ... (extension 484 / the Marketing Department) ..., please?

I'm afraid ... (Patricia's) ... not here at the moment. Can I take a message?

UNIT 8 Preliminary design

INPUT 1 Reading

The following minutes were taken from a meeting at a large publishing company in the initial phase of development of a large new system for computerising an English language dictionary.

Activity 1

When people report what was said in a meeting, the form of the verb often changes. It moves back into the 'past' *form* even when the *function* may still be 'present', or the 'future in the past' *form* even when the *function* may still be 'future'. Some verbs such as *might* and *may* do not change between the reported form and the real form.

Read the text and then try to choose suitable forms of the missing verbs to complete the extracts from the conversations which actually took place in the meeting.

1 Project Manager's report

The following points arose:

- Peter Wellings reported that a photographer had taken a series of photographs of the Computer Group and its equipment at Head Office. He added that he would be discussing internal pubicity for the project with Geraldine Rieux.
- Roland Carlsson mentioned that we had two videos about the dictionary which might be useful for publicity purposes.

2 Computer Group Manager's report

Discussion centred on:

- *Program support*: Geraldine Rieux asked whether the necessary level of support could be provided when the external consultants have gone. The Computer Group were confident that this could be done.

- *Performance*: Geraldine Rieux asked whether performance of the system, when in production, would be covered by a Service Level agreement. Adrian Prentice confirmed that it would.

- *Configuration size*: Geraldine Rieux enquired whether the Computer Group was confident that the capacity of the configuration would be adequate for the project and whether it would be confirmed prior to production. Adrian Prentice said that the manufacturer's experts had been consulted. Their advice, together with the Computer Group's own evaluation of requirements, led him to believe that the planned configuration would be adequate. He added however, that they would be monitoring it as the project progressed and agreed that it would need to be confirmed before production started.

- *Beyond Phase 1*: Brigitte Meadows wondered whether the restriction of the Computer Group to Phase 1 activities might be detrimental to the long-term future of the new dictionary. Tony Banks replied that management was very conscious of the need to plan for future phases. However, he reaffirmed that Phase 1 was currently of paramount importance and that Computer Group activities must be limited to Phase 1 only for the time being.

3 Next phase review

The next phase review will be held on Thursday 3 July in the Main Conference Room at 11.00 a.m. The meeting was reminded that Adrian Prentice would be leaving on 15 July and that Christine McDonnell would be taking over the managership of the Computer Group.

The following sentences are extracts of what was said in the actual meeting to produce the minutes above. Try to complete them from what you have read. For example: 1 = has taken, 2 = will be discussing

PW: On the question of publicity, a photographer ..1.. some photographs of the Computer Group people and the equipment we've got here. I ..2.. internal publicity for the project with Geraldine Rieux.

RC: Did you know that we ..3.. two videos about the dictionary which ..4.. useful for publicity purposes?

GR: One thing I'd like to know is whether you think you ..5.. the necessary support after the external consultants have finished?

AP: I'm quite sure we ..6... There shouldn't be any problem on that.

GR: But when the system is up and running, ..(7).. it ..7.. by a Service Level agreement?

AP: Yes, it ..8...

GR: Just one more point. What about the capacity? ..9.. you sure that the configuration capacity ..10.. adequate for the project?

AP: Well, we ..11.. manufacturer's experts. If we take their advice together with our own findings I've got no reason to believe that the capacity .(12). not ..12.. high enough. But in any case, we ..13.. it as the project ..14.. and we ..15.. to confirm it before production ..16..

BM: I ..17.. whether limiting the Computer Group to Phase 1 activities ..18.. a disadvantage in the long term.

TB: Well we ..19.. very conscious of the need to plan for future phases, but for the moment our main priority ..20.. Phase 1 and we ..21.. ourselves to that.

RC: The next phase review ..22.. on Thursday, the third of July in the Main Conference Room. Can I just remind you all that Adrian Prentice ..23.. on July the fifteenth and Christine McDonnell ..24.. as manager of the Computer Group.

Activity 2

Look through the text and find as many words as you can which are used instead of:

(a) to ask

(b) to say

INPUT 2   Listening

Find the recording for Unit 8, Input 2. The conversation takes place in a large insurance company.

Activity 1

As you listen try to make a note of numbers and codes that you hear. Use the prompts below to help you. If you miss any of the numbers, be ready to ask your teacher to repeat them after the recording. The conversation contains examples of how to ask for repetition.

1 The person who answers Gerry's call: .....
2 Gerry's own extension number: .....
3 The first source code he mentions: .....
4 The system he wants to access: .....
5 The other two source codes he mentions: .....
6 The two terminal numbers he wants to use: .....

7 The identification numbers of the adjustment factors: .....
8 The new values of the two factors: .....
9 The file John's working with: .....
10 The module the change affects: .....
11 The deadline for the Q3 and Q4 changes: .....
12 The time the conversation takes place: .....

Now ask for any you missed.

Activity 2

Did you get the full names of the three people? Ask your teacher to repeat them and make sure you can spell them correctly! ('How do you spell ...?')

1 _____ _____
2 _____ _____
3 _____ _____

Activity 3

The three people you heard on the tape used different ways of checking information and different ways of asking the others to repeat things. Listen to the recording again and try to answer the following questions by noting down the exact words that people used.

1 What did John say to Gerry when he wanted him to repeat his extension number?
2 What did Sally say to check the first source code?
3 What did she say to Gerry to get him to repeat the first terminal number?
4 How did she ask him to repeat the value of the second factor?
5 What did she say to check the sign?
6 How did John get Sally to remind him of the module number?

LANGUAGE PRACTICE

Section 1

When you need to ask for repetition, you can often use a question word such as *who, when, which, where* and then *did you say*. For example, you might miss some of the information in the sentence:

The Norsk Data rep, Torill Asplund, will be at the meeting in Hamburg at 2 o'clock on Friday afternoon.

Sorry, who   did you say?
*   when*
*   where*
*   what time*
*   which company*
*   which meeting*
*   which day*

In Input 1 Activity 1 we saw how the form of the verb often changes when we report things; this often happens when we ask for repetition if we need more information than in the above examples. For example, if you miss part of her name or her job, you need to be more specific:

Sorry, what did you say   her second name is/was?
*   her job is/was?*

Or you can say:

Sorry, who did you say will/would be there?

Sometimes you need to be specific to avoid confusion. For example:

Paul's going on the 14.25 and Paula's leaving on the 15.10.

It is not clear enough to say *Who did you say?* or *Which train did you say?* You need to be more specific:

Who did you say was going on the 14.25?
Which train did you say Paula was catching?

Activity

Now try to form a question in each of the following dialogues so that you get the missing information which is indicated by (?).

1 A: The Q3 factors are stored on the (?) file.

   B: Sorry, ...?

   A: J6.

2 A: Give Linda (?) a ring in the Purchasing Department. She should be able to tell you.
   B: Sorry, ...?
   A: Pankowski.

3 A: The times have been changed. The Group Leaders' meeting's at 2.30 and the (?) meeting's at 4.30.
   B: Sorry, ...?
   A: The steering committee.

4 A: Wakeel will be responsible for the on-line part of the system and (?) will be looking after the batch side of things.
   B: Sorry, ...?
   A: Tchen.

5 A: Phone Andy Barlow in Network Control and ask him what's happening, will you. He's on extension (?).
   B: Sorry, ...?
   A: 593.

Section 2

We can use the verb *to tell*, followed by a person, when people:

- talk about **giving information** to someone:

    'His name is Andrew'
        She told them his name.

    'She's coming tomorrow'
        He told his boss (that) she was coming tomorrow.

- talk about **giving instructions or orders** to someone.

    'Take a backup'
        I told you to take a backup.

    'Don't cancel the job'
        She told the operator not to cancel the job.

We can use the verb *to ask*, followed by a person, when people:

- talk about **requesting information** from someone:

    'When will you arrive?'
        I asked her when she would arrive.

    'Can you come?'
        I asked him whether he could come.

- talk about **requesting action** from someone:

   'Could you confirm it in writing?'
   Sally asked Gerry to confirm the change in writing.

   'I'd like you to make a couple of changes if you could?'
   Gerry asked Sally to make a couple of changes.

We often use *to ask* and *to tell* when we want to leave a message for someone. Look at the examples. The sentences on the left are what you want to say to John himself, but when you phone him, he isn't there, so you use the words on the right:

Giving information:

We've restored the file.	Could you tell him (that) we've restored the file?

Giving instructions:

Use terminal 426.	Can you tell him to use terminal 426?

Requesting information:

Have you contacted Mike Farlow?	Could you ask him whether he's contacted Mike Farlow?

Requesting action:

Could you ring Jenny?	Can you ask him to ring Jenny?

Activity

Now imagine you want to get the following messages to the people in brackets below, but someone else answers the phone. What do you say?

1 (→ Margaret)
   I've sent her a letter.

2 (→ Mr Peterson)
   Can he send me a copy of the report?

3 (→ Allan)
   Don't put the changes in today.

4 (→ Mrs Tarrant)
   Has she sent the test data yet?

5 (→ Anna and Paul)
   The meeting's in room B13.
   Can they bring an overhead projector?
   Is the Apple rep staying for lunch?
   Don't be late!

86 English for Information Systems

DEVELOPMENT 1 Listening

Find the recording for Unit 8, Development 1. The telephone conversation you will hear takes place within the offices of a large travel organisation where two people are trying to arrange a meeting with each other.

Activity 1

As you listen try to make a note of the names and departments of the people involved in the call and fill in as many details as possible in their respective diaries. Today is Wednesday.

Person 1
Name: .....
Department: .....

	Monday	Tuesday	Wednesday (today)	Thursday	Friday
	Monday	Tuesday	Wednesday	Thursday	Friday

Person 2
Name: .....
Department: .....

	Monday	Tuesday	Wednesday (today)	Thursday	Friday
	Monday	Tuesday	Wednesday	Thursday	Friday

Activity 2

Now ask your teacher or your colleague(s) for any information you missed. For example:

Where did he/she say he/she was going on ???day?

What time did he/she say he/she would be free on ???day? etc.

Did you get the full names of the two people? Ask your teacher to repeat them and make sure you can spell them correctly!

Activity 3

Complete the following with suitable phrases. Use the tapescript to help you.

A: Hello Birgitta. Sean here.

B: Hello Sean. What can I ..1..?

A: ..2.. if we could get together sometime tomorrow to talk about the file access security arrangements? ..3.. tomorrow morning.

B: No, sorry ..4.. I won't be here tomorrow morning ..5.. tomorrow afternoon?
A: Well, I've got a meeting from 2.00 till 3.00, but ..6.. after 3.00 ..7.. me fine.
B: ..8.. half past three, then ..9.. come up to your office?
A: Fine.
B: Right. Half past three in your office, then. See you tomorrow.
A: ..10..

DEVELOPMENT 2 Arranging an Appointment

Work with a colleague. Appendix A and Appendix B in the back of the book contain information for two people, A and B. Decide with your partner who is who. Look at the information for Unit 8 for your role only in the appropriate Appendix and follow the instructions there.

LANGUAGE SUMMARY

Sentence types

The manager	reported said mentioned **was** confident **was** sure replied confirmed reaffirmed	that the project **was** on schedule.

The manager	asked enquired wondered **was not** sure	whether the project **was** on schedule.

I told They **asked**					
They They	**didn't**	**ask** **tell**	her the boss	to not to	come.
Could you **tell** **Can** you **ask**					

| I told
I didn't tell
———————
Could you **tell** | him
the boss | that | the report **was finished.**
it **was** important. |

| I asked
I didn't ask
———————
Could you **ask** | him
the boss | whether | the report **was finished.**
it **was** important.
———————
he's coming.
the tape **has arrived.** |

Useful expressions

On the question of ... (X)
One thing I'd like to know is whether ... (you think we've got enough)?
I'm quite sure we ... (have).
(When the system is) ... up and running.
Just one more point.
Can I just remind you that ... (the meeting starts at 10 a.m.)?
Could you ask ... (her) ... to ring me?
What can I do for you?
Could you confirm it in writing?
By the way ... (have you altered the Q3 factors)?
I'll give you a ring.
I'm ringing about ... (the siting of the new equipment).
I wonder if we could ... (have a chat)?

(Thursday / 2 o'clock) ... would be O.K.
(Thursday / 2 o'clock) ... would suit me.
Any time after ... (half past one).
That suits me fine.
Let's say ... (2 o'clock).
Shall we say ... (Wednesday) ... then?
I look forward to seeing you.

Special note

10 a.m. means *10 o'clock in the morning.*

2 p.m./8 p.m. means *2/8 o'clock in the afternoon/evening*

UNIT 9 System development

INPUT 1 Reading

The following extract is from a report by George Meadows, the Data Processing Manager of a fairly small company in the carpet wholesale business. George compares the pros and cons of using a LAN (Local Area Network) or their existing PABX (Private Automatic Branch Exchange) to handle their data communications. Only the 'Conclusions' of the report are given below. The report is from September 1986.

Activity 1

Try to complete the Table 9.1 with the main advantages and disadvantages that George mentions for the two options.

Advantages	Disadvantages
PABX	(none mentioned)
LAN	

Table 9.1

The overall conclusion was that at this particular point in time, the use of the recently installed PABX to handle our data communications would appear to offer a more satisfactory solution than the installation of a LAN. The reasons for this recommendation are as follows.

Although the bulk of the company's data communication requirements are within Head Office, 40% of data traffic occurs within or between the Dundee and Falkirk sites or between those sites and Head Office. The installation of a LAN would not have any effect on that traffic because the distances involved are too great for a LAN to be used.

Despite the fact that 60% of traffic is local to users on the Head Office site the PABX has more than enough capacity to meet needs in the foreseeable future.

While it is certainly true that a LAN would give faster data transfer rates than the PABX, user department feedback indicates that service is satisfactory; response times are not seen to be a problem. Faster data handling would therefore not seem to be in demand.

Installing a LAN would mean significant extra expense in terms of the 'black boxes' that would enable our existing pieces of equipment to communicate with each other. Furthermore, because of the diversity of the equipment which we use, it would be impossible to have a closed system (where the equipment in the network accepts only one manufacturer's equipment). An open system would be necessary and this would be even more expensive.

In addition to the above hardware costs, substantial extra cable installation costs would be incurred whereas a significant amount of cabling for use with the PABX is already in place. The existing network can consequently be expanded more cheaply than with a LAN.

Finally, PABX technology is tried and tested whereas LAN technology presents problems for the inexperienced. These problems are partly due to the lack of widely accepted standards among the different manufacturers. Moreover, we have staff who are familiar with the use of the PABX, but the installation of a LAN would entail extra training costs for network control personnel.

Therefore, taken as a whole, these factors seem to indicate that it would not be worthwhile installing a LAN in the near future since our needs can be adequately met at far less expense. However, the company should continue to monitor developments in LAN technology as it is a rapidly developing field. Future changes may make the installation of a LAN more cost beneficial than it is at present.

Activity 2

Why does George think it would be more expensive to install a LAN?
(Note how George uses the word would *when he explains the extra expense that they* would have *if they installed a LAN.)*

Activity 3

George uses a lot of words which show the connections between different ideas — between parts of sentences, between one sentence and another, or between one paragraph and another.

(a) Showing contrast or difference between two ideas:

PABX technology is tried and tested *whereas* LAN technology presents problems for the inexperienced.

(b) Giving reasons or describing cause/effect connections:

The installation of a LAN would not have any effect on that traffic *because* the distances involved are too great for a LAN to be used.

(c) Giving another, or extra, piece of information:

Finally, PABX technology is tried and tested.

Look through the text again and try to find the sentences where these types of connections are made. Then list the words which are used to make the connection clear under the following headings.

(a) Contrast/difference

(b) Reason; cause−effect

(c) Adding information

You will need to use these words in an exercise in Development 2; take notice of:

- their position
- whether they need a comma before or after them
- whether they link ideas in one sentence or between two sentences.

Activity 4

Try to find other words which would give a similar meaning to the ones in italics in the following phrases from the passage (do not use a dictionary — if you don't understand a word, try to guess the meaning from the context).

1 The *overall* conclusion was that (first paragraph)
2 *the bulk* of the company's data communication requirements (second paragraph)
3 because of the *diversity* of equipment (fifth paragraph)
4 The installation of a LAN would *entail* extra training costs (next to last paragraph/last paragraph but one)

INPUT 2 Listening

Find the recording for Unit 9, Input 2. The conversation takes place in the same medium-sized carpet wholesale company as in Unit 9, Input 1. The manager (George) who wrote the report about the company's data network needs has left the company and has been replaced by Anne Murdoch. In this extract from a management meeting you will hear Anne discussing the network needs with Barry Johnstone, the General Manager, and Alistair Wallace, the Finance Manager. (Barry is the first person you hear).

Activity 1

Make sure you understand the following sentences. Then, as you listen try to choose the most accurate sentence from each of the following groups.

1. (a) George feels that they should discuss the network problem again.
   (b) George is convinced that they should use their PABX.
   (c) George is sure that installing a LAN would be worth it.
2. (a) Anne is in complete agreement with Alistair.
   (b) Anne doesn't entirely agree with Alistair.
   (c) Anne doesn't agree with Alistair at all.
3. (a) Anne has been with the company for six years.
   (b) It only took George four months to find out about the company's needs.
   (c) Anne has been with the company for four months.
4. (a) Anne agrees that George knew a lot about the company.
   (b) Anne is not so sure that George was good at his job.
   (c) Anne doesn't go along with the view that George knew a lot about the company.
5. (a) The way Anne sees it, the merger with Komfy Karpets means that a LAN would be more worthwhile.
   (b) As far as Alistair is concerned, the merger is another reason why they should use their PABX.
   (c) In Anne's opinion it would now be much cheaper to install a LAN.
6. When Anne first mentions the link-up between four local sites:
   (a) Barry doesn't follow Anne's reasoning.
   (b) Barry realises Anne is right.
   (c) Barry feels they're doing things in the wrong order.
7. When Anne talks about whether or not they should stick to their previous decision:
   (a) Barry doesn't suppose a LAN is now a sensible option.
   (b) Barry is inclined to agree provided that they keep an open mind.
   (c) Barry is inclined to disagree unless they reject the idea of a LAN.
8. After hearing the opinions of the others:
   (a) Alistair thinks Anne may be right.
   (b) Alistair feels the discussion has gone far enough.
   (c) Alistair thinks Anne is talking rubbish.

Activity 2

Listen to the discussion again and try to make a note of the expressions that are suggested by the pictures below. What do they mean?

Activity 3

Look at the tapescript in the back of the book. Pick out the expressions that people used in the dialogue to:

1 Express agreement.

2 Express disagreement.

3 Introduce an opinion without showing agreement or disagreement.

Make a note of the expressions so that you can use them yourself.

LANGUAGE PRACTICE

Activity

In Input 1, Activity 3, you made a list of words which connected ideas together. Try to use words from this list to complete the following sentences which report what happened in the meeting in Input 2.

..1.. the idea of using a LAN had been rejected only six months previously, Anne said she wanted to discuss the question again.

Alistair didn't want to discuss it again ..2.. he thought that they should stick to the previous decision.

Anne thought George's arguments had been valid six months ago. ..3.., she wasn't so sure now that the company had merged with Komfy Karpets ..4.., she pointed out that the company was expanding much more now.

..5.. George was with the company for a long time, Alistair felt that he was in a better position to judge the company's needs, ..6.. Anne had only been with the company for four months.

..7.. Barry thought that Anne was right to raise the problem again, he wasn't so sure that they were getting their priorities right. He thought that they were talking about **how** to link the sites together ..8.. they should have been talking about **why** they need to link them together.

At the beginning of the meeting Alistair was quite sure that they should not discuss the issue again ..9.. at the end he was less sure. ..10.. Barry was his boss, maybe he'd changed his mind ..11.. he didn't want to seem to disagree with him. ..12.., perhaps it was more ..13.. Anne's arguments.

9 System development

DEVELOPMENT 1 Listening

Find the cassette recording for Unit 9, Development 1. The conversation you will hear takes place in a small company. The first person, Cathy, has a problem with a new software package. She knows that a colleague, Steve, is familiar with the package, so she goes to ask him for some help.

Activity 1

Look at the following questions and try to answer them as you listen.

1 What sort of software package does Cathy have a problem with?
2 What type of file has she created?
3 What kind of document does she want to use the file with?
4 Which command is used to save the kind of file she created?
5 After the LOAD FORMAT command, which directory does the program look in?
6 To load a format file, what do you include with the filename if the format file is in another directory?
7 How could she put the format file into directory REPORTS?
8 What is the full filename of the file they copy?

Activity 2

Look at the following:

　　　Cathy has a problem. She goes to talk to Steve. She explains the problem.

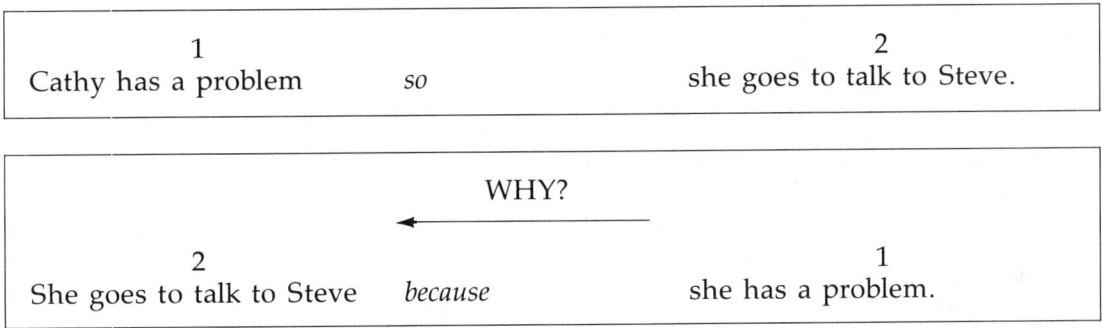

Continued overleaf

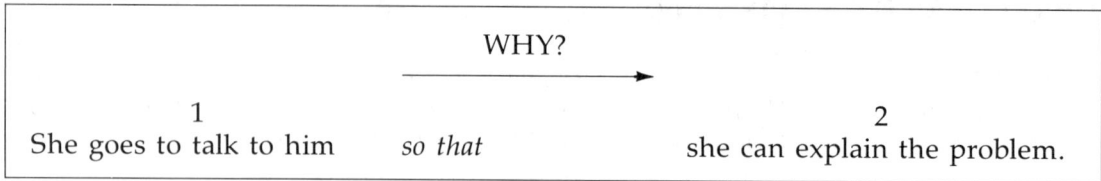

Now complete the sentence below. Use so, so that *or* because.

1 Cathy wants to create a new format file ..... she can use standard paragraph formats in her reports.
2 The program cannot find the new format file ..... she cannot use the new formats.
3 She can't use the new formats ..... the program cannot find the new format file.
4 It cannot find the new file ..... it is in the wrong directory.
5 The SAVE FORMAT command normally puts the format file in the current working directory ..... it can attach it to the same document later.
6 The format file was in a different directory, ... she needed to specify the directory path in the filename.

Activity 3

Listen to the conversation again, and complete the tasks below.

1 Steve asks Cathy why she has come to see him. What does he say?
2 Cathy asks Steve if he has time to help her. What does she say?
3 Steve asks Cathy what the problem is. What does he say?
4 Find two expressions which mean 'Do you understand?'
   (a) .....
   (b) .....
5 Complete the expressions when Steve uses 'let's'
   (a) Let's ..... and the current directory is, for instance, USER/CATHY/LETTERS.
   (b) Let's ..... we do it right.
   (c) Let's ..... we can load it.

DEVELOPMENT 2   Informal Discussion

Discuss one or more of the following:

1 Computer people deliberately use jargon to make users feel insecure.

2 The best systems analysts are people who move into computing from a user department.

3 The only reason why managers of computing departments do not want users to choose their own equipment and software packages is that they are afraid of losing their own little empires.

4 One of the biggest problems with packaged software is that purchasers never give the staff who use it sufficient training — they just sit them at a terminal, tell them to read the manual and expect to see benefits immediately.

5 Computers always deskill the jobs which surround the applications that they are used in.

6 With a lot of software packages, people start spending their time inefficiently doing jobs which are other people's specialisms. With desk top publishing, editors start playing about with design and typesetting; with CAD/CAM, engineers start doing the job of draughtsmen; with word processing, people do their own typing when they should leave it to their typists.

LANGUAGE SUMMARY

Sentence types

If you rename the file it **puts** it in the current directory.
If it can't find the file it **gives** a 'filename not found' message.

It **saves** the formats *so that you can use them again later.*
I **need** a new format file *so that I can change the data display.*

I **can't access** the database *because it can't find my file.*
It **can't find** the file *because it's in the wrong directory.*

When you create a new format file you **use** the SF command.
When you use the SF command it **saves** the new formats.

Useful expressions

The overall conclusion was that ...
At this particular point in time ...
in the foreseeable future.
tried and tested (equipment/methods, etc.).
Taken as a whole ... (these factors indicate that ...).
Why do you think we need to ... (do that)?
It depends what you mean.
With all due respect ...
If I remember rightly ...
Where do we go from here?
What can I do for you?
Could you spare a minute, please?
..., you mean? (e.g. C-A-T, you mean?)
Do you mean ... (C-A-T)?
Alright? Right? OK? Are you with me? = Do you understand?
Let's say you ... = For example, you ...
Let's see if ... (we can do it/it works/it's the right disk).
Let me make sure I can ... (do it).
Let's make sure we can ... (do it).

UNIT 10 System production planning

INPUT 1 Listening

Find the recording for Unit 10, Input 1. The conversation takes place between three members of a computer services department who are working on a new system for the accounts department which combines on-line data entry and enquiry facilities.

Activity 1

Each of the three people suggests different ways of breaking down the coding of the on-line system into subtasks. As you listen, try to summarise the stages which each of them proposes and try to make a note of any reasons they give. The first person to speak is Michelle, the Project Leader.

Michelle

    Step 1
    Step 2
    Reasons?

Jenny

    Step 1
    Step 2
    Reasons?

Mike

    Step 1
    Step 2
    Step 3
    Step 4
    Step 5
    Step 6
    Reasons?

Activity 2

If you were working on the project, which of the three alternatives do you think you would choose? Why? If you can't decide because you don't have enough information, what else would you need to know before you made a decision? Discuss with your colleagues.

Activity 3

The suggestions below are made by different people. Listen to the tape again in short sections and make a note of the way the speakers indicate that they are making a suggestion. Note the exact words they use to introduce the suggestions so that you can use them yourself. (The first one has been done as an example.)

1 Wait until Jenny gets here. → *Why don't we* (wait until Jenny gets here).
2 Do this in small stages. .....
3 Find out about problems with movements between screens. .....
4 Leave that for the moment. .....
5 Discuss it with Jenny as well. .....
6 Find out what she thinks about the timescales first. .....
7 Discuss the other idea at the same time. .....
8 Go away and come back later. .....
9 Code all the screen layouts first and then do the processing later. .....
10 Do what Mike says. .....
11 Start by doing a skeleton system. .....

Activity 4

Look at the tapescript. How many more suggestions can you find after number 11 above? What are they and how are they introduced?

INPUT 2 Reading

The following report is an extract from a technical discussion document on the relative merits of two different cabling systems.

It is a difficult text, so concentrate on developing the reading skill of understanding the main ideas and the connections between them; do not worry if you cannot understand every word. (If language connected with networks is important to you, you will also find the vocabulary very useful.)

Activity 1

Complete the table below with the advantages and disadvantages of the two systems for this company as presented by the writer.

	Advantages	Disadvantages
coaxial cabling		
IBM system		

Background

The ratio of terminals to staff will continue to increase towards a one-to-one situation. A reliable system of cabling is therefore needed that will allow rapid, flexible equipment reconfiguration at low cost whenever required.

Realistically, the only two sensible alternatives which exist for us are a coaxial cabling system or the IBM cabling system.

Briefly, a coaxial system consists basically of lengths of wire between terminals and a mainframe control unit. It can handle dumb VDUs and printers but is not suitable for personal computers, asynchronous printers or certain types of equipment expected in the marketplace in the future. Neither is it suitable for connecting computers together to store or share information. Each new facility has to be directly cabled and a specific port has to be reserved at all times on a control unit of the mainframe computer for each cabled terminal.

The IBM system is more like a flexible switchboard with inbuilt fail-safe facilities. It is wired on a loop basis with outlet sockets at locations where computing facilities are required. Any type of equipment can be connected or disconnected with minimal involvement. The facility itself is then connected to a control unit of the mainframe computer.

As there are likely to be many plug compatible suppliers trading upon the market direction established by IBM, the resultant competition is likely to force down the price of hardware and software available for attachment to the cabling system.

Justification at Head Office

In the long term it is felt that the IBM system will provide a cheaper and more flexible solution.

Even if coaxial cable were employed initially the proliferation of cables and the complexity of maintaining them at their connecting points would force rationalisation to a better system within very few years.

The cost of coaxial removal and replacement in a functioning and occupied building would be something like four times the cost of installing the IBM cabling system at the outset.

The initial saving on coaxial cable installation would therefore only be temporary and would be more than lost on replacement. Moreover, during its life, significant costs would be incurred in the labour of network control staff and electricians (much of it at overtime rates) in setting up and changing facilities. Maintenance and upgrade costs will be much lower with the IBM cabling system.

From a business viewpoint, the IBM solution will give greater flexibility in the different items of equipment which can be plugged in. A prime example is the IBM PC which has a 'twisted pair' connection as opposed to the coaxial connection of dumb VDUs. Under the IBM cabling system the two will be interchangeable but would require separate cabling under the coaxial approach.

Conclusion

Comparative cost estimates indicate that if IBM cabling is used it will cost less than 2.5 times the cost of coaxial. Installing coaxial cabling in the new building would cost some £41 000 while the IBM system would be approximately £93 000. The extra cost of IBM cabling would therefore be £52 000. On that basis it is suggested that installation of IBM cabling at the outset will prove a sound investment.

Activity 2

Which product does the writer talk about most when using the following words:

(a) will: .....

(b) would: .....

Why? What does the use of these words communicate to the reader?

Activity 3

Look at these two pairs of sentences which describe the possible effects of certain actions:

A1 *If they install* the IBM cabling system the long-term costs **will be** lower.

A2 The long-term costs **will be** lower *if they install* the IBM cabling system.

B1 *If they installed* a coaxial cabling system the long-term costs **would be** higher.

B2 The long-term costs **would be** higher *if they installed* a coaxial cabling system.

These types of sentences are useful for connecting ideas together when you want to show the implications of actions. Now use the information from the Development text to complete the following sentences.

1 If they installed a coaxial cable and then found they had to replace it later .....
2 If the company continues to expand .....
3 The cost for the full building would be approximately £40 000 if .....
4 It will pay off in the long run if .....
5 A lot of expense would be incurred later if .....

LANGUAGE PRACTICE

Look at the following summary of the types of *if* sentences we can use with *might, will probably* and *will*. In the speaker's mind, the idea of finishing on schedule is very real, so the Present Tense of *finish* is used in the *if* half of the sentence.

| If we finish on schedule | I might take a week's holiday. you'll probably get promoted. the users will be very happy. |

The words *might, will probably* or *will* are chosen in the second part of the sentence to change how sure the speaker is about the future consequences.

Now look at the following summary of the types of *if* sentences we can use with *might, would probably* and *would*. In the following examples the idea of finishing on schedule is not such a real one, so the past form of the verb *finish* is used in the *if* half of the sentence. (But it is only the **form** of the verb that is **past** — the **idea** is still a **future possibility**.)

| If we finished on time | the boss might buy us a drink! the boss would probably die of shock! it would be the first time ever! |

In the second half of the sentences, *might* is still used when the speaker is not so sure about the possible result of the condition, but *would* is used instead of *will* in the second and third sentences.

Because you can change how strong the idea is, these types of sentences are all very useful when making suggestions. You can vary from very direct or positive:

If we do it that way it'll save time.

to less direct or more diplomatic:

I think the users might feel more involved if we did it that way.

English for Information Systems

Activity

In the following conversation, Joanne, Rick and Dan are discussing the timetable (Figure 10.1) for installing a system in a new office. Joanne is trying to suggest some changes to the timetable.

Try to complete the conversation by using the parts of sentences which are in the box opposite. Match the numbers and letters. For example, 1 = D ('... if Rick stays an extra week').

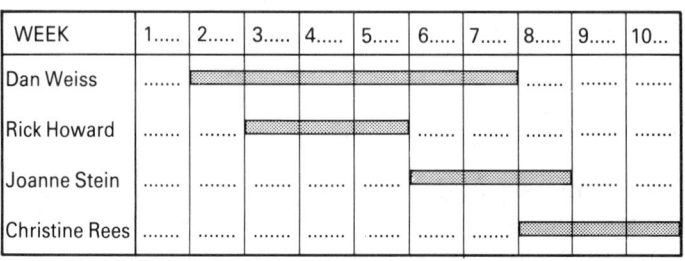

Figure 10.1

Joanne: It might be better (..1..).

Rick: I don't see why.

Joanne: Well, if you do (..2..).

Rick: I don't think my wife would like it (..3..).

Joanne: Well if I started my three weeks a week earlier (..4..).

Dan: No, I'm sorry. If you and Rick were both out there at the same time (..5..).

Joanne: If I promise not to touch you (..6..)?

Dan: I meant that if neither of you were at work here (..7..).

Joanne: I know what you meant; I was just joking.

Dan: In any case, if you moved your three weeks forward (..8..). Anyway, there's really no problem. I'll be there. If Thomas tells me everything that's relevant to your job (..9..).

Joanne: I still think it might be better (..10..). Will it cause problems back here (..11..)? If I do that (..12..).

Dan: OK. We'll do that (..13..).

A	it would give us problems with emergency cover
B	if you think it'll help
C	if I get there for the Friday of week 5
D	*if Rick stays an extra week*
E	it would probably cause problems back home
F	I'll pass the information on to you
G	your wife won't mind, will she, Rick?
H	there'll only be one day when we're both away from here
I	if I can talk to Rick first hand
J	if I stayed an extra week
K	it'd solve the problem, wouldn't it
L	it'll probably help me at the beginning of my stay
M	there wouldn't be anyone there when Christine arrived

DEVELOPMENT 1 Listening

Find the recording for Unit 10, Development 1. A project leader (Ian) in an international manufacturing company is describing the plan for installing hardware and software at a new plant in France. Although four other members of the project team are present (Thomas, Gerry, Julie and Christine) the only other person who speaks during the recording is Julie.

Activity 1

As you listen, mark on the chart in Figure 10.2 (on the next page) the times of the different activities and the periods when the different people are involved. Part of the chart has been completed for you. The conversation takes place in the UK office on the Monday of week 6.

ACTIVITIES	1	2	3	4	5	6	7	8	9	10	11	12	13	14	15	16	17	18	19	20
Power supply and cable planning				▓																
Equipment checking and shipping (Sweden) (UK) (West Germany)						▓														
Production plant equipment installation																				
System software installation																				
Pallet labelling microstation installation																				
Application software installation																				
System tuning																				
Training																				

PERSONNEL	1	2	3	4	5	6	7	8	9	10	11	12	13	14	15	16	17	18	19	20
Ian Watson				▓																
Thomas Patterson				▓																
Julie Wingard																				
Christine Long																				

Figure 10.2

Activity 2

Now imagine the date is exactly three weeks later — Monday at the start of week 9. Use your completed chart and the expressions of time in the box below to complete the following sentences spoken by Ian.

> during
> the week after
> a fortnight ago
> a fortnight later
> in the middle
> this week
>
> two weeks from today
> by the end of
> first two weeks
> last Friday
> next Monday

1 The equipment from Sweden was shipped ..ª.. and arrived at the French site at the beginning of last week. We finished checking the stuff from here ..ᵇ.. and it should arrive at the French site by the end of ..ᶜ...

2 I'm starting my first 3-week stint ..ª... Thomas is joining me ..ᵇ... I'm coming back home for a couple of weeks ..ᶜ.. of Thomas's stay. The pallet labelling micros will be installed ..ᵈ.. the first three weeks that Thomas is there.

3 The system software installation is due to start ..ª.. and should be finished ..ᵇ.. the following week.

4 Julie will now go out instead of Gerry ..ª.. Thomas gets back. Christine is the last person to go out. She's doing her user training sessions the ..ᵇ.. in May.

DEVELOPMENT 2 Informal Discussion

Think of two changes that you would like to make:

1 A change to the way that you have to do your job.
2 A change to the way your department or company is organised.

Prepare to describe the current situation, explaining why you think a change is necessary. Explain how you think the improvements could be made. Ask your colleagues for their opinions and alternative suggestions.

LANGUAGE SUMMARY

Sentence types

Type 1 condition

If the company installs a coaxial system it **will not be** as flexible.

If we install the IBM system it **will give** more flexibility.

It **will be** difficult to expand *if we install a coaxial system.*

We **won't have** as much flexibility *if we don't install the IBM system.*

Type 2 condition

If the company installed a coaxial system it **would not be** as flexible.

If we installed the IBM system it **would give** more flexibility.

It **would be** difficult to expand *if we installed a coaxial system.*

We **wouldn't have** as much flexibility *if we didn't install the IBM system.*

Useful expressions

bound to (used to express certainty)
    There are bound to be some problems.
    He's bound to arrive soon.

likely to (used to express probability)
    There are likely to be a lot of plug compatible suppliers.
    Competition is likely to force down the price of hardware.

worth
    it might be worth ... (looking at).
    it's not worth ... (spending any more time on this).

rather than
    (Let's do it now) ... rather than ... (later).

four times the cost ... (of X).
two and a half times the price ... (of X).

(It will) ... prove a sound investment.
        be a sound investment.

(Installation) ... is due to ... (start in week 12).
              is scheduled to ... (start in week 12).

We've set aside ... (2 weeks) ... for ... (X).
    allowed ... (2 weeks) ... for (X).

a one to one situation:
it's more like a ... (flexible switchboard).
a prime example.
in the long run = in the long term.
some sort of ... (prototype).
it's supposed to ... (be finished).
I'm not supposed to ... (tell you).
That's ... (Thomas's) ... pigeon = Thomas's responsibility.
I'll believe it when I see it.

UNIT 11 System production and testing

INPUT 1 Reading

The document in Figure 11.1 has been completed and submitted to a computer system in order to test some of the error message generation routines.

Activity 1

Look at the form and corresponding messages to see which items have been entered incorrectly; then use the extracts from the user manual to decide how you would enter the six items correctly on a new form.

Suppose that the transaction is for a cash payment of £600.00 per quarter, due on the last day of the appropriate months.

Message code	Message text	Corrected items
PE 413	INVALID OR MISSING START DATE	..1..
PE 416	INVALID ADDITIONAL BENEFITS INDICATOR	..2..
PE 418	INVALID OR MISSING PAYMENT TYPE	..3..
PE 419	INVALID OR MISSING PAYMENT FREQUENCY	..4..
PE 420	INVALID OR MISSING FIRST PAYMENT DATE	..5..
PE 427	INVALID OR MISSING EXPECTED PAYMENT AMOUNT	..6..

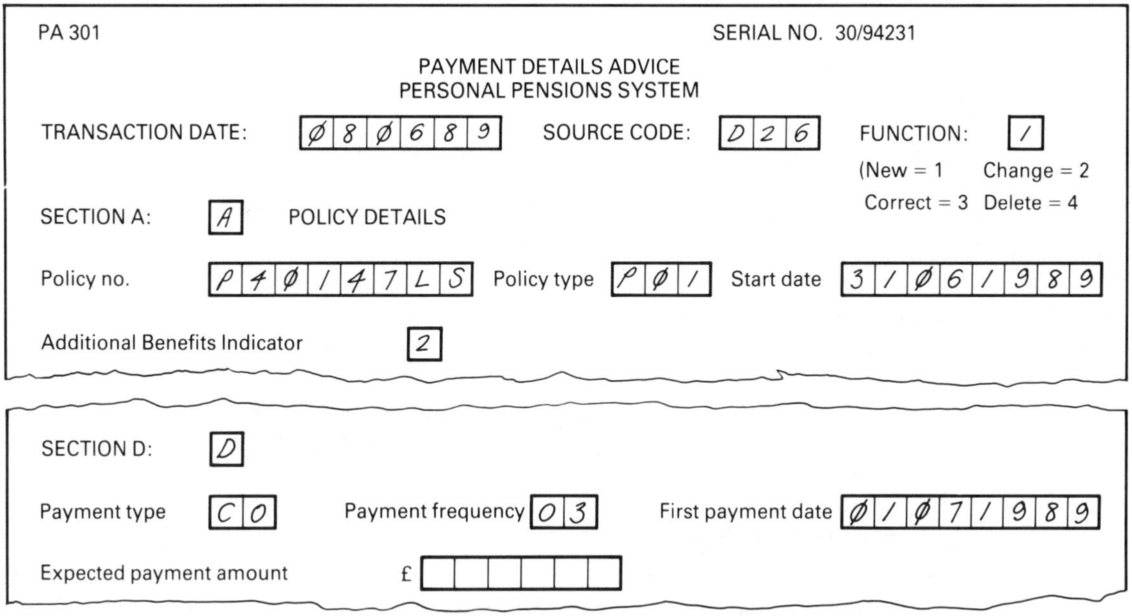

11 *System production and testing* 111

```
PA 301                                          SERIAL NO. 30/94231
                         PAYMENT DETAILS ADVICE
                         PERSONAL PENSIONS SYSTEM
TRANSACTION DATE:  |0|8|0|6|8|9|  SOURCE CODE: |D|2|6|  FUNCTION: |1|
                                                        (New = 1   Change = 2
SECTION A:    |A|    POLICY DETAILS                     Correct = 3  Delete = 4

Policy no.   |P|4|0|/|4|7|L|S|  Policy type |P|0|1|  Start date |3|/|0|6|/|9|8|9|

Additional Benefits Indicator   |2|


SECTION D:   |D|

Payment type  |C|0|   Payment frequency |0|3|   First payment date |0|/|0|7|/|9|8|9|

Expected payment amount    £ |_|_|_|_|_|_|
```

Figure 11.1

ERROR CODE PE 413 : INVALID OR MISSING START DATE

TYPE OF TRANSACTION:

Personal Pensions Payment Details advice (PA301)

REASON FOR ERROR:

The start date has been entered as an invalid date or the date which has been entered is earlier than the transaction date.

ACTION TAKEN BY THE COMPUTER SYSTEM:

Advice rejected.

ACTION REQUIRED:

Ascertain the correct date and submit a complete correct advice.

ERROR CODE PE 416 : INVALID ADDITIONAL BENEFITS INDICATOR

TYPE OF TRANSACTION:

Personal Pensions Payment Details advice (PA301)

REASON FOR ERROR:

Either 1 The indicator has been entered outside the permitted range of 1 to 6

or   2 The item has been entered for policy type P01 or P02.

ACTION TAKEN BY THE COMPUTER SYSTEM:

Advice rejected.

ACTION REQUIRED:

Ascertain the correct value and submit a complete correct advice.

ERROR CODE PE 418 : INVALID OR MISSING PAYMENT TYPE

TYPE OF TRANSACTION:

Personal Pensions Payment Details advice (PA301).

REASON FOR ERROR:

Either 1 An illegal payment type has been entered. The payment type can be blank (if not function NEW) or one of the following:
CA (Cash)
GI (Banker's Giro)
BO (Banker's Order)
DD (Direct Debit).

or 2 The item has not been entered for function NEW.

ACTION TAKEN BY THE COMPUTER SYSTEM:

Section of advice rejected.

ACTION REQUIRED:

Ascertain the correct value and submit a correct section of the advice with function NEW.

ERROR CODE PE 419 : INVALID OR MISSING PAYMENT FREQUENCY

TYPE OF TRANSACTION:

Personal Pensions Payment Details advice (PA301)

REASON FOR ERROR:

Either 1 An illegal payment frequency has been entered. The payment type can be blank (if not function NEW) or one of the following:

01 Annual
02 Half-yearly
04 Quarterly
12 Monthly

or 2 The item has not been entered for function NEW.

ACTION TAKEN BY THE COMPUTER SYSTEM:

Section of advice rejected.

ACTION REQUIRED:

Ascertain the correct value and submit a correct section of the advice with function NEW.

ERROR CODE PE 420 : INVALID OR MISSING FIRST PAYMENT DATE

TYPE OF TRANSACTION:

Personal Pensions Payment Details advice (PA301)

REASON FOR ERROR:

The first payment date has been entered as an invalid date or the date entered is later than the start date.

ACTION TAKEN BY THE COMPUTER SYSTEM:

Section of advice rejected.

ACTION REQUIRED:

Ascertain the correct value and submit a correct section of the advice with function NEW.

ERROR CODE PE 427 : INVALID OR MISSING EXPECTED PAYMENT AMOUNT

TYPE OF TRANSACTION:

Personal Pensions Payment Details advice (PA301)

REASON FOR ERROR:

    1   An illegal payment amount of less than 10 has been entered.

or 2   The item has not been entered for function NEW.

or 3   The item has been entered as non-numeric.

ACTION TAKEN BY THE COMPUTER SYSTEM:

Advice rejected.

ACTION REQUIRED:

Ascertain the correct value and submit a correct section of the advice with function NEW.

Activity 2

Look at the following extracts from the manual.

ACTION TAKEN: . . . . .

ADVICE REJECTED. ACTION REQUIRED: . . . . .

Very often, when making notes or writing brief instructions, people miss out certain parts of passive verbs and also often miss out which, that *or* who. *When words are combined like the three examples above, native speakers of English can usually reconstruct the sentence in their minds to get the correct information. Can you do the same? Pick the correct equivalent meanings from the possibilities on the next page.*

1 ACTION TAKEN: Section of advice rejected.
   (a) Action is taken.
   (b) Action has been taken.
   (c) Action which is taken.
   (d) Action which has been taken.

2 ADVICE REJECTED.
   (a) The advice is rejected.
   (b) The advice has been rejected.
   (c) The advice which is rejected.
   (d) The advice which has been rejected.

3 ACTION REQUIRED: Ascertain the correct value ...
   (a) Action is required.
   (b) Action has been required.
   (c) Action which is required.
   (d) Action which has been required.

Note: You need to be able to understand the real meaning of contractions like the ones above when you see or hear them. However, do not use too many contractions yourself when you are writing because they often cause misunderstanding. **The full forms** may be longer but they **are always clearer**.

Activity 3

Now try to write the full forms of the phrases you see in italics below.

Recruitment campaign status report

1 Number of *new staff required*: 6
2 Number of *applications received* so far: 37
3 Number of *candidates short-listed* to date: 16
4 Number of *interviews already held*: 9
5 Four *candidates offered jobs* so far.
6 Three *offers accepted* to date.
7 Further *interviews scheduled*: 5
8 Two more *staff required*.

INPUT 2 Listening

Find the cassette recording for Unit 11, Input 2. A group leader is talking to a trainee programmer about part of a new on-line order-processing system. The discussion involves a VDU screen layout and the way information is displayed when it is output to the screen.

Activity 1

Look at Figure 11.2 on the next page, which shows what Ian and Peter see on the screen. Make a note of the things which are wrong with items 1 to 8 below as you listen to the recording. To represent high intensity on the screen, bold type is used in the diagram. Italics are used to show unprotected fields — items which can be entered or changed on screen by the user. (Items in standard Roman typeface are output by the program and cannot be changed by the user.)

1 Display number
2 Source code
3 Main heading
4 Order details subheading
5 Address subheadings
   (a) lower/upper case   (b) indentation
6 Net amounts
7 VAT total

Activity 2

Near the end of the conversation the names of all of the special characters below are mentioned. Listen again and write the names of the characters and also make a note of the sequence that appeared in the price field.

1 # .....
2 - .....
3 \ .....
4 . .....
5 * .....
6 & .....
7 / .....

Price field: .....

```
 VP.840                     INVOICE DETAILS DISPLAY                     SOURCE D46

 CUSTOMER DETAILS
 Invoice address                         Delivery address
   B.HOPGOOD AND SONS LTD                  HOPGOOD ENGINEERING
   28 LIVERPOOL ROAD                       UNIT 24
   CHORLTON-CUM-HARDY                      BARTON DOCK INDUSTRIAL ESTATE
   MANCHESTER                              MANCHESTER
   M21 8QT                                 M16 7YB
   Customer A/c No.   13760      Invoice No.   39863/89   Our order No.   89/C/13152
   Customer Order     SL/80146   Invoice Date  08/04/89   Discount Rate   18%
ORDER DETAILS
 Item Code    Item Description           Qty    Price      Gross       Net      VAT
 1 LB 1584    GLOWCO DISHWASHER           1    436.50     436.50    357.93    53.69
 2 WB 7830    T-CONNECTOR                 2      2.70       5.40      4.43     0.66
 3 WB 7831    U-CONNECTOR                 2      1.95       3.90      3.20     0.48
 4 AF 1026    EXTRACTOR FAN HOUSING       1      7.00       7.00      5.74     0.86
 5 AF 1025    EXTRACTOR FAN               1     39.00      39.00     37.98     4.80
 6
 7
                                                                    403.28   060.49
                                                    Carriage         15.50     2.33

 TOTAL AMOUNT DUE:   481.60                                         418.78   062.82
```

Figure 11.2

LANGUAGE PRACTICE

Section 1

When people analyse things that have gone wrong they often use the modal verbs *might, must, could, can't, should* followed by a Present Perfect verb form:

Active

	might		
I/We	must		written
He/She/They	could	have	changed	the program.
You	can't		loaded
	should		

Passive

	might		
	must		been written.
The program	could	have	been changed.
	can't		been loaded.
	should		

Look at the following examples from the conversation you heard in Input 2:

Saying what was wanted or needed:

It **should have been specified** as a protected field.

I **should have seen** that.

Giving possible reasons for the problem (you could also use *could* instead of *might* in these sentences):

You **might have had** items with the same number of digits.

The sales people **could have changed** the price list.

Rejecting certain reasons for the problem:

That **can't have been** in the spec.

Drawing conclusions about why it happened:

I **must have been** asleep when I tested this. I **must have made** a mistake on the spec. You **must have done** something wrong there.

All the sentences above are analysing what went wrong in the past, but we can also use *might, can't, must* and *should* to talk about a current situation:

A: Where's Matthew? He **should be** here by now.

B: Don't know. He **might be** ill.

A: He **can't be**. I saw him in the car park when I arrived.

B: Well he **must be** somewhere around, then. I'll tell him you're looking for him when he comes.

Note: Take care if you use *could* because it changes a lot from the positive to the negative:

It **might be** the cable = It **could be** the cable (= the cable is possibly the cause of the problem).

It **might not be** the problem (= the cable is not necessarily the cause).

It **couldn't be** the cable = It **can't be** the cable (= the cable is definitely not the cause).

It is easier to use *might* and *can't* and avoid the *could* problem altogether for this type of fault analysis situation.

Activity

Try to complete the following conversation between three friends who work in the same team. For example, if you see (1 — do), you need to decide which of the following would be most suitable:

should/might/can't/must	do	(present and active)
	be done	(present and passive)
	have done	(past and active)
	have been done	(past and passive)

Kevin: There (1 — be) something wrong with my terminal. The screen's completely blank.

Anna: It (2 — switch) off at the power socket.

Kevin: No, it (3 — be) the power supply because I can hear it buzzing.

Anna: Check the coax cable, then. It (4 — not be) in properly — somebody (5 — pull) it out accidentally with their feet from under the desk, or something.

Kevin: It (6 — be) that — I've already checked.
No, there (7 — be) something wrong with the monitor.
Do you think I (8 — phone) the network people and ask them to come and look at it?

Daniel: Is it the 2nd of April today Anna?

Anna: No, it was the 31st of March yesterday, so it (9 — be) the 1st today.

Kevin: OK. One of you two (10 — do) something to it. What have you done?

Anna: Would we do something like that to you?

Kevin: Yes. Come on. You (11 — know) what's wrong.

Daniel: Do you think someone (12 — turn) the brightness control down, Anna?

Anna: I doubt it, but I suppose it (13 — be) the brightness control.

Kevin: Thank you. You (14 — use) a lot of imagination to think of that one.

Anna: No, not a lot, but more than you used to try and find the problem. Anyway, you (15 — come) earlier, then we wouldn't have been able to do it.

Section 2

Look at this group of words and how it is built:

error message generation routines = **routines** for the **generation** of **messages** about **errors**
messages about **errors** = *error messages*
generation of *error messages* = *error message generation*
routines for *error message generation* = *error message generation routines*

Look at some of the other groups of words from Input 1 and Input 2:

- missing start date
- invalid payment type
- missing first payment date
- invalid additional benefits indicator
- order details subheading
- new on-line order processing system

The last word in each group is a noun; all the other words before it (adjectives, other nouns, parts of verbs, other groups of words) describe the final noun in more detail.

Activity 1

Try to make compact error messages like the ones in Input 1 for the following problems.

1 The code for the salary of the employee is incorrect.

2 The details of the previous address are missing.

3 The rate of discount for the client is invalid.

Activity 2

Imagine you are completing report sheets. Use the same technique to try to summarise the following reasons for technical failures.

1 There was a failure in the supply of electricity to the main computer.

2 There was damage to the surface of the hard disk unit on the file server.

3 The cable for the connection of the VDU monitor was faulty.

DEVELOPMENT 1 Reading

The following extracts relate to the validation that has to be carried out on the data input from a document containing employee details.

Activity 1

Read the descriptions and enter a value which would be valid for the ten items (a)–(j) below. Assume that the function is 'new' (see item 060). Items (a) and (d) have been done as examples.

(a) 040 '142'   (f) 140 .....
(b) 050 .....   (g) 150 .....
(c) 060 .....   (h) 180 .....
(d) 090 YR 93 43 17 A (i) 190 .....
(e) 120 .....   (j) 200 .....

Item no.	Item description and validation requirements	Length
040	Document number Must be present. Value = 142.	3
050	Serial number Must be present and numeric in range 10000 to 99999.	5
060	Function Must be present and numeric in range 1 to 4. (1 = New 2 = Change 3 = Correct 4 = Delete)	1

(.)		
090	National Insurance Number	9

Must be present.
Must conform to Standard Code List 83.
Validate using general routine GDB210

(.)		
120	Maiden name	20

Can be blank or alphabetic.
Must not be present if item 140 = 'M'.

(.)		
140	Sex	1

Must be present and either 'M' or 'F'.

150	Date of Birth	8

May be blank or numeric.
Must be present for function 1.
If present, must be numeric and a valid date in format DDMMYYYY.
Generate warning if YYYY less than current year minus 65.
Validate using general routine GDB210. (.)

180	Appointment date

May be blank or numeric.
Must be present for function 1.
If present, must be numeric and a valid date in format DDMMYYYY.
Must be greater than or equal to Date of Birth + 16 years.
Validate using general routine GDB210.

190	Current salary	6

Must be present for function 'new', otherwise may be blank.
May be entered with leading or trailing spaces.
To validate, range to right and replace leading spaces with zeros; then check that it is a numeric integer.

(.)	
200	Job grade and level

Must be present for function 'new'.
If present, first two characters must be numeric and less than 16, last character must be alphabetic in range A to E.

Activity 2

In Input 1, we dealt with error messages. Using the details in Input 1 as a model, write error correction procedures for items 120, 150 and 200 above as follows.

- Assume that the above details are from an 'Employee Details Advice', reference number 142.

- All error messages must have a 5-character code consisting of the two letters 'ED' and a 3-digit number.

- For any item which must be present for all functions the advice is rejected, otherwise only the section of the advice in which the error occurs is rejected.

DEVELOPMENT 2   Role Play — Specifying Layout

Design a screen layout for the information below. When you have finished your design, work with a partner. Exchange designs and ideas about the different ways in which you have decided to present the information, modifying the designs where useful suggestions or comments are made.

The screen layout is for a database enquiry and maintenance system in a university. This screen shows current or past student details for one student.

```
A = Alphabetic characters only
N = Numeric only
X = Alphanumeric   X(20) = up to 20 alphanumeric, etc.
```

Screen display reference: 'MU.104'
Screen heading 'Student details'
Three-character operator code: ANN
Student reference number: AAA/NNNNN/NN
Course reference number: AAA/NNNN   Student family name: A(20)
Student given names: A(40)
Title (Mr/Mrs/Miss/Dr) etc.
Degree: X(20)
Date of entry: DD/MM/YYYY
Graduation date: DD/MM/YYYY
Regional education authority code: NNN
Course fees: 9999.99

Addresses:

1. Student term-time address 4*X(40)
   Student term-time post code X(8)
   Student term-time phone number X(12)

2. Student vacation address 4*X(40)
   Student vacation post code X(8)   } If different from 1
   Student vacation phone number X(12)

3. Next of kin address 4*X(40)
   Next of kin post code X(8)   } If different from 1 and 2
   Next of kin phone number X(12)

Next of kin: X(40)
National medical Number: A/NNNNNN/NN/AA

LANGUAGE SUMMARY

Sentence types

Modal Active (Present and Past)

	might			
	must			
X	could	do	Y	(*Present*)
	can't	have done	Y	(*Past*)
	should			

Modal Passive (Present and Past)

	might		
	must		
Y	could	be done	(*Present*)
	can't	have been done	(*Past*)
	should		

Message and note forms

Complete sentence: The advice **has been rejected.**
Message or note form: Advice **rejected.**

Complete sentence: The action which **was taken** by the computer system was as follows:
Message or note form: Action **taken** by the computer system:

Complete sentence: The action which **is required** is as follows:
Message or note form: Action **required:**

Useful expression

(£600) per quarter
due on ... (the last day of the month)
one of the following: ... (a, b, c)
outside the permitted range ... (of 1 to 6)
in the range ... (900 to 999)
(it must) ... conform to a standard
a 5-character code
a 3-digit number

UNIT 12 System implementation

INPUT 1 Listening

Listen to the cassette recording for Unit 12, Input 1. It is a recording of part of a training session for end users in an insurance company. Someone is presenting part of a new accounting system to a group of supervisors in the accounts department.

Activity 1

Complete the following summary of the part of the presentation that you hear.

INTRODUCTION TO THE PRESENTATION

1 Self-introduction

   (a) Name: .....
   (b) Job: .....
   (c) Responsibilities: .....

2 Training session plan
   System overview:

   (a) summary of .....
   (b) similarities / differences between ..... and .....
   (c) Estimated time for overview: .....

   Main session activities:

   (d) .....
   (e) .....
   (f) Estimated time: .....

3 Other information

MAIN BODY OF THE PRESENTATION

System overview

1 Names of main system facilities:

    (a) .....
    (b) .....
    (c) .....

2 Capabilities of main system facilities:

    (a) .....
    (b) .....
    (c) .....

Activity 2

In her introduction Alison uses certain words and phrases to give a structure to her presentation. The language signals that she uses help the listener to understand: the purpose of the training session; her intentions; the content of the session; the order/sequence of information and activities.

A lot of expressions are useful for presentations on any subject. Use the tapescript in the back of the book and pick out the general phrases which help her to introduce the specific information below. You can then use the general part of the sentences in your own presentations. The first one is done for you.

1 Self-introduction

    (paragraph 1) *For those of you who don't know me, my name's* (Alison McLeod).

2 Explaining the purpose of a meeting/presentation

    (paragraph 2) ..... (how the first phase ..... is going to work).

3 Starting off

    (a) (paragraph 2) ..... (explaining a little bit about the order that I'm going to do things in).

    (b) (paragraph 6) ..... (the system as a whole).

4 Describing a planned sequence

    (a) (paragraph 3) ..... (a brief overall picture of the first phase).

    (b) (paragraph 3) ..... (some of the main similarities and differences).

    (c) (paragraph 4) ..... (the main part of the training session).

    (d) (paragraph 4) ..... (the different parts of the system on the terminals).

(e) (paragraph 4) ..... (talking you through the different screen displays).

(f) (paragraph 4) ..... (doing some practical exercises).

5 Finishing a point/summarising

(last paragraph) ..... (the three main facilities, then).

6 Moving to a new point

(last paragraph) ..... (some of the advantages they give you).

Activity 3

Use the summary from Activity 1 and the expressions from Activity 2 to give a brief introduction to Alison's presentation.

INPUT 2 Reading

The following letter concerns the installation of a new cabling system for a network in a company's new office block. The cabling was installed by a contract firm, not by the equipment manufacturer. Because the Computer Services Manager had doubts about the way the cabling was installed he asked the manufacturer to check the installation. This letter presents the findings of the equipment manufacturer's engineers.

Dear Graham

Further to the concerns that have been expressed about the cabling system in your new building, we have now had an opportunity to review the installation. I therefore think it is appropriate to document our view of the system as it has been implemented.

With regard to the work done by the subcontractors in terms of the physical installation, our engineers are of the view that this has been done to the highest standard.

There are, however, one or two aspects of the design that we feel might be limiting in the future, or detrimental to the use of the cabling system as a vehicle for a Local Area Network. However, I would like to stress that these comments are made without detailed knowledge of the architecture of the building.

Continued

In summary, our consultants felt that the design has achieved the physical wiring of a number of separate floors rather than the logical wiring of an entire building which would cater for a terminal user community whose communication requirements would extend beyond the physical boundaries of a floor, or beyond the building itself. There are in addition a number of specific points which we felt might lead to some difficulties later.

At a number of points the trunking passes over radiators in the building. We would strongly advise that the trunking should be installed either below radiator level, or in the ceiling. The heat from the radiators will be transmitted through the cables, not only affecting the conductivity, but also potentially creating problems with the connector baluns whose components are made of a variety of materials which of course expand at different rates.

In addition to the point about the positioning of the baluns, it was also noted that cableless baluns had not been used to provide the cabling interface between the system and coaxial supported cables. Such baluns are certainly easier to use and also have the advantage of being much neater.

In the event of you wishing to add new outlets for expansion and additional flexibility, it appears to us that holes will have to be drilled through a fairly heavy steel trunking, directly behind which is the cabling itself. Apart from the risk of hitting and damaging existing cable, one of the primary objectives of the cabling system is to provide sufficient outlets for easy expansion: these have not been provided.

The positioning of the floor points was also of some concern to our engineers who felt that since these are not flush with the floor, desks have been placed over them to avoid creating a hazard. This in turn seems to have dictated the positioning of the desks.

Finally, our consultant noticed a tendency for the outlet cables to be dislodged by the heavy flaps at the outlet points when the flaps were lifted. It was felt that this may be the cause of some operational difficulty. We would like to point out that our cabling system provides locking mechanisms to avoid accidental fall-out of cables from outlets. However, these do not appear to have been implemented. Use of these may avoid future difficulties in this area.

I make these points because we are aware that you intend to extend this cabling system to your old building as part of a refurbishment and I hope the comments may prove useful in enhancing the system which is to be installed. As you are aware, we were not consulted in the installation of the system in the new building although we do provide an installation design service of our own. If we can be of assistance with the project ahead, please do not hesitate to contact us.

Yours sincerely

Bill Norman.

Bill Norman
Account Representative

Activity 1

As you read the text try to complete the table below as follows. Make a note of the problems found by the equipment manufacturer in the left-hand column. Say what should have been done in the right-hand column.

Problems discovered	What should have been done
1 **Wiring design** Floors have been wired as separate physical units. Later expansion may be difficult.	.....
2 **Trunking routes** Trunking	Trunking should have been installed either: (a) ..... or: (b) .....
3	Cableless baluns .....
4	Additional outlets .....
5	.....
6	.....

Activity 2

The job of the writer is to evaluate the situation, identifying problems and suggesting solutions. As an external consultant his job is not to criticise or to find someone to blame. The tone of the letter is very diplomatic, largely as a result of two language strategies.

1 He points out problem areas very tactfully by using the passive or a neutral idea to avoid saying *you* or *your company*. For example, he does not say:

(a) You have not used cableless baluns.
(b) You have not designed the wiring properly.

He says:

(a) Cableless baluns have not been used.
(b) The design has achieved the physical wiring of a number of separate floors rather than the logical wiring of the building.

Find three more examples of how he avoids saying you, etc.

(a) .....
(b) .....
(c) .....

2 He expresses opinions very tactfully and avoids committing himself totally because he has not seen the installation himself. For example he often uses words and expressions with *might, may, would like to, appear, feel, seem* to 'soften' his opinion or recommendation.

Find at least one example in the text of each of these items:

(a) might: .....
(b) may: .....
(c) would like to: .....
(d) appear: .....
(e) feel: .....
(f) seem: .....

LANGUAGE PRACTICE

Look at the following sentences:

1 Recommended alternative:
They *should have installed* the floor points flush with the floor.

2 Reason for recommended alternative:
Then they *would have been* able to put the desks wherever they wanted.

3 Condition necessary for improvement:
If they *had installed* the floor points flush with the floor they *would have been* able to put the desks where they wanted.

Notice that we are talking about what went wrong in the past, not making suggestions for future actions — compare these sentences with the ones in Unit 10 which are for very different situations.

Activity

Read the following description of the problems which faced a small project team during a 10-month period; then, at the end of each paragraph, try to write groups of three sentences like the ones above (except for the first paragraph, which just gives the background).

Catherine had five other people in her team when they started work on a new internal mail and document production system in week 4. The project finally finished in week 48, but the original target date for completion was week 30.
   When they started, there were only three terminals between her five staff. They often had to wait for each other to finish before they could use a terminal. She had requested two extra terminals the previous November when her staff had increased from three to five. She didn't get them until the beginning of April — a 6-month wait.

1 (a) They should ..... more terminals.

   (b) Then they wouldn't ..... for each other.

   (c) If ......

12 System implementation 131

In April, when they finally got another two terminals, the most experienced member of the team, Lynne, left the company. Although she gave three months' notice and wanted to leave in June, as soon as she handed in her resignation the company gave her three months' salary and asked her to leave.

2 (a) The company shouldn't ......

(b) Then she would ..... in June.

(c) If ..... in June they ..... her experience for an extra three months.

Catherine wanted to get someone who had similar experience of internal systems quickly from another project team, but she was told that nobody could be made available. About six weeks after Lynne left, a new recruit joined from outside the company who wasn't very experienced and needed a lot of initial training in the company's systems and procedures.

3 (a) Either they should ..... or they should ......

(b) He ..... so much training.

(c) If ......

At the beginning of May they also had to start doing a lot of conversion work on old programs so that they would run under a new operating system which was going to be installed in October. Catherine asked for a contract programmer with experience of this kind of conversion to be recruited to do this fairly routine but time-consuming work. She was told it was out of the question.

4 (a) ..... a contract programmer.

(b) ..... the conversion work.

(c) If .....

When they started testing and asking the users to check results in August it was a very busy time for the users, who were short-staffed during the summer holidays. It took a long time for test results to be checked.

5 (a) ..... before the summer period.

(b) ..... short-staffed.

(c) If ......

Her boss had been so uncooperative, refusing to listen to any suggestions that she made, that when Catherine got the chance of another job she had no hesitation in handing in her notice. She left at the beginning of September. Her skill as a team leader was badly missed and the project was delayed even further.

6 (a) .....

(b) .....

(c) .....

132 English for Information Systems

DEVELOPMENT 1 Listening

Listen to the cassette recording for Unit 12, Development 1. It is a recording of part of a meeting concerning the computerisation of an English dictionary. One person has just finished what he wanted to say; the Chairman is about to ask the Computer Group Manager to report on progress now that they have come to the end of Phase 1 of the project.

Activity 1

Complete the following summary of the part of the presentation that you hear.

1 In the introduction, the speaker says he aims to cover:

  (a) Achievements so far
  (b) Project shedules
  (c) ..... estimates
  (d) ..... estimates

2 Achievements during first six months

  (a) .....
  (b) .....
  also: .....

3 Project plan

  (a) Staff:
     (i) Nature of problem: .....
     (ii) Effect on schedules: .....
  (b)

Lexicographic system	Original target date	Revised target date
Limited editing facilities	.....	.....
Full-function system	.....	.....
Start entering new words	.....	.....

Activity 2

Listen to the beginning of the recording again until Alan begins speaking.

1 What does the first speaker say to indicate that he has finished?

2 What language does the chairman use to:

  (a) take back control?
  (b) give others the chance to ask questions?
  (c) go on to the next speaker?

Activity 3

In Input 1 you picked out words and phrases which Alison used in her training session to help the listener to understand:

- the purpose of the session;
- her intentions;
- the content of the session;
- the order/sequence of information.

Alan is speaking in a very different kind of situation, but he still uses similar words and expressions to present his information in a clearly structured way. Listen again to the part of the cassette where he speaks and try to pick out useful phrases which help him to do the following:

1 Explaining the main purpose of his report: .....
2 Starting off: .....
3 Indicating the sequence of information: .....
4 Avoiding unimportant detail: .....
5 Moving to a new point: .....
6 Finishing a point/summarising: .....

DEVELOPMENT 2 Formal Presentation

Alan said he was going to talk about four things:

1 Achievements so far
2 Project schedules
3 Cost estimates
4 Code estimates

However, we only heard the part of the meeting where he talked about 1 and 2.

The information which Alan prepared relating to points 3 and 4 is given below. Put yourself in his position and prepare to present either part 3 or part 4 to your colleague(s). You do not necessarily need to explain all the details — details are given to make sure you have enough background information to explain the reasons for changes. Just use what you feel you need. Look carefully at language from the rest of this unit for examples of how to structure and present your information clearly.

Optional Presentation 1

Use the following information if you want to prepare part 3 of Alan's presentation. When you are ready, continue the presentation from the point where Alan said: 'Right, let's move on to the cost estimates, then.'

Cost estimates

Original estimated costs

Estimated costs are for building and running the computer system within the calculated timescales. Estimates are in pounds sterling at 1985 values.

Summary

1985–6	436 000
1986–7	698 000
1987–8	265 000
1988–9	228 000
TOTAL	1 627 000

Detail

People	273 000	69 000	163 000	131 000
Equipment	70 000	95 000		
Maintenance	55 000	89 000	89 000	89 000
Other	38 000	45 000	13 000	8 000
	436 000	698 000	265 000	228 000
GRAND TOTAL	1 627 000			

Revised estimated costs

Estimated costs are for building and running the computer system within the calculated timescales. Estimates are in pounds sterling at current (Jan. 1986) values.

Summary

1985–6	376 000
1986–7	732 000
1987–8	258 000
1988–9	212 000
TOTAL	1 578 000

Detail

People	254 000	383 000	146 000	113 000
Equipment	44 000	204 000	5 000	5 000
Maintenance	23 000	89 000	89 000	89 000
Other	55 000	56 000	18 000	5 000
	376 000	732 000	258 000	212 000
GRAND TOTAL	1 578 000			

Overall reduction in costs compared with original estimate approx. £50 000.

Reasons:

1 Lower manpower costs (current external consultant manager to be replaced by in-company manager).
2 Lower maintenance costs (the equipment manufacturers still have title to equipment — the publishing company is therefore not yet responsible for maintenance).

Optional Presentation 2

Use the following information if you want to prepare part 4 of Alan's presentation. When you are ready, continue the presentation from the point where Alan might say: 'Right, let's move on to the code estimates, then.'

Code estimates

The table below gives information on the development effort required according to revised estimates.
Sizes of software components are given in *lines of executable code* — LOCs (excluding comments).
Required effort is given in *man months* — mm.
Productivity rates are given in LOCs per man month — LOCs/mm.
Total estimated LOCs are 30% higher than original estimates.

Original estimates

Subsystem	LOCs	mm	LOCs/mm
Data capture and validation	1 050	3	350
Proofing	4 350	10	425
Database system	4 150	14	300
Lexicographic system	9 450	38	250
Cross-reference system	1 050	6	200
TOTALS	20 050	71	

New estimates and LOCs completed to date

Real productivity experience to date indicated by *; required productivity indicated by **.
Productivity should increase as staff become more knowledgeable.

Subsystem completed	LOCs	mm	LOCs/mm	LOCs
Data capture and validation	1 750	6	280*	1 750
Proofing	3 300	9	370*	1 900
Database system	6 200	15	410**	0
Lexicographic system	12 600	17	660*	11 000
Cross-reference system	2 400	6	400**	0
TOTALS	26 250	53		14 650

LANGUAGE SUMMARY

Sentence types

It **might have been** a good idea.
They **might not have received** it.

You **should have told** me.
He **shouldn't have said** anything.

It **would have made** a big difference.
It **wouldn't have made** any difference.

If her boss had been more helpful she   **might not have left**
      probably **wouldn't have left**
      wouldn't have left

She **might not have left**
She *probably* **wouldn't have left**   *if her boss had been more helpful*
She **wouldn't have left**

Useful expressions

first/firstly/first of all
second/secondly
third/thirdly

Right then.
I think we'll make a start.
For those of you who don't know me already, my name's . . . .
If you have any questions, please feel free to interrupt.

I'm going to start	by explaining	. . . (the benefits).
I'd like to start	by looking at	. . . (how we can benefit).
Let's start	with	
I'm going to	move on to	. . . (the problems).
I'd like to	go on to	. . . (how we can solve them).
Let's		
What I'd like to do is	summarise	. . . (the problem).
	describe	
	talk about	
	start with	

APPENDIX A Simulation and role play information for participant A

UNIT 2 Development 2, Participant A

Simulation 1

You are a new user on a file enquiry system. Find out from your colleague which keys you use for the following functions:

Roll-through from one part of a record to the next.

Roll-back within the same record.

Return to the subsystem menu.

Return to the first screenfull of data.

Display the start of the next logical record.

Sign off.

Simulation 2

Use the following information to answer your colleagues questions about a new word-processing package.

1 Mark the beginning and end of a block for DELETE, COPY and MOVE operations as follows:

   Position cursor at start position.
   Hold down function key 7 and type '1'.

Move cursor to where you want the block to end.
Hold down function key 7 and type '2'.

2 Delete a block of text as follows:

Mark the beginning and end of a block (see 1 above).
Hold down CONTROL and press function key 1.

3 Move a block of text as follows:

Mark the beginning and end of a block (see 1 above).
Hold down CONTROL and press function key 2.

4 Copy a block of text as follows:

Mark the beginning and end of a block (see 1 above).
Hold down CONTROL and press the COPY key.

UNIT 3   Development 2, Participant A

Task 1

Look at the flowchart opposite (Figure A.1) which shows how a microcomputer-based training package works. Your partner has the same flowchart but without the information in the boxes. Your task is to describe the process (NOT to give instructions).

Start your description with 'The program menu is loaded automatically from the program disk when the user presses SHIFT and BREAK'.

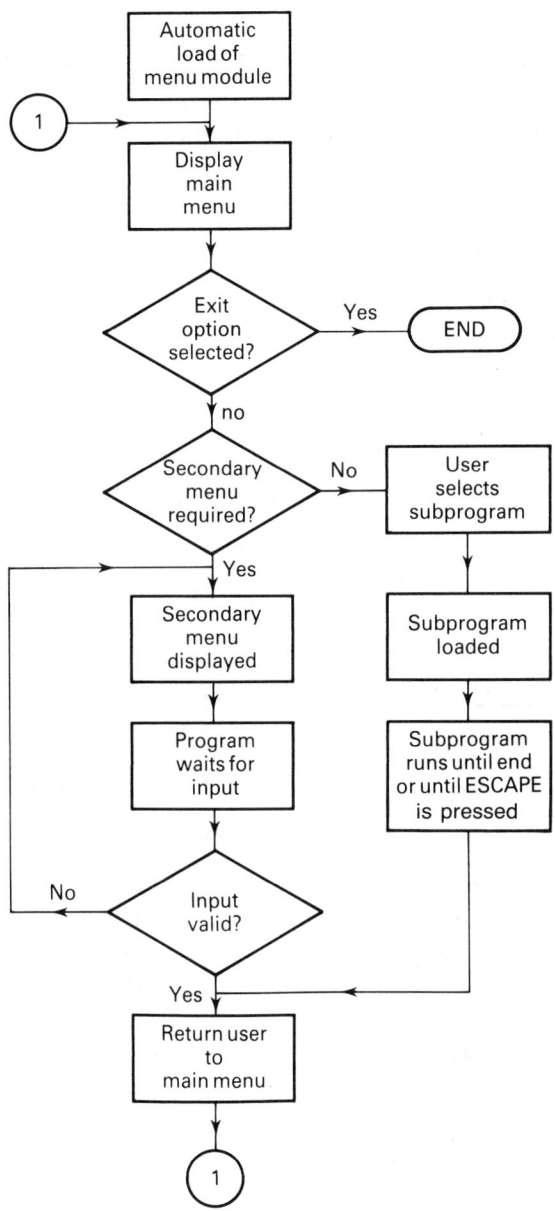

Figure A.1

Task 2

Listen to your partner's description of the process which is shown in the diagram below (Figure A.2) and fill in the boxes in the flowchart with the information you hear. Ask questions if you do not understand the explanation.

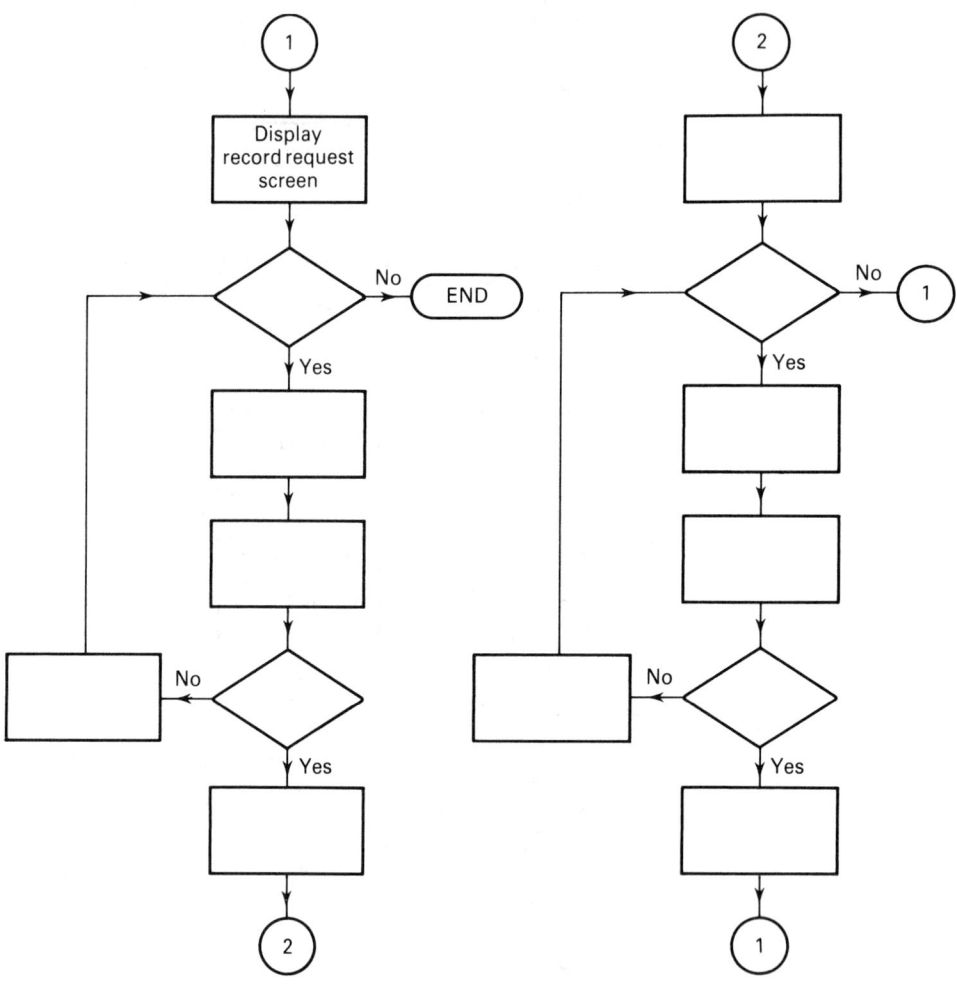

Figure A.2

UNIT 7   Development 2, Participant A

Simulation 1

Call 1

You will receive a phone call from a Mr Kowalski. He wants to speak to Mr Adams at Office Futures. Your company is called Future Offices. Because people often make this mistake, you know that the number of Office Futures is 623381.

Call 2

Switchboard: First of all, play the part of the switchboard operator. Just greet the caller and give the name of your company, Office Futures, then connect the caller to the person he/she wants (Mr Adams).

Mr/Ms Adams: Play the part of Mr/Ms Adams. You deal with the account of Wider Travel and you know Mr/Ms Kowalski, who often orders supplies from you. Make a note of the order. Delivery will probably take about a week.

You will also be asked about something else, but you are not sure if you will be free yourself on Friday afternoon, although you can probably arrange for someone else to do what is required.

Simulation 2

Your name is Chris Gilling and you work for KTB Services. Phone Les/Lisa Barret at Hard and Soft Limited. If he/she is not there and you are asked if you want to leave a message, say you will phone back later.

Subject 1: You would like a quotation for an Epson GQ3500 6PPM laser printer.

Subject 2: You also placed an order two weeks ago for 50 3.5" double-sided density Sony disks. You have been invoiced for 50, but only 20 were sent. Your order reference number was HT/56892-89. Their invoice number was L-68430.

142 *Appendix A*

UNIT 8   Development 2, Participant A

Simulation

Your name is Jo Adebiyi and you are the Data Network Services Manager for Wiz-Com, a telecommunications company. You want to arrange a meeting with Miko Takumi, the North Eastern Regional Manager some time next week. Here is your diary for next week.

Phone Miko Takumi and try to arrange a time which suits you both.

Mon		13.00 Appointment with Mr. Baker	15.00 meeting with Sales people
Tue	08.05 train to London arrive 11.40	13.00 meeting	17.35 return train to Newcastle
Wed			19.00 train to Birmingham
Thu	Annual Regional Managers Conference In Birmingham all day		
Fri	Day 2 of ARM Conf.	14.00 Return to Newcastle	

APPENDIX B Simulation and role play information for participant B

UNIT 2   Development 2, Participant B

Simulation 1

Use the following information to answer your colleagues questions about a new file enquiry system.

Key	Function
PA1	Return to the subsystem menu.
PF1	Return to the first screenfull of data.
PF2	Display the start of the next logical record.
PF7	Sign off.
PF11	Roll-back within the same record.
PF12	Roll-through from one part of a record to the next.

Simulation 2

You are a new user of a word-processing package. Find out from your colleague how to do the following operations.

Move a block of text from one place to another.

Copy a block of text (so that the same block appears twice).

Delete a block of text.

UNIT 3 Development 2, Participant B

Task 1

Listen to your partner's description of the process which is shown in the diagram below and fill in the boxes in the flowchart with the information you hear. Ask questions if you do not understand the explanation.

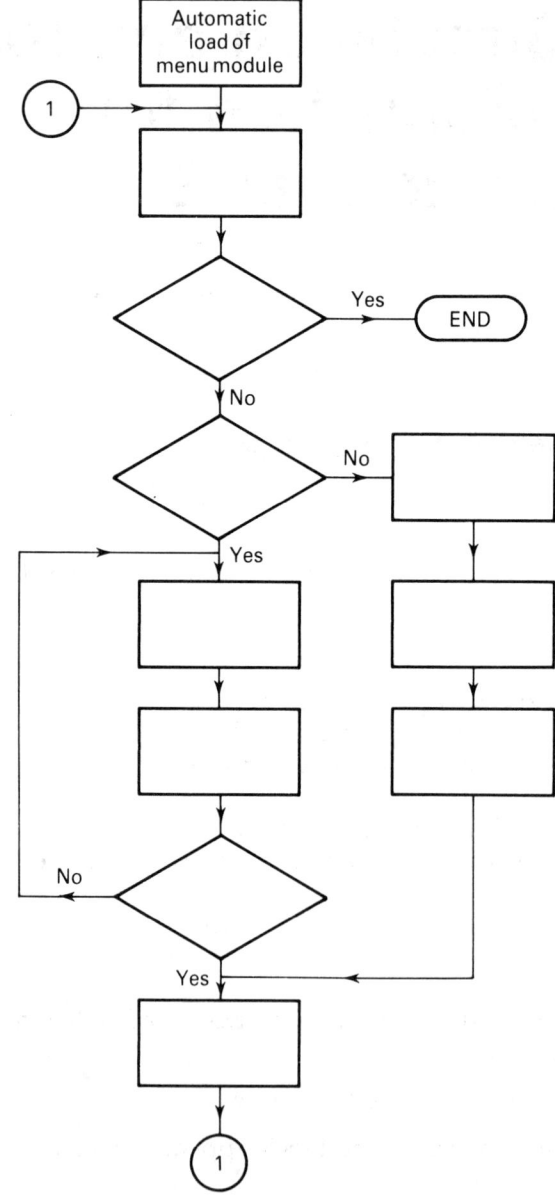

Figure B.1

Task 2

Look at the flowchart below. Your partner has the same flowchart but without the information in the boxes. Describe the process which shows how to obtain and update a single record from an on-line database system. Start your description 'First of all the Record Request screen is displayed'.

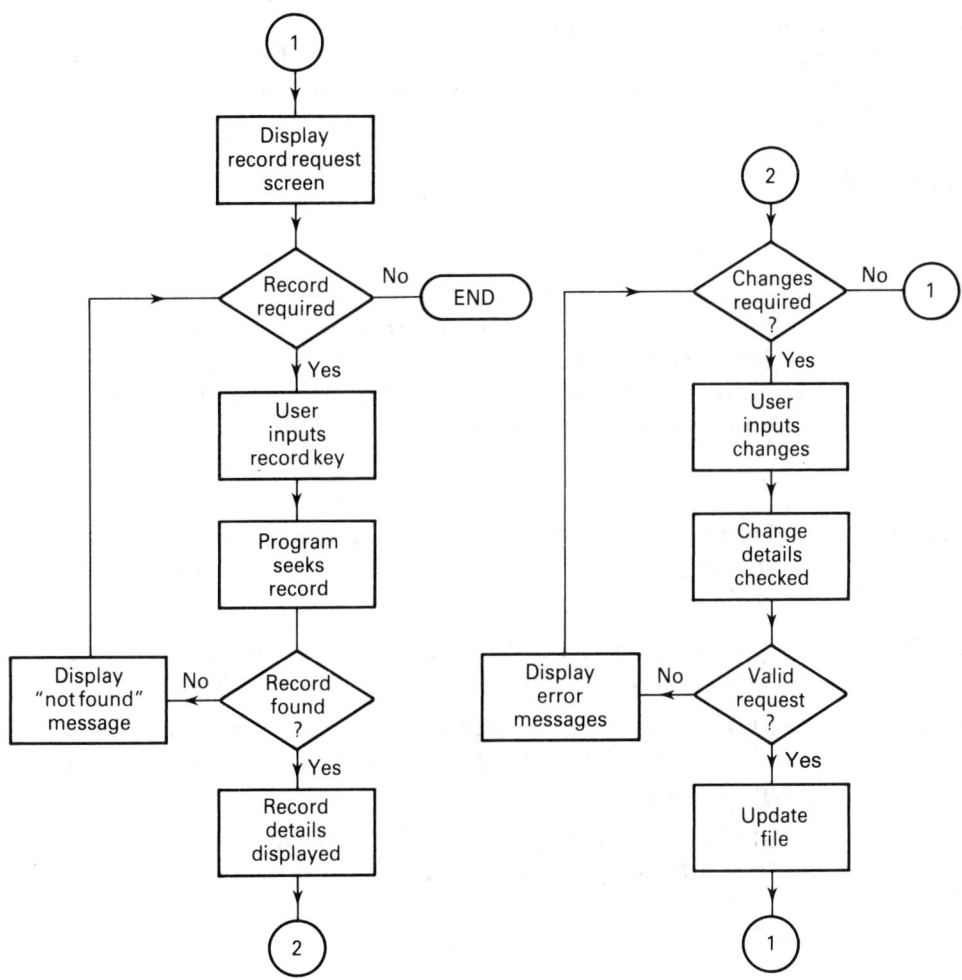

Figure B.2

UNIT 7 Development 2, Participant B

Simulation 1

Call 1

You are Ms/Mr Kowalski of Wider Travel. Phone Mr/Ms Adams at Office Futures. Place an order for 10 000 sheets of true A4 90GSM stationery and 2000 3.5" by 1.5" labels (two across). Ask how soon you will get them.

You want to know if he/she will give you a demonstration of the Canon 110 and 120 fax machines if you go to their office on Friday afternoon.

Simulation 2

Call 1

Switchboard:	First of all, play the part of the switchboard operator. Just greet the caller and give the name of your company, Hard and Soft Ltd. Then try to connect the caller to the person he/she want (Les/Lisa Barret). Unfortunately, he/she is not there at the moment. Ask if you can take a message.

Call 2

Switchboard:	First of all, play the part of the switchboard operator again. Then connect the caller to the person he/she wants (Les/Lisa Barret), who is there this time.
Les/Lisa Barret:	Play the part of Les/Lisa Barret and answer the caller on the two subjects that he/she mentions with the information below.
Subject 1:	Make a note of the equipment for which a quotation is required. You do not have the prices available. Promise to send a quote immediately.
Subject 2:	Make a note of the problem and ask for the invoice number. Promise to send the goods immediately.

UNIT 8 Development 2, Participant B

Simulation

Your name is Miko Takumi and you are the North Eastern Regional Manager for Wiz-Com, a telecommunications company. You are about to receive a call from Jo Adebiyi, the Data Network Services Manager at Head Office. Here is your diary for next week.

Mon	0.900 Project Leaders' Meeting	11.00 Appointment and lunch with Mr. Simms	
Tue			14.00 Fly to Dusseldorf
Wed	0.900 Meeting in Dusseldorf	12.30 return flight to Manchester arriving 15.00	
Thu	10.00 Dentist's appointment		
Fri	11.30 meet Costa Rican visitors	Lunch with visitors	Meeting & Negotiations

APPENDIX C Key to activities

UNIT 1

INPUT 1

Activity 1

Documentation co-ordinator / Jenny Long
Technical author / Peter Holmes
Technical author / Sandra / technical manuals
Technical author / Brian / database documentation
Technical author / Les Barton / end user procedure manuals and training materials
IS manager / Mr Blakely

Activity 2

Peter:	Good morning. My name's (Peter Holmes) / I'm (Peter Holmes)
Jenny:	(... You) must be (Peter Holmes)
Jenny:	I'm / my name's (Jenny Long.) Pleased to meet you. / How do you do?
Peter:	How do you do? / Pleased to meet you.
Mr B:	Hello (Jenny).
Jenny:	Can I introduce you to (Peter Holmes)?
Peter:	How do you do? / Pleased to meet you.
Mr B:	Pleased to meet you / How do you do?
Les:	Hello. (Les Barton).
Peter:	Hi.
Jenny:	(And) this is (Sandra).
Peter:	Nice (to meet you.)
Sandra:	Glad (to meet you.)
Brian:	Hello there.
Peter:	Hello. (Do you all do the same sort of thing?)

Appendix C 149

INPUT 2

Activity 1

1 Training courses
2 Customer support
3 User groups
4 Compatible environments
5 Only the best

Activity 2

	Verb	Noun
1		backing
2	to maintain	
3	to provide	
4	to install	
5		training
6		support
7		enhancement
8	to optimise	
9	to implement	
10		requirement
11	to communicate	
12		development
13		improvement
14	to discuss	
15	to compare	
16	to decide	

Activity 3

(a) decides
(b) discuss
(c) requirements
(d) discuss / compare
(e) requirements
(f) comparison
(g) provide
(h) training
(i) install/implement
(j) support
(k) communication
(l) enhance/improve
(m) improve/enhance

LANGUAGE PRACTICE

Section 1

1. is starting; is showing; is introducing
2. is going
3. handles/deals with/looks after; handles/deals with/looks after
4. are working
5. visit
6. provide
7. provide

Section 2

F = Formal; N = Natural; F/N = both

1. F/N
2. N
3. N
4. N
5. N
6. F
7. F/N
8. N
9. F
10. N
11. F/N
12. F
13. F
14. N
15. N

DEVELOPMENT

Activity 1

A1 General Manager
B1 Planning
B2 Processing
C1 Existing
C2 Strategic
C3 Computer Production
C4 Technical Support
C5 Liz Campbell
D1 Telecoms software support
D2 Systems programming

Appendix C   151

Activity 2

(Free format exercise)

Activity 3

1(a) hardware compatibility
1(b) staffing
2(a) integrated systems
2(b) Management Information requirements
3(a) (review) development proposals
3(b) (monitor) parallel runs
3(c) hardware (planning)
3(d) capacity (planning)

UNIT 2

INPUT 1

Activity 1

1 (Shift-click)
2 Double-click
3 Drag
4 Click
5 Press

Activity 2

1 (To select) MacPaint, position the pointer on the MacPaint icon and click the mouse.

2 (You can) choose 'Close' from the file menu by positioning the pointer on 'File', dragging to the 'Close' command and releasing the mouse button.

3 (To close MEMO1) position the pointer on the MEMO1 icon and click the mouse. Then position the pointer on 'File', drag to the 'Close' command and release the mouse button.

4 (You can) open MEMO2 by positioning the pointer on the MEMO2 icon and double-clicking the mouse button.

INPUT 2

Activity 1

1 a Same field, preceding record
  b Preceding screenfull of records
  c First record in display sequence

2 a Preceding field, same record
  b First field, same record
  c Previous character, same field
3 a Next field, same record
  b Last field, same record
  c Next character, same field
4 a First field, next line/Start of next sequential record
  b Next screenfull of records
  c Last record in display sequence
5 Press downward cursor key
6 Press upward cursor key

Activity 2

Example questions are given for numbers 1 and 2. For numbers 3 to 7, only the answers are given.

1 How do I get to ...
  How do you get to ...
  Which key do I use to ... get to the next record? etc.
  Press the downward cursor key.
2 How do I move to the start of the last field in the record?
  Hold down the SHIFT key and press the 'right' cursor key.
3 Hold down the CTRL key and press the 'down' cursor key.
4 Press the upward cursor key.
5 Hold down the CTRL key and press the 'right' cursor key.
6 Hold down the SHIFT key and press the 'left' cursor key.
7 Hold down the CTRL key and press the upward cursor key.

Activity 3

1 Let's look at ...
2 Can we come back to that in a second ...
3 There's just one more thing ...
4 Right, that covers ...
5 Let's look at ...

LANGUAGE PRACTICE

Section 1

1 ... does 'clicking' ...   ... an application or a document
2 What does ...   ... positioning the mouse on something, pressing the mouse button and holding it down while moving to another position, then releasing the mouse.

Appendix C   153

3 What does 'dragging' do?   ... lets ...
4 What does 'WIMP' mean?   It means ....
5 What does 'cursor right' do?
6 What does 'cursor up' do?
   It takes you to the same field in the previous record.

Section 2

1 ... allows you to go back to the first record in the display sequence.
2 ... enables you to move around the database.
3 ... lets you see ...
4 ... allow you to use the program ...
5 ... enables you to open MEMO2 in one operation.

Section 3

1 You can display the previous screenfull of data by holding down SHIFT and pressing 'up'.
2 If you want to go back to the previous field in a record, hold down SHIFT and press 'left'.
3 To get to the last record in a display sequence, hold down CONTROL and press 'right'.
4 If you want to select MacWrite, position the pointer on the MacWrite icon and click the mouse.
5 You can choose an application by dragging the mouse.

DEVELOPMENT 1

Activity 1

(a) Place a copy of Accounts program disk in drive A
(b) Put Ledgers disk in drive B
(c) Wait for system prompt A>
(d) Type ACCOUNTS, press RETURN
(e) Ledgers disk in drive B?
(f) Insert Ledgers disk in drive B
(g) Input password
(h) Password correct?
(i) Program locks and returns user to system prompt
(j) Select option
(k) Option 11, 12, 13 or 14?

Activity 2

(Free format exercise)

UNIT 3

INPUT 1

Activity 1

A1:
1 pass
2 check
3 initial
4 collect
5 fill in

B1:
1 are passed
2 (are) checked
3 (are) initialled
4 are grouped
5 is (also) completed

A2:
1 includes
2 identifies
3 take
4 hand
5 distributes
6 key in
7 use

B2:
1 is identified
2 is (also) entered
3 are (then) taken
4 are (then) keyed in
5 (are) stored
6 are processed
7 are used

Activity 2

A3:
1 consists
2 makes
3 matches
4 performs
5 updates
6 deletes

Appendix C 155

7 changes
8 assembles
9 prints

B3:
1 is checked
2 are carried out
3 are validated
4 are added
5 are amended
6 is extracted
7 are output
8 is handled
9 are sorted

INPUT 2

Activity 1

1 console terminal
2 log printer
3 microstations
3a VDU
3b keyboard
3c local printer
4 channel controller
5 ATP ports
6 X.25 switch
7 multiplexor
8 cross-connection cabinets
9 terminals
10 local printers

Activity 2

1 provide
2 has
3 control/handle
4 are linked/are connected
5 includes/incorporates/has
6 includes/consists of
7 includes/consists of
8 connect/link

Appendix C

LANGUAGE PRACTICE

Section 1

1 works
2 enable
3 are not limited
4 licenses
5 allow
6 is needed
7 consists
8 is designed
9 does not depend
10 provides
11 are not forced

DEVELOPMENT

Activity 1

1 (b)
2 (e)
3 (a)
4 (f)
5 (d)
6 (c)

Activity 2

1 do you get
2 are transactions rejected
3 are most of the mistakes made
4 do you find out
5 does Paul do
6 is a rejected transaction resubmitted

UNIT 4

INPUT 1

Activity 1

1 OE100 (can be obtained from DL100, can obtain OE120)
2 AC100 (can be obtained from DL100, can obtain AC900)
3 SE110 (can be obtained from SE100, links up with OE120)
4 OE110 (can be obtained from OE100, can obtain OE120)
5 OE120 (can be obtained from OE100, can obtain SE110, can be obtained from AC900)

Activity 2

1 F
2 ? (not specified for SE100, only for SE110)
3 T
4 F
5 T
6 T
7 F
8 T
9 F
10 ? (not mentioned)

Activity 3

(Free format exercise)

Input 2

Activity 1

1 ? (Not specifically mentioned)
2 T
3 T
4 F
5 F
6 ? (Not specifically mentioned)
7 T
8 ? (Not specifically mentioned)

Activity 2

(Free format exercise)

LANGUAGE PRACTICE

1 first of all
2 produces
3 comprises
4 after (possibly 'once')
5 are separated
6 is sent
7 until
8 is used
9 prepare

158 Appendix C

10 once/as soon as/when
11 after/once/when
12 is filed
13 then
14 when
15 are delivered
16 are (then) passed
17 at this point
18 invoices

DEVELOPMENT 1

Activity 1

1 48 metres per minute
2 600 to 700 a minute
3 between two and three hundred per minute
4 reasonable quality
5 very flexible
6 extremely high
7 fairly inexpensive
8 A3-sized (A3)
9 A4
10 fairly thick (card)
11 very thin (foils)
12 medium-sized
13 small
14 very few
15 often

Activity 2

1 What we've got here is a very serious problem.
2 All you need is just two levels for most applications.
3 What you can do is use different cassettes for different departments.
4 What you've got is a lot of flexibility.
  What the machine gives you is a lot of flexibility.
5 What the machine does is put the two images side by side.

Appendix C   159

UNIT 5

INPUT 1

Activity 1

1 Strawman requirements
2 Woodenman requirements
3 Tinman requirements
4 Ironman requirements
5 Selection of four teams
6 Selection of Green and Red
7 Final choice: Green language
8 Drawing up of proposed standard
9 Production of standardised language

Activity 2

1 (e)
2 (b)
3 (f)
4 (g)
5 (j)
6 (a)
7 (c)
8 (i)
9 (d)
10 (h)

Activity 3

(Free format exercise)

INPUT 2

Activity 1

1 (c)
2 (c)
3 (c)
4 (c)
5 (a)
6 (c)
7 (b)

Activity 2

(Free format exercise)

Activity 3

(Free format exercise)

LANGUAGE PRACTICE

Activity

1 intended
2 went
3 spent
4 was being installed
5 were trying
6 were taking
7 sorted
8 was disconnected
9 did
10 was reconnected
11 was refitted

DEVELOPMENT 1

Activity 1

1 Efficiency of code; maximisation of hardware usage
2 Quicker to write; more readable code
3 Readability; maintainability
4 Use by non-experts; more end user involvement
5 (Programming):
  Advantages: technical knowledge; familiarity with program specifications.
  Disadvantages: lack of business knowledge and/or communication skills.
6 User department staff who are good communicators:
  Advantages: sensitive to business needs and user department frustration.
  Disadvantages: lack of technical knowledge; lack of appreciation of technical problems.
7 Graduate trainees:
  Advantages: ability to communicate; well educated.
  Disadvantages: lack of experience of both business and computing.

Appendix C 161

Activity 2

Paragraphs 2, 3 and 4: *were, were written, was, maximised, were developed, enabled, allowed, was, made, encouraged, affected, fell, began, was, took, had, wrote, moved, were, influenced.*

Paragraphs 6, 7, 8 and 9: *have had, have become, (meet), has increased, have become, have started, has created, (has).*

The first group relate to finished events and activities. The second group have some connection with the present.

Activity 3

1 have worked
2 have been invented
3 was made
4 received
5 were introduced
6 have become

UNIT 6

INPUT 1

Activity 1

1 (Fred)
2 (Alan)
3 Alan
4 Fred
5 (Sonja)
6 Sonja
7 Fred
8 Fred
9 Sonja
10 Fred
11 Sonja
12 Sonja
13 Alan
14 Sonja

Activity 2

1 (b)
3 (b)
4 (a)
5 (b)
7 (b)

162 Appendix C

9 (b)
11 (a)
14 (a)

Activity 3

(Free format exercise)

INPUT 2

Activity 1

Post reference number: **?**   Date of application: **23 - 9 - 90**
Advertised in: **COMPUTING**   on: **17 - 9 - 90**
First name of applicant: **ANNE**   Family name: **BLANSHARD**
Address: **WATER LANE, FLAXBY, YORK**   Post code: **YO7 3OZ**
Experience: (tick the appropriate boxes)
Computing:

Applications programming	✓	Telecommunications	☐
Systems programming	☐	Supervisory	☐
Systems analysis	✓	Management	☐
Operations	☐	Training	✓

Other (specify): **WRITING CONSULTANCY, LINGUISTICS**
Current employer name: **N/A**   Current employer address: **N/A**
Present salary: **?**   Period of notice required: **N/A**
Availability date: **1 - 11 - 90**   Foreign languages spoken: **NORWEGIAN**

Activity 2

natural language interface products
microcomputer-based educational software
commercial data processing
software training manuals
programmer training materials

Appendix C   163

LANGUAGE PRACTICE

Activity 1

1 they have launched
2 they have not decided
3 has arrived
4 have been
5 have only been
6 has extended
7 they have introduced
(a) just
(b) just/already
(c) yet
(d) for
(e) already
(f) since

Activity 2

1 have you met
2 we've met
a already
3 we've known
b for
4 it's been
5 we've not had/we haven't had
6 have you seen
7 has she left
c yet (or already)
d already

DEVELOPMENT 1

Activity 1

1 (a)   Training
2 (b)/(c)   IBM/Lloyds Bank
  (d)/(e)/(f)/(g) cashiering/welding/safety training/telephone techniques
2 (a)/b)   Point of Sale (POS)/Point of Information (POI) markets
  (c)/(d)   banks/other financial insitutions
  (e)/(f)   selling/internal training
3 Shorter product life cycles, more sophisticated products, faster production methods

Activity 2

1. (a) committed
   (b) was
   (c) 've spent
2. (a) use
   (b) 's (also) been used
   (c) use
3. (a) have (actually) tried
   (b) 're trying
   (c) walk
   (d) interact
4. (a) are (generally) getting
   (b) are becoming
   (c) know
   (d) are being asked

Activity 3

(a) is or *was* if (b) is *emerged*
(b) has emerged or *emerged* if (a) is *was*
(c) has established
(d) includes
(e) supplies (= 1 company) supply (= people in VideoLogic)
(f) was
(g) enables
(h) placed
(i) has become
(j) has penetrated (possibly *is penetrating*)
(k) are sold (possibly *are being sold*)
(l) is growing
(m) has reached
(n) is estimated (possibly *has been estimated*)

UNIT 7

INPUT 1

Activity 1

1. (a) No
   (b) Too big, too costly in time and human resources.

Appendix C

2 (a) No
  (b) Same as Gerry, but also a question of hardware resourses.
3   The kind of relationship they want with a supplier.
4   An outside supplier who can produce the whole system.
      An outside supplier who can do a discrete part of the project.
      A partnership on all aspects of the project.
5   Draw up an invitation to tender.
6   Copyright and ownership agreements.

Activity 2

(Free format exercise)

Activity 3

(Free format exercise)

Activity 4

1 (Costly) in what way exactly?
2 What do you mean by (resources)?
3 Do you mean (we haven't got enough staff or we haven't got the right kind of staff)?
4 You mean whether we should (subcontract the whole thing or just part of it)?
5 So you're saying we should (draw up an invitation to tender).

INPUT 2

Activity 1

 1 !!
 2 (!!)
 3 !
 4 !
 5 (!)
 6 !!
 7 !!
 8 !
 9 + + +
10 + +?
11 +??
12 !!
13 + +?
14 !

Activity 2

1 capture
2 description
3 completion
4 submission
5 statement
6 identify
7 specify
8 produce
9 distribute
10 provide
11 occur

LANGUAGE PRACTICE

Activity 1

1 will (therefore) continue
2 will (soon) be solved
3 should note
4 must (not) be submitted
5 should (only) be submitted
6 must (not) be submitted
7 must (not) be submitted
8 should avoid
9 will (not) apply
10 might delay
11 will (definitely not) decrease
12 will be reviewed
13 will probably be (able to ...)
14 should monitor
15 might cause

DEVELOPMENT 1

Activity 1

1 5982
2 Andrew Holland
3 Jill Daniels
4 Computer Services
5 Paula Braganza
6 His flight has been delayed
7 impossible

8 probable
9 possible
10 probable
11 To postpone the meeting until 2 p.m.
12 To send a car to meet him at the airport.
13 He has booked a hire car.

Activity 2

1 Hello, could I speak to
2 Hold the (line)
3 (KK) speaking
4 (Hello,) this is (GR)
5 Could I speak to (LA, please)?
6 (they've put you) through to (the wrong extension)
7 Could/can you (just ...)
8 (... hold the) line
9 (to) put you (through)
10 extension (548)
11 is that (you, Leif)
12 Hello

Activity 3

(Free format exercise)

UNIT 8

INPUT 1

Activity 1

1 (has taken)
2 (will be discussing)
3 have
4 might be
5 can provide
6 can
7 will ... be covered
8 will
9 are
10 will be
11 have consulted
12 will not be
13 will be monitoring

14 progresses
15 will need
16 starts
17 wonder
18 may be
19 are
20 is
21 must limit
22 will be held
23 will be leaving
24 will be taking over

Activity 2

(a) ask: enquire, wonder
(b) say: report, add, mention, confirm, reply, reaffirm, remind

INPUT 2

Activity 1

1 John Bateson
2 8143
3 K14
4 PRA
5 A22 and A26
6 425 and 436
7 Q3 and Q4
8 -0.1865 and $+0.025$
9 J3
10 EGI300
11 four o'clock
12 3.30

Activity 2

John Bateson, Gerry Cook, Sally Wetherall

Activity 3

1 Sorry, what was the number again?
2 Sorry, did you say K14 or K40?
3 Sorry, could you give me the first one again?
4 Sorry, I didn't catch the second one.
5 Is that plus or minus?
6 Which module did you say it was in?

LANGUAGE PRACTICE

Section 1 Activity

1 (Sorry), which file did you say?
2 (Sorry), Linda who did you say?/what did you say her surname was?
3 (Sorry), which meeting did you say was at 4.30?
4 (Sorry), who did you say will be looking after the batch side?
5 (Sorry), which extension did you say?

Section 2 Activity

1 Could you tell Margaret that I've sent her a letter?
2 Could you ask Mr Peterson to send me a copy of the report?
3 Could you tell Alan not to put the changes in today?
4 Could you ask Mrs Tarrant whether she's sent the test data yet?
5 Could you tell Anna and Paul that the meeting's in room B13 and ask them to bring an overhead projector? And could you ask them whether the Apple rep is staying for lunch? Can you tell them not to be late?

DEVELOPMENT 1

Activity 1

Mr Benson, Bookings Administration

Wednesday (today):	Afternoon meeting; 4 p.m. train to London
Thursday	(in London)
Friday	Return from London
Monday	Interviewing
Tuesday	Free in afternoon
Wednesday	Entertaining visitors
Thursday	Free
Friday	

Pamela Knight, Computer Services

Wednesday (today)	
Thursday	
Friday	
Monday	
Tuesday	Meeting at 2 p.m.
Wednesday	
Thursday	Going on holiday
Friday	

170 Appendix C

Activity 2

(Free format exercise)

Activity 3

1 (What can I) do for you?
2 I wonder/was wondering (if we could ...)
3 How about/Are you free/would you be free (tomorrow morning)?
4 I'm afraid
5 How about/Are you free/would you be free (tomorrow afternoon)?
6 any time (after 3)
7 (after 3) suits/would suit (me fine)
8 Let's say (half past three, then)
9 Shall I (come up to your office)?
10 'Bye

UNIT 9

INPUT 1

Activity 1

PABX advantages:
    sufficient existing capacity
    suitable for long distance traffic
    cheaper — already in place
    a lot of cabling already in place
    tried and tested technology
    staff already trained

LAN advantages:
    faster data transfer

LAN disadvantages:
    not suitable for long distance traffic
    extra expensive hardware needed
    extra cable installation costs
    lack of standards between suppliers
    extra training costs

Activity 2

    'black boxes' would be required
    extra cable installation costs would be incurred
    an open system would be necessary
    a LAN would mean additional training costs

Activity 3

(a) Contrast/difference
   although
   despite the fact that
   while
   whereas
   however
   but
(b) Reason; cause—effect
   the reasons are as follows
   because
   therefore
   because of
   consequently
   due to
   since
   as
(c) Adding information
   furthermore
   in addition to
   finally
   moreover

Activity 4

1 (the) general (conclusion)
2 Most of (the company's)
3 (the) variety (of equipment)
4 (would) involve (extra training)

INPUT 2

Activity 1

1 (b)
2 (b)
3 (c)
4 (a)
5 (a)
6 (c)
7 (b)
8 (a)

Activity 2

1 putting the cart before the horse
2 go back to square one
3 sticking to a decision
4 where do we go from here

Activity 3

(Free format exercise)

LANGUAGE PRACTICE

Activity

1 although/despite the fact that
2 because/since/as
3 however
4 furthermore/moreover/in addition
5 because/since/as
6 whereas/while/but
7 although/despite the fact that
8 whereas/while
9 but/whereas
10 since/as
11 because
12 however
13 because of/due to

DEVELOPMENT 1

Activity 1

1 a word-processing package
2 a format file
3 reports
4 SF/Save Format command
5 the current working directory
6 the directory path
7 by using the operating system COPY command
8 FORMAT1.FMT

Activity 2

1 so that
2 so
3 because
4 because
5 so that
6 so

Activity 3

1 What can I do for you?
2 Could you spare a minute?
3 What's the problem?
4a Are you with me?
 b Alright?
5a Let's say you start doing something else (and the ...)
 b Let's make sure (we do it right)
 c Let's just see if (we can load it)

UNIT 10

INPUT 1

Activity 1

Michelle:
    Step 1: Code the screen layouts
    Step 2: Do the processing later
    Reasons: It's the way they've always done it

Jenny:
    Step 1: Skeleton system with movements between dummy screens
    Step 2: Code one display, plus associated processing, at a time
    Reasons: More user involvement

Mike:
    Step 1: Do the skeleton
    Step 2: Do the menu panel
    Step 3: Do one of the data entry panels
    Step 4: Do one of the detailed enquiry panels
    Step 5: Do one of the summaries
    Step 6: Do the rest
    Reasons: Highlight problems as early as possible to minimise changes

Activity 2

(Free format exercise)

Activity 3

2 It might be a good idea (to do this in small stages)
3 If we did that we'd (find out ...)
4 Shall we (leave that ...)?
5 Wouldn't it be better if we (discussed it with her)?
6 Let's (find out)
7 Don't you think we should (discuss the other idea)?
8 Maybe I should (go away)
9 I suggest we just (code all the screen layouts)
10 It might be worth (doing what Mike says)
11 We could (start by doing a skeleton system)

Activity 4

(Free format exercise)

INPUT 2

Activity 1

Coaxial cabling:
advantages:
    cheaper initially
disadvantages:
    unsuitable for PCs, asynchronous printers and other types of equipment
    no good for connecting computers together
    direct cabling required for each facility
    specific port required for each facility
    difficult and expensive to maintain
    expensive to replace
IBM system:
advantages:
    any type of equipment can be connected
    easy expansion capability
    lower maintenance and upgrade costs
    cheaper in the long term
disadvantages:
    more expensive initially

Activity 2

(a) IBM system
(b) coaxial cabling

Reasons:
Will is a more real possibility to him because he is in favour of the IBM system. *Would* is more hypothetical — it is not the one he recommends. There are so many disadvantages that the possibility of installing it is not a very real possibility in the writer's mind.

Activity 3

Your half sentences should contain basically the same information as the following example answers. If the first half sentence uses the past simple, your half must use *would*; if the first half uses the present simple, yours should use *will*.

If the first half sentence uses *would*, your half must use the past simple; if the first half uses *will*, yours should use the present simple.

1 it would be very expensive.
2 they will need a reliable and flexible system of cabling.
3 they installed coaxial cabling.
4 they install IBM cabling at the outset.
5 they installed coaxial cabling.

LANGUAGE PRACTICE

Activity

1 D
2 L
3 J
4 K
5 E
6 G
7 A
8 M
9 F
10 I
11 C
12 H
13 B

DEVELOPMENT 1

Activity 1

See completed Figure 10.2.

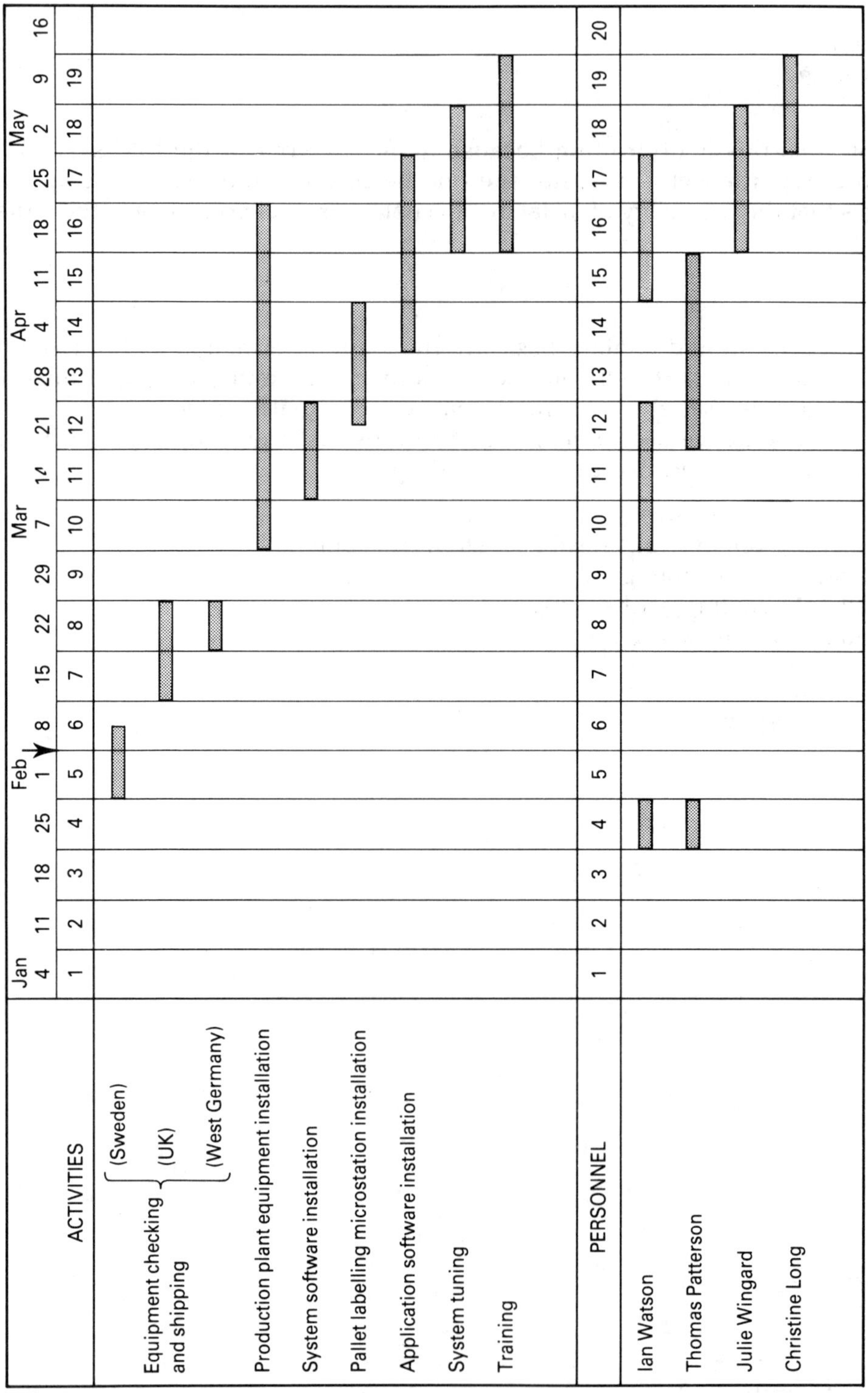
ACTIVITIES
Jan 4 11 18 25
Feb 1 8 15 22 29
Mar 7 14 21 28
Apr 4 11 18 25
May 2 9 16
1 2 3 4 5 6 7 8 9 10 11 12 13 14 15 16 17 18 19
Equipment checking and shipping
(Sweden)
(UK)
(West Germany)
Production plant equipment installation
System software installation
Pallet labelling microstation installation
Application software installation
System tuning
Training
PERSONNEL
1 2 3 4 5 6 7 8 9 10 11 12 13 14 15 16 17 18 19 20
Ian Watson
Thomas Patterson
Julie Wingard
Christine Long

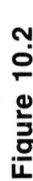

Figure 10.2

Activity 2

1. (a) a fortnight ago
   (b) last Friday
   (c) this week

2. (a) next Monday
   (b) a fortnight later
   (c) in the middle
   (d) during

3. (a) two weeks from today
   (b) by the end of

4. (a) the week after
   (b) first two weeks

UNIT 11

INPUT 1

Activity 1

1. The date shown is not a valid date (31st of June!). Change to e.g. 30/06/89.
2. Should be blank for policy type P01.
3. Should be CA (for cash payment as specified in the exercise instructions)
4. Should be 04 (for quarterly payment as specified in the exercise instructions)
5. Should be less than or equal to start date.
6. Should be entered for function new (£600.00 as specified in the exercise instructions)

Activity 2

1. (d)
2. (b)
3. (c)

Activity 3

1. Number of new staff who/that are required:
2. Number of applications which/that have been received:
3. Number of candidates who/that have been short-listed:
4. Number of interviews which/that have already been held:
5. Four candidates have been offered jobs.
6. Three offers have been accepted.
7. Further interviews that are scheduled (OR that have been scheduled):
8. Two more staff are required.

INPUT 2

Activity 1

1. 'VP.840' should be in high intensity.
2. 'D46' (Source code) should be protected against being overwritten.
3. 'INVOICE DETAILS DISPLAY' should start in column 29 instead of column 27.
4. 'Order details' should start on line 12 in column 2 instead of in column 1.
5. (a) 'Delivery address' should be 'Delivery Address' (capital 'A').
   (b) 'Invoice Address' should start in column 4 and 'Delivery Address' should start in column 43.
6. The Net amounts should be aligned on the decimal point as follows:
   ```
   357.93
     4.43
     3.20
     5.74
    37.98
   ```
7. The VAT total should be 62.82 (not 062.82).

Activity 2

1. hash
2. hyphen
3. backslash
4. full stop
5. asterisk
6. ampersand
7. slash

Price field = #\5.-&

LANGUAGE PRACTICE

Section 1 Activity

1. must be
2. might be switched, might have been switched
3. can't be
4. might not be
5. might have pulled
6. can't be
7. must be
8. should phone
9. must be
10. must have done
11. must know

12 might/could have turned
13 might/could be
14 must have used
15 should have come

Section 2

Activity 1

1 incorrect employee salary code
2 missing previous address details
3 invalid client discount rate

Activity 2

1 main computer electricity supply failure
2 file server hard disk unit surface damage
3 faulty VDU monitor connection cable

DEVELOPMENT 1

Activity 1

(a) 040 given
(b) 050 e.g. 23485
(c) 060 1
(d) 090 (given)
(e) 120 Should be blank if 5 = M. If 5 = F, can be blank or any surname
(f) 140 M or F
(g) 150 e.g. 15/8/59
(h) 180 e.g. 16/3/83 (must be 15 years later than g)
(i) 190 e.g. 15000
(j) 200 e.g. 09B

Activity 2

(Free format exercise)

UNIT 12

INPUT 1

Activity 1

INTRODUCTION
1. (a) Alison McLeod
   (b) Systems analyst
   (c) End user training
2. (a) summary of first phase of new system
   (b) similarities and differences between existing and new systems
   (c) 10 minutes
   (d) explanations
   (e) practical exercises
   (f) 3 hours
3. Can ask questions during presentation
   Coffee break half way through

MAIN BODY
1. (a) suspense accounts enquiry facility
   (b) on-line data entry
   (c) link to personal pensions enquiries
2. (a) request detailed information; request summarised information
   (b) submit transactions from the keyboard
   (c) transfer from new system to personal pensions enquiries and back again to original display

Activity 2

2. we're here to see ...
3. (a) I'd like to start by ...
   (b) Let's start by looking at ...
4. (a) I'll be starting with ...
   (b) I'll also be pointing out ...
   (c) Then we'll move on to ...
   (d) We'll be looking at ...
   (e) Some of the time I'll be ...
   (f) Some of the time you'll be ...
5. Those are ...
6. Now let's look at ...

Activity 3

(Free format exercise)

INPUT 2

Activity 1

1 The building should have been wired as a logical unit.
2 Problem: Trunking passes over radiators.
   → Trunking should have been installed either (a) below radiator level or (b) in the ceiling.
3 Problem: Cableless baluns have not been used.
   → Cableless baluns would have been neater and easier to use.
4 Problems: A heavy steel trunking has been used. Outlets have not been provided for expansion.
   → Additional outlets should have been provided from the beginning.
5 Problem: Floor points are badly positioned.
   → Floor points should have been placed flush with the floor.
6 Problem: Outlet cables are easily dislodged.
   → The locking mechanism should have been implemented.

Activity 2

1 the trunking passes over radiators
   (expansion outlets) have not been provided
   desks have been placed over floor points
   locking mechanisms do not appear to have been implemented
   etc.
2 See text for the full range of possibilities.

LANGUAGE PRACTICE

The following answers are provided as examples of the types of sentence which are possible. Others may be equally acceptable.

1 (a) (They should) have had (more terminals).
  (b) (Then they wouldn't) have had to wait (for each other).
  (c) (If) they had had more terminals they wouldn't have wasted so much time.
2 (a) (The company shouldn't) have made her leave so soon.
  (b) (Then she would) have left (in June).
  (c) (If) she had left (in June they) would have benefited from (her experience for an extra three months).
3 (a) (Either they should) have made someone available from another team (or they should) have recruited someone with more experience.
  (b) (He) wouldn't have needed (so much training).
  (c) (If) they had found someone with more experience they wouldn't have needed to do so much initial training.
4 (a) They should have taken on (a contract programmer).
  (b) He or she would have done (the conversion work).

(c) (If) they had used a contract programmer they would have had more time for the project.
5 (a) They should have started testing (before the summer period).
  (b) Then the users wouldn't have been so (short-staffed).
  (c) (If) they'd started testing before the summer period it probably wouldn't have taken so long to check the test results.
6 (a) Her boss should have been more cooperative.
  (b) Then she wouldn't have felt fed up with the job.
  (c) If she hadn't felt so fed up she might have stayed.

DEVELOPMENT 1

Activity 1

1 (c) cost
  (d) code
2 (a) Prototype lexicographic system on schedule.
  (b) Data capture and validation subsystem.
  also Editing and proof production work.
3 (a)
    (i) Long time to obtain staff and train them to the required levels.
    (ii) Six weeks later than original target date but still earlier than 'latest' date.
  (b) 2/1/87 —
      1/7/87   28/2/87
      31/5/87 31/5/87

Activity 2

1 I think that covers everything.
2 (a) Thank you Tim.
  (b) Does anyone have any questions?
  (c) We can move on to item 4 on the agenda.

Activity 3

1 What I'd like to do while we're all here is ...
  Then I'd like to ... and finally to ...
2 Right, let's look at ... to start with.
3 Two things basically ...
  Second thing is, ...
4 I won't go into that at the moment.
5 Let's move on to ...
  As far as the Lexicographic System is concerned, ...
6 That's all I have to say about ...

APPENDIX D Tapescripts

UNIT 1

Input 1

Receptionist:	Good morning.
Peter:	Good morning. My name's Peter Holmes. I'm starting today as a technical author in the Information Services Department.
Receptionist:	Oh, yes, Mr Holmes, Miss Long's expecting you. I'll just let her know you're here.
Jenny:	Jenny Long speaking.
Receptionist:	Hello, Miss Long, Reception here. Mr Holmes has arrived and is waiting in reception.
Jenny:	Right, thank you. I'll be down in a second.
Receptionist:	Miss Long's coming down now, Mr Holmes. Would you like to take a seat.
Peter:	Thank you.
Jenny:	(*footsteps*) Good morning, you must be Peter Holmes.
Peter:	That's right.
Jenny:	I'm Jenny Long. Pleased to meet you.
Peter:	Pleased to meet you.
Jenny:	I'm the documentation co-ordinator so we'll be working quite a lot together. Would you like to come this way and I'll show you round and introduce you to the other people in the documentation section. Have you met Mr Blakely, the Information Services Manager?
Peter:	No, I was interviewed by the Assistant Manager.
Jenny:	Right, let's see if he's in, then. Good morning, Mr Blakely.
Mr Blakely:	Hello, Jenny.
Jenny:	Can I introduce you to Peter Holmes, the new Technical Author? Peter, Mr Blakely.
Peter:	How do you do?
Mr Blakely:	Pleased to meet you, Peter, I hope you'll be happy here.
Peter:	Thank you. I'm sure I will.
Mr Blakely:	Is Jenny just showing you round?
Peter:	Yes, that's right.
Mr Blakely:	Look, I don't mean to be rude, but I'm afraid I'm just going to a meeting. I'll come round and talk to you later.
Jenny:	Right. We'll go and meet the others, then, Peter.
Mr Blakely:	'Bye for now.
Peter:	'Bye.

184   *Appendix D*

Jenny: Right, this is our section. Morning.
Three voices: Hi.
Hello.
Morning.
Jenny: Can I introduce you all to Peter Holmes, our new technical author.
Les: Hello. Les Barton.
Peter: Hi.
Jenny: And this is Sandra ....
Peter: Nice to meet you.
Sandra: Glad to meet you.
Jenny: And last but not least, Brian.
Brian: Hello there.
Peter: Hello. Do you all do the same sort of thing?
Les: Well, we're all involved in documentation production as technical authors, but each of us has different special areas. Sandra looks after the technical manuals side of things, Brian deals with database documentation and I handle end user procedure manuals and training materials. In theory, anyway. In practice we overlap quite a lot. In fact I'm working with Sandra at the moment on a technical manual. Have you seen the rest of the department?
Peter: No, Miss Long's just showing me round now.
Jenny: Please call me Jenny, Peter. Everybody calls Mr Blakely by his surname but everybody else in the department uses first names. Now then, would you like a coffee?

Development 1

Keith: Right, Paul, I'm going to show you where you fit in in a minute, but I think it's best if I start by telling you a bit about the Information Services Division in general. Basically it's split up into three departments now, and each one has its own manager who is accountable to the General Manager for Information Services in the UK.
Paul: Is he actually based in the UK or at Headquarters in Hines Brussels?
Keith: Well, it's 'she' actually. No, she's based here at the UK Head Office. There's also a General Manager IS for Europe as a whole, so Margaret Rothwell — the UK IS manager — reports to him. So, to get back to the three departments. First of all there's the Planning Department, which comes under Andrew Meredith. They're involved in long-term planning. They're concerned with things like security arrangements, hardware compatibility, staffing, compatibility between different sites and so on.

Then there's the Development Department which is divided up into two main areas, as you can see on the diagram. There's the Existing Systems section — which is broken down into various project teams and another fairly new section called Strategic Systems. They're the people who are in charge of developing new systems.
Paul: What sort of things are they doing at the moment, then?
Keith: In Strategic Systems, do you mean?
Paul: Yes.
Keith: They're involved in developing new systems using fourth generation languages and producing more integrated systems. At the moment, for example, they're trialling DBase IV, which we're just starting to use. So they look into Management Information requirements and what have you. They're also looking at one or two security packages.

Anyway, let's look at the Processing Department, which is where we are. As you can see, my job title is Manager of Computer Processing and as the Assistant Manager in charge of Computer Production you report directly to me. The other two Assistant Managers who come under me look after the Technical Support and Operational Support sections.

Paul:	What do they do exactly, then?
Keith:	Well, Bill Larkin in Technical Support looks after the Telecoms software support and the systems programming side of things. The Operations Support section is headed by Liz Campbell and they deal with things like change management.
Paul:	For new systems, you mean?
Keith:	Well, for new systems and for changes to existing systems. They do all the co-ordination for interfaces between different systems, and review development proposals. They also check that security arrangements conform to standards and when we put new systems in they monitor parallel runs and look after handover arrangements, things like that. And they liaise with Technical Support and the Planning Department on hardware and capacity planning as well. And then of course we come to you and your role ...

UNIT 2

Input 2

Rachel:	Right, let's look at how you use the cursor control keys, then. We've got a screenfull of records in a display format that looks like a spreadsheet, right?
Martin:	Mmm.
Rachel:	Now, you use the cursor control keys to move to different records, to different fields within a record and to different characters within each field. If you press the down cursor key, the cursor moves to the next line — that's the start of the next sequential record in alphabetical order of manufacturer. To get to the start of the next field in that record, press the right cursor key. So now you're at the start of the second field in the second record. If you press the upward cursor key, it takes you to the corresponding field in the preceding record.
Martin:	So does the left cursor take me back to the first field in the first record?
Rachel:	That's right. Now you can also use the cursor keys together with the SHIFT and CONTROL keys for other types of movement. At the moment, we can't see all the fields in each record. Now if you press SHIFT and the right key, the cursor jumps to the start of the last field and the screen display shifts left.
Martin:	Ah, ah.
Rachel:	Now if you want to page through to the next screenfull of data, you use the SHIFT and down keys together.
Martin:	I see. So SHIFT and left cursor take me back to the first field in a record and SHIFT together with the upward cursor take me back to the previous screenfull.
Rachel:	Correct.
Martin:	What do you use the CONTROL key for, then?
Rachel:	Well if you use it with the cursor right and cursor left keys it goes left or right within a field, one character at a time.
Martin:	What about up and down?
Rachel:	That's a bit different. CONTROL and up takes you to the first record in the display sequence, CONTROL and down take you to the last one — I mean the final one.
Martin:	Do you mean the end of the file?
Rachel:	Not exactly. At the moment we're looking at records in alphabetical order of the manufacturers; if we look at the records in ascending order of price or descending order of maximum speed, the last record in the display will be different.
Martin:	How do you change the order, then?
Rachel:	Can we come back to that in a second? There's just one more thing I'd like to show you about moving through the records. Just move to the last record on the screen. OK. Now press the downward cursor key. Now you see that the screen just scrolls upwards by one line.

Martin: Right, so you can just roll forwards by one record at a time instead of paging through a screenfull at a time. And does it scroll downwards if you're on the top line of the display?

Rachel: Yes, it does. You can get the previous record by pressing the upward cursor key. Right, that covers the cursor movements. Let's look at how to change the display sequence shall we? ...

UNIT 3

Development 1

A: What does the system give you at the moment, then?
B: We get a daily printout which lists all the rejected payment transactions.
A: How many are rejected on average?
B: I don't know. We don't keep any statistics.
A: Are they rejected because of clerical errors?
B: It's mostly to do with clerical errors on the input advices, yes.
A: Are most of the mistakes made when the data preparation clerks key the details in?
B: Sometimes, but our people in the accounts section sometimes enter the wrong payment amount or they get the policy number wrong.
A: So how do you use the details on the printout to find out what's wrong?
B: Well, Paul tries to find out why the computer has rejected them by looking at information on the Personal Pensions Enquiries system. You can see that the printout shows the policy number, the name of the policy holder, the payment amount, the transaction date, actual payment date and the payment due date.
A: So what does he do? Does he just look at the details for that customer's policy and then fill in a new form with the correct details?
B: It's not quite as simple as that. We can only find policies by policy number or client name on the enquiries system. If the payment details don't match that policy the enquiries system doesn't help us to find other policies with similar payment due dates or similar payment amounts.
A: So what happens if they don't match?
B: We have to ask DP to run a program that searches the file and prints a list of policies with the same payment date or payment amount or whatever.
A: But how often do you need to do that? I mean, aren't most of the problems sorted out by using the enquiries system?
B: Most of them, yes, but we have to ask DP to do a search four or five times a week.
A: Who decides that you need to ask?
B: John.

UNIT 4

Development 1

Paul: What we've got here with the 1000 model is the first of a range of microfilmers that are what we call intelligent microfilmers. It's very fast — the film transport will work at up to 48 metres per minute. That means it'll film up to about six or seven hundred cheque-sized documents a minute. With A4 it's around two to three hundred. But the documents need to be reasonable quality to reach those speeds. If they haven't got a very good edge, quite often they jam.

Now you've got a lot of flexibility. You can choose whether you want it to film at 24 or 40 times reduction, or you can tell it to film double sided documents so that the images are side by side or you can actually film down one side of the film, turn the film cassette over and then film back up the other side again. That's more useful for archiving purposes when you want to fit more on the film but you don't need to access the images very often.

So it's very flexible and potentially, you have an extremely high capacity on each cassette. The nice thing about using cassettes is that they're fairly inexpensive, which means that a company or department can use just one of the machines, but different cassettes for different departments or sections.

You can film up to A3-sized documents, but A4 is the largest size that people normally want to use. For different thicknesses, all you need to do is adjust a lever under the front of the machine and that makes the gap between the rollers on the automatic feed slightly larger or smaller. It'll take anything from fairly thick card to those very thin foils that you get as a receipt when you use a credit card.

Now the indexing of the microfilmer is very very flexible. The microfilmer itself is capable of putting what we call blips or small image marks on a film. A blip is basically a small mark next to a document on a film which the retrieval terminal uses to get to the document that you want. So what the microfilmer does is it actually puts those marks on the film while it's filming the document.

If you look at this sample, you can see the blips down the left-hand edge of the film and the documents are just to the right of them. All right? Now what you can do with this microfilmer is put different sizes of blips on. The reason why we do this is so that you can get back to the document quickly when we come to retrieval time.

On this sample it puts on one of these smaller blips for each document that it films. But you've also got these slightly larger blips which identify the start of a batch. Now if you look at the next sample, the other thing we can do is put on what we call a large blip. There are very few people who use a large blip. Most of the time, batch and item are enough. It just gives you an extra level of indexing but as I said it's very unusual — I've only got one customer who uses it and that's a very large travel organisation. They use the largest blips for indexing by day and the medium-sized and small blips for batches and items within the day.

So that's the 1000 model. Now with the 2000, we've got a very sophisticated machine. It can do everything that the 1000 can do, but it can also do things that . . .

UNIT 5

Input 2

Fred: Let me start by giving you a bit of background. Basically I work as a freelance sales consultant and in particular I've got quite a lot of experience of handling database products. About a year ago I came across a company in the States called Ontologic who're based in Massachusetts.

They were developing a product called VBASE, which was an object-oriented database. In fact I'd rather not call it a database because it's more of an environment. What it is is a programming language which is integrated with what they call an object-oriented database.

They decided — Ontologic that is — to market this product in the UK with a company called Smalltalk Express who handle this type of software product. So they were appointed as the UK distributors about a month ago and I got myself involved with them on a freelance basis via Ontologic right from the start.

Alan:	Now they have a very novel way of seeding the marketplace. What they decided to do was to allow Smalltalk Express five licences in the UK at quite a phenomenal discount of 80% on the current commercial list price.
Alan:	So what does that come to in actual figures?
Fred:	Right. The commercial price is £23 000 for a single Sun licence. Then it goes up to double for a network of Suns attached to a file-server, then if you double that you can go up to a site licence for any user within the university. OK that's pretty expensive, but if you're one of the first five what you're looking at is an 80% discount on the commercial price of the product, which is an extremely good deal, I think.
Alan:	So we're talking about four and a half thousand for a single user.
Fred:	Something like that, yes. Which is pretty good. I mean, this is a very interesting piece of software for research establishments like yourselves. Then it's twice as much for a cluster and twice as much again for a site licence. But after the first five licences are taken up you're looking at a standard educational discount of 50%. Obviously it's much cheaper if you take one of the first five.
Alan:	And what about maintenance?
Fred:	Ah, if you want you can take out a maintenance contract which is ... 50% of the commercial price.

UNIT 6

Input 1

Fred:	So as I say, the people in Leeds have decided to go with it now. They've had about three months' experience of using it and think it has a lot of potential as a research tool. The people in Glasgow have just come back from the States where they've had a closer look at it and the people in Strathclyde have shown quite a lot of interest. I mean I've been in this business since the sixties but I haven't seen so much interest in a product for a long time. Things are really moving.
Alan:	I certainly think that if we want to be at the forefront of this new technology we need some kind of experimentation vehicle. Now I've discussed a few possibilities of how we can do that ourselves, but really I think it's much better if we can actually buy something in to give us a starting point.
Fred:	I couldn't agree more. I mean, why re-invent the wheel. This gives you a jump-off point.
Sonja:	Well, it sounds very interesting, but I think the basic problem is the money. We've just spent £4000 on Ingress and I don't think we can really go back and ask for another four-and-a-half straight away.
Fred:	Well, you never know. This is a completely different product. You might get some help with funding from another department. Personally, I don't think there's any doubt that you have to get into this. People are already saying that the eighties was the age of the relational database but in the nineties it's going to be object-oriented databases. Really we're seeing this already and you have to move with it.
Sonja:	Yes I accept that, but you see, what we teach the students is our first priority. We have to consider what is more useful to them. And when they finish the course, Ingress is more useful because it's more widely available. Apart from which the textbooks are already written so it's easier from that point of view as well.
Fred:	But that's right now. Things are definitely changing and at a cost of 4000 for a Sun it's probably a worthwhile acquisition.
Sonja:	Yes I take your point that it's an interesting area to get into but as always there's a limited amount of money available.

Fred:	But the people who've already used it are looking at both areas. They're saying they want to use it as a research tool and as a teaching tool.
Sonja:	I certainly think you're right and this is something we have to move into one way or another. The question is how we do it. How do we fund it?
Alan:	I think our best way forward is to have a much more thorough look at the documentation to get a better idea of what it offers. Then I think we can go across to Leeds and see how they've found it.
Sonja:	Oh I certainly agree that it's worth looking into, yes.
Alan:	Well, ... Come in. Hello, have you come along to hear about this relational database thing?
Ann:	Yes, sorry, we're late. We've been looking for you for about twenty minutes — the doorman didn't know who you were.
Alan:	Well I've only been here a week and I've only been in this office since yesterday — he probably hasn't heard of me yet!

Development 1

Alistair:	Training has virtually built the UK interactive video industry. People like Lloyds Bank, back in 1985, committed themselves to 1500 systems which was an investment of some £4 000 000 plus in the technology and since then they've spent about another 12 million or so on applications.
Steve:	That's quite an investment.
Alistair:	It certainly is. In fact through that investment they have sponsored the whole industry. IBM themselves are a major contributor. They actually have systems throughout Europe for dealer training, etc. and they also sell IV courses about their products.
Steve:	It is mostly the financial and high-tech sectors that use it then?
Alistair:	Not only, no. It's also been used for skills such as welding. British Nuclear Fuels use it for safety training. Basically I think that as long as there is a procedure that can be broken down and split into tasks, the subject matter itself is largely irrelevant. It can be cashiering, welding, safety training, telephone techniques — whatever.
Steve:	What about other uses apart from training?
Alistair:	Well training has been the main use so far but the Point of Sale and Point of Information markets have also started to use this much more. Most of the major banks have actually tried these things called information kiosks, for example, because they're trying to get into things like stocks and shares, mortgages, insurance, etc. — new areas for the bank. People walk up to a stand-alone terminal in the bank and they interact with it via a touch-screen, etc. and learn about the services. In fact not only the banks but the whole of the finance sector is taking this technology to heart both in selling and in internal training. I feel that one of the key reasons for the development of IV in selling is because with computers in manufacturing and design, people are producing smaller faster widgets that can do twice as many things and they can produce them in half the time. So product life cycles are generally getting shorter the products are becoming more sophisticated and the potential users know less and less about the equipment that they are being asked to use, etc.
Steve:	So there is a kind of training element there, isn't there.
Alistair:	Absolutely. I think to a certain extent the marketing problems of today are virtually the same problems as training — how to put across the information and educate people so that they feel confident enough to buy the product.

UNIT 7

Input 1

Graham:	The basic question really is whether we should do the system entirely in-house. Is it feasible to do it ourselves? What do you think, Gerry?
Gerry:	I think it's out of the question. It's a huge project and I think it'll be far too costly for us to do it all ourselves.
Graham:	Costly in what way exactly?
Gerry:	In terms of time and resources.
Graham:	What do you mean by resources? Personnel?
Gerry:	Yes. I don't think we've got the staff to handle it.
Graham:	Do you mean we haven't got enough staff or we haven't got the right kind of staff?
Gerry:	Oh I think we've got people who are capable of doing the work but we definitely won't be able to meet our existing commitments and take on a project of this scale.
Graham:	What about you, Shirley? What do you think?
Shirley:	I agree with Gerry, basically. But I don't think it's just a question of manpower resources, it's hardware resources, too. There'll be certain types of equipment that'll only be used in the initial stages of the project — we won't have any need of them after that — so it'll probably be much better to subcontract the parts of the project where that type of hardware is needed. Personally I don't think it's a question of whether we should do it ourselves — I'm quite sure we can't — it's what sort of relationship we want with an outside supplier who can provide a system. And that's what we should look at.
Graham:	You mean whether we should subcontract the whole thing or just part of it?
Shirley:	Well, I think there's a whole range of possibilities. If we invite people to tender for the work we might find a supplier who can produce the whole system with us just paying for it. Or we might produce certain parts while a supplier produces other parts, or we may be able to form a different sort of partnership with all of us working together on all of the system components.
Graham:	So you're saying we should draw up an invitation to tender and ask people to submit proposals.
Shirley:	Yes. But whatever the relationship is with an outside supplier we should be particularly careful to get the right sort of copyright and ownership agreements. In fact Gerry and I have already had a chat about inviting tenders and come up with a few ideas about what we should include in the document.
Graham:	Oh, have you?

Development 1

Operator:	Inter Accident Insurance, good morning.
MD:	Hello, could I have extension 5982, please.
Operator:	Hold the line, please. Trying to connect you.
AH:	Extension 5982, Andrew Holland speaking.
MD:	Hello, this is Maurice Damoiseau from the Brussels office. Could I speak to Jill Daniels please?
AH:	I'm sorry, who did you say?
MD:	Maurice Damoiseau, from ...
AH:	No sorry, I meant who did you want to speak to?
MD:	Jill Daniels.
AH:	I'm sorry, I think you've got the wrong number. There is no Jill Daniels here. Which department did you want?

MD:	She works in Computer Services.
AH:	OK if you just hold the line a second I'll ask the switchboard to put you through.
Operator:	Switchboard.
AH:	Hello, could you put this through to Jill Daniels in Computer Services, please.
PB:	Computer Services.
MD:	Hello, is that Jill Daniels?
PB:	No, this is Paula Braganza, Ms Daniel's secretary. I'm afraid Ms Daniels won't be here until about 10.00 this morning. Can I take a message?
MD:	Yes, this is Maurice Damoiseau from the Brussels office. I'm supposed to be meeting Jill Daniels and Brian Faulkner at 11 a.m. but my flight to Manchester has been delayed because of technical problems so I won't be able to make it for 11 o'clock. They say the plane will probably be ready in about an hour so I should be there between 12 and half past but you never know; it might take them longer.
PB:	Right.
MD:	I wonder if it might be better to put the meeting off until about 2 p.m. and then Ms Daniels and Mr Faulkner won't waste any time waiting for me.
PB:	Right, I'll tell them Mr Damoiseau.
MD:	Thank you. Look I'll ring from Manchester airport to find out about the new time for the meeting, because it'll probably take about an hour to get from there to your office.
PB:	Well if you give me your flight number we'll find out the new time of arrival and send a car to pick you up at the airport.
MD:	Well, thank you very much, but that won't be necessary. I've booked a hire car.
PB:	Oh, I see. Right Mr Damoiseau, I'll make sure Ms Daniels gets the message. I hope you won't have to wait much longer. Thank you for ringing.
MD:	Thank you, goodbye.
PB:	Bye.

UNIT 8

Input 2

John:	Information Services, John Bateson speaking.
Gerry:	Hello, is Sally Wetherall there please. It's Gerry Cook from Pensions.
John:	Sorry, she's not here at the moment.
Gerry:	Right well could you ask her to ring me on extension 8143 as soon as she gets back.
John:	Sorry, what was the number again?
Gerry:	8143.
John:	Oh, just a second, she's here now. Sally, Gerry Cook from Pensions for you.
Sally:	Hello Gerry, what can I do for you?
Gerry:	Hello Sally. There are a couple of changes I'd like you to make if you could. We'd like to allow source code K14 (*fourteen*) to get onto the PRA system.
Sally:	Sorry, did you say K14 (*fourteen*) or K40 (*forty*)?
Gerry:	Fourteen: one four. Also we'd like to be able to use that source code and the ones that are valid already — that's A22 and A26 — from terminals 425 (*four twenty five*) and 436 (*four thirty six*).
Sally:	Sorry, could you give me the first one again?
Gerry:	Do you mean the source code or the terminal number?
Sally:	The terminal number.
Gerry:	425.

Sally:	OK, but could you confirm it in writing?
Gerry:	Yes, sure. By the way, have you altered the Q3 and Q4 adjustment factors for tomorrow?
Sally:	For tomorrow? You're joking. Look I've told Ron Gibson before that we need notification a lot earlier than half past three on the day before the new ones come into force. Could you tell him to send them down at least 2 days before you want them in.
Gerry:	Well I've got a memo with the new ones here.
Sally:	Yes, but he should tell us, Gerry. What are they? I'll have to ask John to do them.
Gerry:	Right, −0.1865 (*minus nought point one eight six five*) and 0.025 (*oh point oh two five*).
Sally:	Sorry, I didn't catch the second one.
Gerry:	0.025 (*oh point oh two five*).
Sally:	Zero point zero two five. Is that plus or minus?
Gerry:	Plus.
Sally:	And which one's which?
Gerry:	The first one's the Q3.
Sally:	Right, but I can't put them into the production system for tomorrow unless I get written confirmation before four o'clock. Could you tell Gibson to bring them down?
Gerry:	I certainly will. Will you let me know when you've done the source code changes?
Sally:	Yes, we should be able to do them tomorrow morning. I'll give you a ring as soon as they're done, OK?
Gerry:	Thanks. 'Bye.
Sally:	'Bye. (...) John, are you busy?
John:	I'm just going to start that J3 validity change that you asked me to do yesterday. Which module did you say it was in?
Sally:	EGI300 (*three hundred*), but leave that for now, will you. The Q3 and Q4 factors need to be changed before four o'clock.
John:	When did you say? It's half past three now! Don't tell me — Ron Gibson.
Sally:	How did you guess!

Development 1

Benson:	Bookings Admin., Benson.
Pamela:	Hello, is that Mr Benson?
Benson:	Speaking.
Pamela:	Hello, this is Pamela Knight from Computer Services. I'm ringing about the siting of the equipment you're getting for the new on-line bookings system that we're putting in next month.
Benson:	Oh, yeh.
Pamela:	Yes. I erm ... I wonder if we could have a chat some time about exactly where you want to put the various terminals and printers because we need to plan the cabling and so on.
Benson:	I'm sorry, I'm very busy today. I've got a meeting this afternoon then I'm leaving for London on the 4 o'clock train and I probably won't be back until late on Friday.
Pamela:	Well, I wasn't thinking of today, actually. I was wondering if we could get together towards the beginning of next week. Would you be free on Monday or Wednesday?
Benson:	I'm afraid I'm interviewing job applicants all day Monday and some visitors are coming on Wednesday, so I think I'll be with them most of the day. Let me just check my diary. Mmmm. Thursday would be OK, though, I'll be free all day.
Pamela:	It's no good for me, I'm afraid. I'm going on holiday for a fortnight on Thursday.
Benson:	Lucky you. Maybe we should leave it until you come back from holiday then.
Pamela:	Well, I'd rather we didn't if you don't mind. I'd really like to get things moving on this before I go away. How about Tuesday morning? Are you free then?

Benson:	I'm sorry, when did you say?
Pamela:	Tuesday morning.
Benson:	If you could make it Tuesday afternoon it would be more convenient. Any time after half past one.
Pamela:	Well, 3 o'clock would suit me. I've got another meeting at 2.00.
Benson:	OK. Let's say 3 p.m. Shall I come over to Computer Services?
Pamela:	Well actually, I'd rather come over to you. It would be better if we could actually look at where you want to put things.
Benson:	Oh, yes I suppose it would.
Pamela:	So shall we say I'll meet you in your office at 3 o'clock next Tuesday then?
Benson:	That suits me fine.
Pamela:	Right, thank you. I look forward to seeing you. 'Bye.
Benson:	'Bye.

UNIT 9

Input 2

Barry:	Why do you think we need to look at the question of Local Area Networks again Anne?
Alistair:	I'm sorry but I really don't see any point in raising this again. George looked at our networking needs before he left and convinced us that we should use our PABX. Don't you think his investigations were thorough enough?
Anne:	It depends what you mean, Alistair. If you're saying that his arguments were convincing at the time, I would agree with you. But I'm afraid I don't agree that his study took into account the company's needs in terms of ...
Alistair:	With all due respect, Anne, after six years with the company George knew a lot more about our needs than you do after only four months.
Anne:	Look, I'm not disputing the fact that George knew a lot more about the company, what I'm saying is that ...
Alistair:	Well you certainly seem to be trying to say that. You keep saying that ...
Anne:	What I'm trying to say is — if you'll let me finish (*pause to collect thoughts*) ... Look, the point is that George left four months ago. I realise that's not such a long time, but since he left, the company has made several decisions that affect our long-term needs. It's partly to do with decisions about expansion but it's especially because of the merger with Komfy Karpets and the fact that they already use a LAN.
Barry:	But surely that doesn't stop us using our PABX to link up with them.
Anne:	No, it doesn't, you're right. But the point is it makes the cost of us using a LAN ourselves more justifiable.
Alistair:	I don't really see how. It doesn't make it any cheaper, does it? If I remember rightly, one of the main reasons for rejecting the idea of a LAN was that it was far more expensive than the PABX.
Anne:	I didn't say it would make it any cheaper, I said it would make it more justifiable. Previously most of our traffic was with Dundee and Falkirk, right? But the Komfy Karpets warehouse and main office are both within a mile of here. And the other thing is that the decision to expand our other office here means that a link-up between the four local sites would be more worthwhile.
Barry:	I can see what you're getting at, Anne, but don't you think we're putting the cart before the horse?
Anne:	How do you mean?

Barry: Well, it appears to me that we're talking about linking together four sites without having looked at why they need to be linked together yet. We seem to be talking about choosing A or B so that we can do X more efficiently but we haven't even identified what X is, have we?

Anne: I quite agree, but what I'm saying, basically, is that we need to go back to square one and look at our networking needs again. We shouldn't be sticking to a decision that was based on 6-month-old recommendations when our situation has changed so much since.

Barry: In that case, I would tend to agree with you, so long as we don't presuppose that a LAN is now the only sensible option. What about you Alistair?

Alistair: (*grudgingly*) Fair enough, yes. I can see that Anne might have a point I suppose. Question is, where do we go from here?

Development 1

Cathy: Hello, Steve.

Steve: 'Morning, Cathy. What can I do for you?

Cathy: I've got a problem with this word-processing package. Could you spare a minute?

Steve: Sure. What's the problem?

Cathy: Well, you know how you can create different format files to create standard paragraphs and things . . .

Steve: Yes . . .

Cathy: Well, I've created a new format file for reports, but every time I try to load it it says 'File not found'. So I can't use my new formats because it can't find the format file. Can I show you on the machine?

Steve: Sure.

Cathy: Right. ATTACH FORMAT1 — that's the format file — and RETURN. You see? FORMAT1 NOT FOUND.

Steve: Mm . . . Mm. Can you just come out of the word processing package and display the disk directory . . .
Mmmm. It's not there, is it. Maybe it's because . . . um, were you working on the training files when you created the format file?

Cathy: Yes. Why?

Steve: Ah! That's the problem, then. When you create a format file you save it with the SF command, right?

Cathy: Yes.

Steve: Well, when you use the SAVE FORMAT command, the program puts the format file in the same directory as the document that you're working on so that it can attach it automatically when you try to load the document again. Are you with me?

Cathy: Not exactly!

Steve: Well, um, suppose you're working on a document called MYREP in a directory called REPORTS and you call your format file FORMAT1; when you use the SAVE FORMAT command, the program saves the file in that directory as FORMAT1.FMT (*format one dot f-m-t*).

Cathy: So it stores it in directory REPORTS.

Steve: That's right. Now, let's say you start doing something else and the current directory is, for instance, USER CATHY LETTERS — that's your personal default directory; if you use the LOAD FORMAT command to load FORMAT1.FMT, it can't find it in the current directory. Alright?

Cathy: Ah, I see. OK. So when I want to load the format file I have to include the directory path in the filename if it's not in the current directory.

Steve: That's right. Or you can copy the file to your reports directory before you go into the word-processing package.

Cathy:	Ah, I see. Yes, now I'm with you. So I can just use the operating system COPY command.
Steve:	Yes. But let's make sure we do it right. Um. You see the current directory is USER CATHY REPORTS and your format file is in USER CATHY TRAINING.
Cathy:	So I type

        COPY USER CATHY TRAINING FORMAT1

        OK?

Steve:	Almost. Format files have a suffix of .FMT, so FORMAT1.FMT is the full filename.
Cathy:	Dot F-M-T.
Steve:	Right — and press RETURN.
Cathy:	Great, thanks a lot.
Steve:	Well, before you thank me, let's just see if we can load it ....

UNIT 10

Input 1

Michelle:	So there are ten displays altogether. How long do you think it's likely to take?
Mike:	Why don't we wait until Jenny gets here. She'll be able to give you a better idea than I can. You know I still think it might be a good idea to do this in small stages and involve the users in testing each stage instead of waiting till the end. If we did that we'd find out early on whether there were any problems with movements between screens.
Michelle:	There shouldn't be any problems with that, should there?
Mike:	Come on Michelle, there are bound to be some changes. There always are. It'd save a lot of time in the long run if we found out at the beginning.
Michelle:	Well, shall we leave that for the moment? Jenny's here now.
Mike:	Wouldn't it be better if we discussed it with her as well?
Michelle:	Let's find out what she thinks about the timescales first, shall we? Hi Jenny.
Jenny:	Hello.
Michelle:	Jenny, you've seen the specs for the IP system. If you did the coding for the screen displays, how long do you reckon it would take you?
Mike:	Michelle, I'm sorry but don't you think we should discuss the other idea at the same time? They're not really separate issues, are they?
Jenny:	Maybe I should go away again and come back later!
Michelle:	No, no. Mike thinks we should do some sort of prototype but I suggest we just code all the screen layouts first and then do the processing that goes with them later, which is the way we've always done it before.
Jenny:	It might be worth doing what Mike says, actually. We could start by doing a skeleton system with movements between dummy screens. I think the users might feel more involved if we did it that way, too — there wouldn't be such a big delay before they saw something.
Michelle:	But what about after that?
Jenny:	Once the movements between screens were OK we could do one display at a time with all its associated processing and ask them to test it out before starting the next one.
Mike:	Well ... OK, do the skeleton first, but then, rather than doing just one after the other in sequence, wouldn't it be better if we then did one of each of the main types of display?
Jenny:	How do you mean?

Mike:	Well, there's the menu panel — so that would obviously have to be done first. Then there are the two data entry screens, aren't there? So we could do one of those to show them how the data entry and validation procedures would work. Then there are the four detailed enquiry panels for the different account types. If we did one of those next it would highlight most of the problems that we might get on any of the other three details panels. Then there are the weekly, monthly and annual summaries; the responses and movements to other screens are similar on each of them, so if we did one of those, again it would give us some idea of any changes that we might need to make to the other two.
Jenny:	Mmmm. Sounds reasonable.

Development 1

Ian:	So the first of the equipment that needs to be shipped to France is due to arrive here at the beginning of next week and various other bits and pieces will be coming during the rest of that week and the following week. Pia Gullbery rang me from Gothenburg yesterday to confirm that the stuff that's going from Gothenburg was checked last week and leaves for France the day after tomorrow. The Dusseldorf people are doing the same sort of thing the week after next. They haven't got as much to do so a week should be plenty.

At our end, Gerry will be responsible for checking equipment as it comes in here. Once it's all been checked it'll be shipped to the French plant. All of it must be ready for shipping by the end of week 8 at the latest as it has to be at the French plant by the beginning of March. Sorry, that's not quite right — I should say by the start of the first full week in March. |
Julie:	So that's the beginning of week 10.
Ian:	That's right — in 4 weeks' time. That's when they start to install the equipment in the production plant. The production plant equipment installation should be completed by the end of week 16.
Julie:	So it's all supposed to be finished within 7 weeks?
Ian:	If you mean within 7 weeks of starting to install it, yes. That's 11 weeks from now. Some of the equipment installation doesn't concern us, of course, but we are going to be involved throughout that period on one thing or another.

As you all know, Thomas and I were over at the new site the week before last to talk to the site engineers and the people from Hewlett Packard about the power supply to the computers, cabling requirements and so on. The Hewlett Packard people are installing the system software in weeks 11 and 12.

Now there are one or two changes to the scheduling of the different activities and the people who'll be responsible for them. Originally I was going to be there for 8 weeks starting in week 10. Instead of that I'm now going to be there for 6 weeks altogether, but in two blocks of three. I'm still going out 4 weeks from today, but I'll be coming back here after 3 weeks. Then I'll be going out again a fortnight later for a further 3 weeks. The idea is that I'll be there for the start of the equipment installation and stay until the Hewlett Packard people have installed the system software.

Right. As far as the pallet labelling microstations are concerned, installation is scheduled to start in the middle of week 12. We've allowed $2\frac{1}{2}$ weeks for that. As that's Thomas's pigeon, he's going out at the beginning of that week but he's going to stay for 4 weeks instead of the 3 we intended so that he can ask as a link between my two periods there. That also means that he can take on some of the applications software installation work which we plan to start in week 14. That should be finished by the time I leave at the end of my second 3 weeks there. |

	That just leaves the fine tuning and training activities. Julie will now be responsible for the fine tuning as Les is moving to another project. We've set aside 3 weeks for that Julie, so you'll be there from the beginning of week 16 until the end of week 18. You and I will also be doing some training from week 16 onwards, but Christine is going out for a couple of weeks starting week 18 as originally planned to look after the user training for the applications side with the sales order processing and financial systems.
Julie:	So everything should be in perfect working order by the end of week 19.
Ian:	That's the plan!
Julie:	I'll believe it when I see it!

UNIT 11

Input 2

Ian:	I'm just looking at this VP 840 display and there are a few things that aren't quite right. Not too serious — just a few indentation and highlighting problems, mainly.
Peter:	Uh uh.
Ian:	Mmm. First thing is, the reference number in the top left-hand corner.
Peter:	But that's where it should be according to the spec.
Ian:	Oh yes, it's in the right place but it should be highlighted and it's appearing in low intensity.
Peter:	Oh, sorry, yes.
Ian:	The other thing on the top line is the source code that's picked up from when you sign on ...
Peter:	Yes?
Ian:	Well, I can overwrite it and I shouldn't be able to.
Peter:	Oh, I thought you should be able to change that. It was specified as unprotected.
Ian:	Oh, I must have made a mistake on the spec, then. Sorry. It should have been specified as a protected field.
Peter:	Right, that's easy enough to change.
Ian:	OK. Now this main heading isn't quite centred. I think it needs to go a couple of characters further to the right.
Peter:	Um. Can you just move the cursor to the start of it to see what column it starts in at the moment? Yes. Hang on. 27. Right so I'll alter that to start in column 29.
Ian:	OK. Now the subheading just below it is alright but the corresponding subheading for 'Order details' — that's on line, let's see, line 12 — that should be left aligned with the first one but you've got it starting at the left margin in column 1.
Peter:	So it should start in column 2.
Ian:	Yeh. And just a small point on the 'Invoice Address' and 'Delivery Address' subheadings, you've got a capital 'A' for the first 'Address' and a lower case one on the second; can you make them both upper case? The other thing about those subheadings is — I know you've done it the way it was specified, but seeing it on screen it doesn't look so good — I wonder if you could indent the heading so that it lines up with the address details below it instead of lining up with the customer details heading. And can you do the same thing with the 'Delivery Address' subheading over on the right.
Peter:	Ah. Do you want the 'Delivery Address' subheading to move right or the address details to move left?

198 Appendix D

Ian: You'll have to move the heading, otherwise you'll be taking space from the 'Invoice Address' details fields.
Peter: Oh, yes, that's true.
Ian: Just a couple more things here with the order details. The net amounts should be aligned on the decimal point but they're 'left aligned' ...
Peter: Sorry, I should have seen that. I must have been asleep when I tested this.
Ian: Well, you might have had items with the same number of digits before the decimal point when you tested it. Anyway, it's not a disaster. There's another slight problem with the 'Total VAT' on the bottom line ...
Peter: Oh, yes I can see I've not suppressed the leading zeroes.
Ian: That's right.
Peter: Right, is that the lot?
Ian: Not quite, I'm afraid. The biggest problem is if I decide to alter the quantity field and enter something that's not valid. If I key in ampersand slash, for example. Look. It puts an asterisk just before the field to show it's incorrect, but then it puts garbage in the price and gross amount fields — you can see — we've got hash, backslash, five, full stop, hyphen, ampersand as the price! And it's also altered the whole of the rest of that line to high intensity. That can't have been in the spec — I think you must have done something wrong there, Peter!
Peter: Oh, I don't know, the sales people might have changed the price list!

UNIT 12

Input 1

Alison: Right then. If we're all here I think we can make a start. Janice and Malcolm know me already, but for those of you who don't my name's Alison McLeod. I work in Information Services as a systems analyst and I have special responsibility for end user training.

Obviously we're here to see how the first phase of the new on-line accounting system is going to work, but I'd like to start by explaining a little bit about the order that I'm going to do things in.

I'll be starting with a brief overall picture of the first phase of the new system: what the different parts are, what they can do for you and how they fit together. I'll also be pointing out some of the main similarities and differences between the new system and the existing batch systems. Altogether this part should only take about 10 minutes.

Then we'll move on to the main part of the training session where we'll be looking at the different parts of the system on the terminals. Some of the time I'll be talking you through the different screen displays and explaining how you use them, some of the time you'll be doing some practical exercises which will give you some hands on experience of the system.

The session is supposed to last 3 hours, but we'll have a short break for coffee about half way through. If you have any questions please feel free to interrupt.

Right, let's start by looking at the system as a whole. There are three main facilities: first, there's a suspense accounts enquiry facility, second, an on-line data entry facility and third a link with the existing personal pensions enquiry system.

The first of these allows you to request information from the different suspense accounts. As we'll see later, you can display all entries within an account on a specific date, all entries for a specified cash amount or all entries for a policy holder name or a policy number. It's also possible to obtain summaries of the different suspense accounts by account number; and you can specify whether you want weekly, monthly or yearly summaries. Once you have a particular display on the screen you are allowed to page forward or backwards a screenfull at a time. So if you have an annual summary on screen you can roll forwards to the next year and so on.

The second of the facilities — on-line data entry — enables you to submit transactions at the keyboard that you normally do on the cancellation and alterations advice. I'll explain some of the advantages for you in a minute.

Thirdly, I mentioned the link with the existing personal pensions enquiry system. Basically, the system lets you transfer to personal pensions enquiries from an accounting system screen and then transfer back again. Your original data is redisplayed automatically.

Those are the three main facilities then. Now let's look at some of the advantages they give you.

First of all ... when you key in ...

Development 1

Tim: Right, I think that covers everything.

Christine: Thank you Tim. Does anyone have any questions? Right, if there are no questions we can move on to item 4 on the agenda which is the Computer Group Manager's report. Alan.

Alan: Right. Well, you should all have received a copy of the Phase 1 report, but what I'd like to do while we're all here is just summarise some of the more important points about what we've achieved so far. Then I'd like to explain a little bit about why we've had to alter the project plan slightly for the next phase and how this will affect schedules, and erm ... and finally to give you a brief run-down on what the new cost estimates and code estimates are.

Right, let's look at what we've done in the first 6 months, then, to start with.

Two things basically. We've produced a prototype lexicographic system on schedule. We've put it through a very comprehensive user trial that shows it can do the editing work on the text of the dictionary successfully. So we're satisfied that it provides a very suitable nucleus for building the final product within the original timescale.

Second thing is, we've completed the data capture and validation subsystem, so we can now handle the data that we get from the agency tapes, validate and normalise them, carry out certain other basic operations and load the data on to the source database.

We've also got quite a long way with other aspects of editing and proof production work, but I won't go into that at the moment. It's all in the report.

Right. Let's move on to the project plan. Not everything has gone according to plan, I'm afraid. It took us a lot longer than we thought to find the right quality staff and it also took quite a while before the new people reached a stage where they were fully productive. So I'm afraid we won't be able to provide you with processed text ready for editing until about six weeks later than the original target date. However, having said that, it's still earlier than the latest date we set, so it shouldn't actually cause you any problems.

Now, as far as the Lexicographic System is concerned, there's been a significant change to the plan. Originally we were going to provide two builds of the system with Build 1 providing limited facilities by the second of January 1987 and Build 2 providing full facilities by July the first '87. In fact, the work has gone so well on this subsystem that it won't be necessary to do it in two stages. Instead, we'll be able to provide you with a full-function system by February the twenty-eighth, which is 5 months earlier than originally promised.

There is a slight problem, though: the previous plan stated that you would have had limited editing facilities by the first of January if Build 1 had been completed on schedule. But because we're now doing the two builds in one, you won't have any facilities at all until you get the full-function system at the end of February. In fact, since you didn't intend to start entering new words into the database until the end of May anyway, you'll have a full system in plenty of time for that. So we feel that the advantages of getting the full system earlier outweigh the disadvantages of having to wait a little longer before you get anything at all.

OK, that's all I have to say about the revised project plan. Any questions? Right, let's move on to the cost estimates, then.

According to the original plan . . .

Appendix E Unit by unit vocabulary

n: noun, v: verb, adj: adjective, p: preposition as used in the context of this text. NB some words may, of course, be used in different ways in other contexts.

UNIT 1

Input 1

assistant (n)
assistant manager (n)
co-ordinator (n)
department (n)
documentation (n)
expect (v)
first name (n)
in fact (adv)
in practice (adv)

in theory (adv)
interview (v)
introduce (v)
manager (n)
manual (n)
meet (v)
meeting (n)
procedure manual (n)
production (n)

reception (n)
reference manual (n)
section (n)
surname (n)
technical author (n)
technical manual (n)
training manual (n)
training materials (n)
wait [for] (v)

Input 2

applications software (n)
available (adj)
client (n)
client site (n)
communicate (v)
company (n)
efficient (adj)
enhancement (n)
environment (n)
feedback (n)
financial applications (n)
hands-on training (n)

hotline (n)
implement (v)
install (v)
integrated (adj)
mainframe (n)
maintain (v)
minicomputer (n)
optimise (v)
product development (n)
product line (n)
provide (v)
requirements (n)

Research and Development (n)
response (n)
site (n)
software (n)
support (n)
system (n)
system improvement (n)
telephone (n)
up-to-date (adj)
user (n)

202 Appendix E

Development 1

accountable [to] (adj)
arrangement (n)
based: to be based [at/in] (v)
break broke broken (v)
broken: to be broken down into (v)
capacity (n)
capacity planning (n)
change (n)
charge: in charge of (p)
co-ordinate (v)
compatibility (n) between sites
compatibility (n)
conform (to) (v)
develop (v)
development proposal (n)
divide (v)
divided: to be divided [into] (v)
division (n)
existing systems (n)
fourth generation language (n)
general manager (n)
handover (n)
handover arrangements (n)
hardware (n)
hardware compatibility (n)
head office (n)
headquarters/HQ (n)
in charge of (p)
interfaces (n)
involve (v)
language (n)
liaise (v)
long-term (adj)
long-term planning (n)
look after (v)
monitor (v)
operational support (n)
package (n)
parallel (adj)
parallel run (n)
planning (n)
processing (n)
project (n)
project teams (n)
proposal (n)
provision (n)
report to (v)
requirement (n)
review (v)
security (n)
security package (n)
software support (n)
split (up) (v)
staffing (n)
standards (n)
support (n)
systems programming (n)
team (n)
technical support (n)
trial (n)

UNIT 2

Input 1

activate (v)
allow (v)
application (n)
button (n)
choose (v)
click (v)
document (n)
double-click (v)
drag (v)
extend (v)
feature (n)
hold (v)
hold down (v) [a key]
item (n)
let (v)
menu (n)
mouse (n)
pointer (n)
position (n)
press (v)
release (v)
select (v)
selection (n)
shorten (v)
technique (n)
user (n)

Input 2

alphabetical (adj)
alphabetical order (n)
ascending order (n)
change the order (v)
character (n)
control keys (n)
cursor (n)
cursor control (n)
cursor control key (n)
cursor key (n)
cursor left/down key (n)
cursor movement (n)
data (n)
descending order (n)
display (n)
display format (n)
display sequence (n)
down cursor key (n)
field (n)
file (n)
format (n)
in alphabetical order (adv)
in ascending order (adv)
in descending order (adv)
in order of [price/importance] (adv)
key (n)

manufacturer (n)
move through (v)
next line (n)
next sequential record (n)
order: in order (of) (adv)
page through (v)
preceding (adj)
preceding record (n)
press (v)

previous (adj)
previous record (n)
previous screenfull (n)
record (n)
roll forwards (v)
screen (n)
screen display (n)
screenfull (n)
scroll (v)

scroll downwards (v)
scroll upwards (v)
sequential record (n)
shift (v) left/right
SHIFT key (n)
spreadsheet (n)
upward cursor key (n)

Development 1

accounts (n)
accounts program (n)
appear (v) on the screen
appear (v)
attempt (n)
automatic loading (n)
automatic loading facility (n)
computer (n)
copy (n)
disk (n)
diskette (n)
display (v) a menu
display (v)
drive (n)
enter (v)

feature (n)
input (v)
insert (v) a disk into a drive
insert (v)
instructions (n)
key in (v)
load (v)
loading (n)
loading facility (n)
lock (v) [someone] out
lock (v)
main menu (n)
message (n)
option (n)
option number (n)

password (n)
press (v) a key
program (n)
program disk (n)
prompt (n)
reset (v)
RESET button (n)
return (v)
RETURN key (n)
run (v) a program
run (v)
secondary menu (n)
system prompt (n)
today's date (n)
type (v)

UNIT 3

Input 1

account number (n)
add (v)
advice (n)
amend (v)
assemble (v)
bank sort code
batch (n)
batch control (n)
batch number (n)
batch type (n)
carry out (v)
change (v)
check (v)
clerk (n)
code (n)
collect (v)

computerised (adj)
computerised system (n)
consist of (v)
contents (n)
control document (n)
control item (n)
cross-check (v)
data entry (n)
data item (n)
data prep(aration) (n)
database (n)
delete (v)
destination (n)
distribute (v)
document (n)
dump file (n)

enter (v)
extract (v)
file (n)
fill in (v)
hand (v)
handle (v)
identify (v)
include (v)
initial (v)
input advice (n)
item (n)
key in (v)
keyboard (n)
keyboard operators (n)
match (v)
messenger (n)

obsolete (adj)
output (v)
pass (v)
post code (n)
preformatted (adj)
preformatted screen (n)
print (v)
print record (n)
printing (n)
process (v)

processing (n)
screen (n)
section supervisors (n)
sort (v)
sort code (n)
source (n)
source code (n)
stage (n)
submission date (n)

supervisor (n)
system (n)
transaction (n)
transaction details (n)
update (v)
use (v)
valid (adj)
validate (v)
working day (n)

Input 2

bar code (n)
bar code reader (n)
central processor (n)
channel controller (n)
computer room (n)
computing (n)
computing facilities (n)
connect (v)
connected to (p)
connection (n)
console (n)
console terminal (n)
contain (v)
control (v)
cross-connection cabinets (n)
data network (n)
equipment (n)
facilities (n)
handle (v)
incorporate (v)

installation (n)
interface (n)
keyboard (n)
label (v)
labelling (n)
link (n)
link (v)
linked to (p)
local (adj)
local area network (n)
local printer (n)
local sales office (n)
log (n)
log printer (n)
long distance (adj)
main processor (n)
microstations (n)
multiplexor (n)
network (n)
packaging (n)

packet switched data
  network (n)
port (n)
printer (n)
processor (n)
production (n)
production plant (n)
provide (v)
relay (v)
RS232C interface (n)
sales office (n)
screen (n)
system printer (n)
terminal (n)
traffic (n)
VDU (n)
VDU screen (n)
via (p)
X.25 switch (n)

Development 1

clerical (adj)
clerical error (n)
customer (n)
daily (adj)
do (v) a search
enquiries system (n)
error (n)
fill in (v) a form
fill in (v)
form (n)
get (v) [something] wrong
get (v) a printout

input advice (n)
keep statistics (v)
key (v) [the details] in
list (v)
match (v)
mistake (n)
payment amount (n)
payment date (n)
payment transaction (n)
policy number (n)
print (v)
printout (n)

reject (v)
rejected (adj)
rejected transaction (n)
run (v) a program
search (n)
search (v)
statistics (n)
transaction date (n)
wrong (adj)
wrong amount (n)

UNIT 4

Input 1

accept (v)
acceptance (n)
access (n)
access (v)
accounting system (n)
adjust (v)
alternative (n)
amend (v)
approval (n)
approve (v)
availability (n)
by mail (adv)
cancellation (n)
check (v)
comprise (v)
confirmation (n)
consignment (n)
contact name (n)
credit limit (n)
customer account (n)
customer details (n)
database (n)
despatch (n)
despatch documents (n)
display (n)
display (v)
enquiry (n)
enquiry system (n)
exceed (v)
finance department (n)
hold back (v)
in stock (adv)
input data (n)
invoice (n)
mail (n)
make (v) an enquiry
master menu (n)
obtain (v)
on-line (n)
on-line [sub]system (n)
order (n)
order entry (n)
order processing (n)
order quantity (n)
out of stock (adj)
over the phone (adv)
panel (n)
part number (n)
part order (n)
pending orders (n)
place (v) an order
process (v)
processing (n)
quantities on hand (n)
receive (v) an order
re-order (v)
re-order level (n)
re-order quantity (n)
request (n)
request (v)
retrieve (v)
return (v)
sales assistant (n)
sales department (n)
sales order processing (n)
screen display (n)
select (v)
stock (n)
stock availability (n)
submit (v) an order
subsystem (n)
summarise (v)
summary (n)
supply (v)
validate (v)

Input 2

accuracy (n)
allocation (n)
allow (v)
by-product (n)
capability (n)
check-out (n)
check-stands (n)
code (n)
connected to (p)
considerably (n)
corporate headquarters (n)
cost reduction (n)
data capture (n)
design (v)
determine (v)
development (n)
division (n)
eliminate (v)
employee (n)
headquarters (n)
identify (v)
improve (v)
increase (v)
input (n)
inventory (n)
item movement (n)
item number (n)
keep track of (v)
label (n)
labour activity (n)
labour scheduling (n)
look-up (n)
look-up data (n)
merchandise (n)
point of sale (n)
price (n)
procedure (n)
productivity (n)
profits (n)
provide (v)
remarking (n)
reorder (v)
reordering (n)
result in (v)
retrieve (v)
savings (n)
scanner (n)
scanning unit (n)
scheduling (n)
set up (v)
shelf label (n)
shipment (n)
simultaneously (adv)
stock (v)
summarised data (n)
supervise (v)
supply (v)
symbol (n)
symbol-marked (adj)
test (n)
throughput (n)
transaction data (n)
transfer (v)
transmit (v)
warehouse (n)

Development 1

access (v)
adjust (v)
archiving (n)
automatic feed (n)
batch (n)
capacity (n)
cassette (n)
cheque (n)
company (n)
credit card (n)
department (n)
double-sided (adj)
extra level of indexing (n)
film (n)
film (v)
fit (v)
flexibility (n)
gap (n)
high capacity (n)
indexing (n)
inexpensive (adj)
intelligent microfilmer (n)
item (n)
jam (v)
level (n)
level of indexing (n)
lever (n)
mark (n)
medium-sized (adj)
microfilmers (n)
per minute (adv)
purpose (n)
quality (n)
range (n)
reduction (n)
retrieval (n)
sample (n)
section (n)
side by side (adv)
size (n)
speed (n)
terminal (n)
thickness (n)

UNIT 5

Input 1

agree (v) a standard
agree (v)
applications (n)
assess (v)
bid (n)
bidder (n)
capabilities (n)
computer language (n)
consequence (n)
consult (v)
costs (n)
decision (n)
definition (n)
design (v)
develop (v)
development costs (n)
dialect (n)
do (v) a study (n)
draw (v) a conclusion
drawback (n)
evaluate (v)
evaluation (n) existing applications (n)
expert (n)
fall (v)
findings (n)
hardware (n)
hardware costs (n)
improvement (n)
increase (n)
investment (n)
invite (v) bidders
involve (v)
language (n)
maintain (v)
production costs (n)
productivity (n)
productivity tools (n)
programmer (n)
programming (n)
programming methodology (n)
proposed standard (n)
prototype (n)
record (v)
refinement (n)
required (adj)
requirements (n)
research (n)
result (n)
rise (v)
select (v)
set (n)
set of requirements (n)
software (n)
software development (n)
software production (n)
software production costs (n)
specify (v)
spend [money] (v)
stage (n)
standard (n)
study (n)
team (n)
testing (n)
testing phase (n)
tool (n)

Input 2

allow (v)
appoint (v)
based in (p)
cluster (n)
consultant (n)
contract (n)
current (adj)
current price (n)
database (n)
database products (n)
develop (v)
discount (n)
distributors (n)
double (adj)
educational discount (n)
environment (n)
file-server (n)
freelance (adj)
freelance basis (n)
freelance consultant (n)
get involved (v)
handle (v)
integrated (adj)
licence (n)
list price (n)
maintenance (n)
maintenance contract (n)
market (n)
marketplace (n)
network (n)
object-oriented (adj)
object-oriented database (n)
on a freelance basis (adv)
price (n)
product (n)
programming language (n)
research (n)
research establishment (n)
single user (n)
site (n)
site licence (n)
software product (n)
standard discount (n)
take out a maintenance contract (v)
user (n)

Development 1

adapt (v)
affect (v)
allow (v)
analyst (n)
applications (n)
approach (n)
assembly language (n)
authoring packages (n)
business awareness (n)
code (n)
coding (n)
commercial data processing (n)
commercial requirements (n)
communicative ability (n)
computer-literate (adj)
data processing (n)
demand (n)
design (n)
design process (n)
develop (n)
diplomacy (n)
distributed processing (n)
effect (n)
enable (n)
factor (n)
fall fell fallen (v)
fourth-generation languages (n)
graduate (n)
graduate trainee (n)
hardware costs (n)
high-level languages (n)
increased (adj)
influence (v)
information centre (n)
involved (adj)
job (n)
lack (v)
language (n)
low-level languages (n)
maintain (v)
maintainability (n)
maximise (v)
meet (v) requirements
modularity (n)
operations staff (n)
personnel (n)
priority (n)
program design (n)
program specification (n)
programmer (n)
promote (v)
prototyping (n)
readability (n)
readable (adj)
representatives (n)
requirements (n)
rise rose risen (v)
role (n)
software costs (n)
specification (n)
systems analyst (n)
task (n)
technical knowledge (n)
technical training (n)
testing (n)
tools (n)
trainee (n)
user department (n)
user representatives (n)
write (v) code

UNIT 6

Input 1

acquisition (n)
available (adj)
buy (v) [something] in
buy bought bought (v)
database (n)
forefront (n)
fund (v)
funding (n)

jump-off point (n)
new technology (n)
object-oriented database (n)
office (n)
potential (n)
priority (n)
reinvent (v)
relational database (n)

research tool (n)
spend spent spent (v)
starting point (n)
teaching tool (n)
thorough (adj)
widely available (adj)
worthwhile (adj)

Input 2

advertise (v)
advertisement (n)
applicant (n)
application form (n)
applications programming (n)
authorship (n)
available (adj)
CV (curriculum vitae) (n)
career (n)
complete (v)
documentation (n)
educational software (n)
employer (n)
enclosed (adj)
experience (n)

family name (n)
first name (n)
foreign language (n)
freelance (adj)
management (n)
microcomputer-based (adj)
natural language (n)
natural language interface (n)
notice (n)
on a freelance basis (adv)
operations (n)
package (n)
period of notice (n)
post code (n)
project leader (n)

referee (n)
reference number (n)
salary (n)
software producer (n)
supervisory (adj)
systems analysis (n)
systems programming (n)
telecommunications (n)
textbook (n)
training (n)
training consultant (n)
training manual (n)
training materials (n)
training package (n)

Development 1

bank (n)
break down (v)
contributor (n)
dealer (n)
design (n)
financial sector (n)
high-tech sector (n)
industry (n)
information kiosk (n)
insurance (n)
interact (v)
interactive video (n)
investment (n)
irrelevant (adj)

IV (interactive video) (n)
key reason (n)
life cycle (n)
major contributor (n)
manufacturing (n)
marketing (n)
mortgage (n)
point of information (n)
point of information applications (n)
point of sale (n)
point of sale applications (n)
procedure (n)
product life (n)

product life cycle (n)
safety (n)
sector (n)
selling (n)
skill (n)
split into (v)
sponsor (n)
stand-alone (adj)
stand-alone terminal (n)
stocks and shares (n)
task (n)
terminal (n)
touch screen (n)
training (n)

UNIT 7

Input 1

capable (adj)
commitment (n)
copyright (n)
copyright agreement (n)
costly (adj)
draw up (v)
existing commitments (n)
hardware resources (n)
in-house (adv)
initial stage (n)
invitation to tender (n)

invite (v) [someone] to tender
manpower (n)
manpower resources (n)
meet (v) a commitment
outside supplier (n)
ownership (n)
ownership agreement (n)
partnership (n)
personnel (n)
project (n)
proposal (n)

range (n)
range of possibilities (n)
relationship (n)
resources (n)
scale (n)
staff (n)
subcontract (v)
submit (v) a proposal (n)
supplier (n)
system component (n)
tender (n)
tender (v)

Input 2

business relationship (n)
capture (v) data (v)
capture (v)
commitment (n)
complete (v) a questionnaire (v)
contribution (n)
copyright (n)
distribute (v)
end user (n)
establish (v)
feedback (n)
identify (v)
implementation (n)

initial phase (n)
layout (n)
long-term (adj)
long-term commitment (n)
long-term project (n)
machine-readable (adj)
marketing rights (n)
method of operation (n)
minimise (v)
nature (n)
normal working hours (n)
obtain (v) feedback
output (n)
ownership (n)

phase (n)
proposal (n)
proposed system (n)
questionnaire (n)
rights (n)
secondary phase (n)
selling rights (n)
state (v)
statement (n)
submit (v) a proposal
supplier (n)
support (n)
support staff (n)
working hours (n)

Development 1

airport (n)
arrival (n)
book (v)
connect (v)
delay (v)
department (n)
extension (n)
flight (n)
flight number (n)
hire car (n)
hold (v) the line

hold held held (v)
line (n)
meet met met (v)
meeting (n)
message (n)
number (n)
office (n)
pick (v) someone up
plane (n)
put (v) [someone] through
put (v) a meeting off

ring (v)
ring rang rung (v)
secretary (n)
switchboard (n)
take (v) a message (n)
technical problems (n)
time of arrival (n)
waste (v) time
waste (v)
wrong number (n)

UNIT 8

Input 1

add (n)
adequate (adj)
advice (n)
agree (v)
arise arose arisen (v)
ask (v) whether [X is true]
ask (v)
capacity (n)
confident (adj)
configuration (n)
configuration size (n)
confirm (v)
consult (v)
consultant (n)
currently (adv)
detrimental (adj)
discuss (v)
enquire (v) whether [X is true]
evaluation (n)
external consultant (n)
future (n)
future phase (n)
group manager (n)
hold (v) a meeting (n)
in production (adv)
leave (v)
level of support (n)
limit (n)
long-term (adj)
long-term future (n)
mention (v)
monitor (v)
performance (n)
plan for (v)
planned (adj)
planned configuration (n)
point (n)
prior to (p)
progress (v)
project manager (n)
provide (v) support
publicity (n)
reaffirm (v)
remind (n)
reply (v)
report (n)
report (v)
restriction (n)
support (n)
take (v) a photograph
take over (v)
wonder (v) whether [X is true]
wonder (v)

Input 2

adjustment (n)
allow (v)
alter (v)
catch (v)
change (n)
come (v) into force
confirm (v) [something] in writing
confirm (v)
extension (n)
factor (mathematical) (n)
force (n)
get back (v)
guess (v)
memo (n)
minus (n)
module (n)
notification (n)
nought (n)
plus (n)
production system (n)
ring (v)
source code (n)
terminal (n)
valid (n)
validity (n)
written confirmation (n)

Development 1

applicant (n)
be back (v)
bookings (n)
busy (adj)
cabling (n)
chat (n)
check (v) [my/your] diary
check (v)
convenient (adj)
diary (n)
equipment (n)
fortnight (n)
free (= not busy) (n)
have (v) a chat [about X]
interview (v)
job applicant (n)
leave for (v)
meeting (n)
on-line (adj)
on-line system (n)
plan (v)
printer (n)
ring (v)
siting (n)
terminal (n)
visitor (n)

UNIT 9

Input 1

beneficial (adj)
black box (n)
bulk (n)
cable (n)
cable installation (n)
cable installation costs (n)
cabling (n)
capacity (n)
closed system (n)
communicate (v)
communication requirements (n)
conclusion (n)
cost beneficial (adj)
data communication requirements (n)
data communications (n)
data handling (n)
data traffic (n)
data transfer rate (n)
development field (n)
developments (n)
diversity (n)

enable (v)
entail (v)
existing equipment (n)
expand (v)
expense (n)
factor (n)
feedback (n)
foreseeable (adj)
foreseeable future (n)
handle (v)
hardware costs (n)
Head Office (n)
Head Office site (n)
indicate (v)
inexperienced (adj)
install (v)
installation (n)
installation costs (n)
LAN (n)
local (adj)
meet (v) a need
monitor (v)
network (n)

network control (n)
open system (n)
PABX (n)
piece of equipment (n)
rapidly developing field (n)
rate (n)
recommendation (n)
response (n)
response time (n)
satisfactory (adj)
service (n)
site (n)
solution (n)
staff (n)
standards (n)
training costs (n)
transfer (n)
transfer rate (n)
widely accepted (adj)
worthwhile (adj)

Input 2

agree (v)
argument (n)
choose chose chosen (v)
convince (v)
convincing (adj)
convincing argument (n)
cost (n)
dispute (v)
efficiently (adv)
expansion (n)
identify (v)
investigation (adj)
justifiable (adj)

LAN (= Local Area Network) (n)
link together (v)
link up (v) [with X]
link-up (n)
Local Area Network (n)
local sites (n)
long-term needs (n)
main office (n)
merger (n)
needs (n)
networking (n)
networking needs (n)
option (n)

PABX (n)
presuppose (v)
realise (v)
recommendations (n)
reject (v)
situation (n)
study (n)
take (v) into account
thorough (adj)
thorough investigation (n)
traffic (n)
warehouse (n)
worthwhile (adj)

Development 1

attach (v)
command (n)
copy (v)
create (v) a file (n)

create (v)
current directory (n)
default (n)
default directory (n)

directory (n)
directory path (n)
disk directory (n)
display (v)

document (n)
file (n)
filename (n)
format (n)
format file (n)
include (v)
load (v) a file
load (v)
open (v)
operating system (n)
operating system command (n)
package (n)
paragraph (n)
path (n)
press (v)
program (n)
report (n)
save (v) a file
save (v)
spare (v) [a minute]
standard paragraph (n)
store (v)
suffix (n)
type (v)
word processing (n)
word-processing package (n)
work (v) on [something] (v)

UNIT 10

Inut 1

annual (adj)
annual summary (n)
change (n)
coding (n)
data entry (n)
data entry screen (n)
delay (n)
detailed enquiry (n)
details (n)
display (n)
dummy screen (n)
enquiry (n)
highlight (v)
in sequence (adv)
involve (v)
layout (n)
menu (n)
menu panel (n)
monthly (adj)
monthly summary (n)
movement (n)
processing (n)
prototype (n)
response (n)
screen (n)
screen display (n)
screen layout (n)
sequence (n)
skeleton system (n)
spec (n)
stage (n)
test (v)
testing (n)
timescale (n)
user (n)
validation (n)
validation procedure (n)
weekly (adj)
weekly summary (n)

Input 2

alternative (n)
approximately (adv)
asynchronous (adj)
asynchronous printer (n)
at low cost (adv)
at the outset (adv)
attachment (n)
basis (n)
cable (n)
cabling (n)
cabling system (n)
coaxial cable (n)
coaxial cabling (n)
coaxial connection (n)
coaxial system (n)
compatible (adj)
competition (n)
computing facilities (n)
connect (v)
connecting point (n)
control unit (n)
cost estimates (n)
disconnect (v)
dumb (adj)
dumb terminal (n)
dumb VDU (n)
electrician (n)
equipment (n)
equipment reconfiguration (n)
establish (v)
estimate (n)
facility (n)
fail-safe (adj)
fail-safe facilities (n)
flexible (adj)
force (v)
force down (v)
handle (v)
hardware (n)
in the long term (adv)
inbuilt (adj)
inbuilt facilities (n)
inbuilt fail-safe facilities (n)
increase (v)
incur (v) [costs]
indicate (v)
initial saving (n)
install (v)
interchangeable (adj)
investment (n)
item (n)
labour (n)
location (n)
loop (n)
mainframe (n)
mainframe computer (n)

mainframe control unit (n)
maintenance (n)
maintenance costs (n)
market place (n)
network control (n)
on that basis (adv)
one to one (adj)
outlet socket (n)
outset (n)
overtime (n)
overtime rates (n)
personal computer (n)
plug compatible (adj)
plug compatible supplier (n)
plug in (v)
port (n)

printer (n)
rapid (adj)
rate (n)
ratio (n) [of X to Y]
rationalisation (n)
reconfiguration (n)
reliable (adj)
removal (n)
replacement (n)
reserve (v)
saving (n)
sensible (adj)
set up (v)
share (v)
socket (n)

software (n)
solution (n)
sound investment (n)
store (v)
suitable (adj)
switchboard (n)
terminal (n)
trade (v)
twisted pair (n)
twisted pair connection (n)
unit (n)
upgrade (n)
upgrade costs (n)
wire (n)
wire (v)

Development 1

applications software (n)
be involved (v)
bits and pieces (n)
cabling (n)
cabling requirements (n)
check (v)
concern (v)
due (adj)
due to
equipment (n)
equipment installation (n)
financial system (n)

fine tuning (n)
in working order (adv)
install (v)
label (v)
labelling (n)
microstation (n)
pallet (n)
pallet labelling (n)
plan (n)
plant (n)
power (n)
power supply (n)

production plant (n)
responsible (adj) [for]
sales order processing (n)
sales order processing system (n)
scheduling (n)
ship (v)
site (n)
site engineers (n)
software installation (n)
system software (n)
user training (n)

UNIT 11

Input 1

advice (n)
amount (n)
annual (adj)
ascertain (v)
blank (adj)
code (n)
computer system (n)
details (n)
enter (v)
error code (n)
following (adj)
frequency (n)
function (n)
half-yearly (adj)
illegal (adj)

indicator (n)
invalid (adj)
invalid date (n)
item (n)
message (n)
message text (n)
missing (adj)
monthly (adj)
non-numeric (adj)
payment (n)
payment amount (n)
payment date (n)
permitted (adj)
permitted range (n)
quarterly (adj)

range (n)
reason for error (n)
reject (v)
rejected advice (n)
rejected transaction (n)
require (v)
section (n)
start date (n)
submit (v) an advice
submit (v)
transaction (n)
transaction date (n)
value (n)

Input 2

according to (adv) the spec
according to (adv)
address details (n)
align (v)
alter (v)
alter (v)
ampersand (n)
asterisk (n)
backslash (n)
bottom line (n)
capital (n)
centre (n)
centred (adj)
character (n)
column (n)
corner (n)
corresponding (adj)
cursor (n)
customer details (n)
decimal point (n)
delivery address (n)
digit (n)
display (n)
enter (v)
field (n)
full stop (n)

garbage (n)
gross amount (n)
hash (n)
heading (n)
high intensity (n)
highlight (v)
highlighting (n)
hyphen (n)
indent (v)
indentation (n)
invoice address (n)
item (n)
key in (v)
leading zeroes (n)
left aligned (adj)
left-hand corner (n)
line (n)
line up (v) [with X] (v)
line up (v)
low intensity (n)
lower case (n)
main heading (n)
margin (n)
net amount (n)
on screen

order details (n)
overwrite (v)
price (n)
price list (n)
protected (adj)
protected field (n)
reference number (n)
right aligned (adj)
right-hand corner (n)
screen (n)
sign on (v)
slash (n)
source code (n)
subheading (n)
suppress (v)
test (v)
top left (adj)
top line (n)
top right (adj)
unprotected (adj)
unprotected field (n)
upper case (n)
valid (adj)
Value Added Tax (VAT) (n)
VAT (Value Added Tax) (n)

Development 1

alphabetic (adj)
blank (adj)
characters (n)
check (v)
code list (n)
conform (v) [to X]
current year (n)
delete (v)
description (n)
equal to
format (n)
function (n)

general routine (n)
generate (v)
greater than
integer (n)
item (n)
leading spaces (n)
length (n)
less than
maiden name (n)
National Insurance Number (n)
numeric (adj)

numeric integer (n)
otherwise
present (adj)
range (n)
range (n)
replace (v)
routine (n)
serial number (n)
trailing spaces (n)
validate (v)
validation requirements (n)
warning (n)

Appendix E 215

UNIT 12

Input 1

account (n)
account number (n)
accounts (n)
advantage (n)
allow (v)
alteration (n)
amount (n)
annual/yearly (adj)
batch systems (n)
cancellation (n)
cash (n)
data entry facility (n)
difference (n)
display entries (n)
end user (n)
end user training (n)
enquiry facility (n)
enquiry system (n)
entries (n)

existing (adj)
explain (v)
facilities (n)
fit together (v)
hands on (adj)
hands on experience (n)
interrupt (v)
keyboard (n)
link (n)
main facilities (n)
monthly (adj)
obtain (v)
obtain a summary (v)
on-line (adj)
on-line system (n)
order (n)
original data (n)
overall (adj)
page (v) backwards

page (v) forward
phase (n)
practical exercise (n)
redisplay (v)
request (v)
request information (v)
screen display (n)
session (n)
similarities and differences (n)
similarity (n)
specified amount (n)
submit (v) transactions
systems analyst (n)
terminal (n)
training session (n)
transfer (v)
user training (n)
weekly (adj)
yearly/annual (adj)

Input 2

affect (v)
appropriate (adj)
architecture (n)
at different rates (adv)
at the same rate (adv)
building (n)
cable (n)
cabling (n)
cabling interface (n)
cabling system (n)
cater for (v)
comments (n)
communication requirements (n)
component (n)
concern (n)
conductivity (n)
connector (n)
consult (v)
consultant (n)
create (v) problems
damage (v)

design (n)
detrimental (adj)
document (v) (n)
drill (v) a hole
drill (v)
engineer (n)
enhance (v)
expand (v)
expansion (n)
express (v) concern
extend (v)
extend (v)
flexibility (n)
floor point (n)
flush (with) (adj)
implement (v)
install (v)
installation (n)
installation design (n)
interface (n)
knowledge (n)
limiting (adj)

Local Area Network (n)
locking (n)
locking mechanism (n)
logical (adj)
material (n)
objective (n)
outlet (n)
outlet cable (n)
outlet point (n)
physical (adj)
physical installation (n)
positioning (n)
potentially (adv)
provide (v)
radiator (n)
rate (n)
review (v) (n)
steel trunking (n)
sub-contractors (n)
terminal user (n)
trunking (n)
wiring (v)

Development 1

according to plan (adv)
achieve (v)
advantage (n)
affect (v)
agency (n)
agenda (n)
alter (v)
carry out (v)
code (n)
comprehensive (n)
copy (n)
cost estimates (n)
data (n)
data capture subsystem (n)
database (n)
disadvantage (n)
editing (n)
estimate (n)
facilities (n)

handle (v)
limited facilities (n)
load (v)
on schedule
operation (n)
original plan (n)
original target date (n)
original timescale (n)
outweigh (v)
previous plan (n)
processed text (n)
productive (adj)
project plan (n)
prototype (n)
prototype system (n)
report (n)
revised (adj)
revised plan (n)
revised project plan (n)

rundown (n)
satisfied (adj)
schedule (n)
staff (n)
stage (n)
sub-system (n)
subsystem (n)
successfully (adv)
summarise (v)
tape (n)
target date (n)
text (n)
timescale (n)
trial (n)
user trial (n)
validate (v)
validation (n)
validation subsystem (n)

APPENDIX F Vocabulary index

Unit and section references are given after each word. For example: 4/I1 = Unit 4, Input 1; 5/D1 = Unit 5, Development 1.

accept (v), 4/I1, 6/I1, 9/I1
acceptable (adj), 6/I2, 7/I2
acceptance (n), 4/I1
access (n), 4/I1
access (v), 4/D1, 4/I1
according to plan (adv), 12/D1
according to the spec, 11/I2
according to, 11/I2
account number (n), 3/I1, 12/I1
accountable [to] (adj), 1/D1
accounts (n), 12/I1, 2/D1
accounts program (n), 2/D1
accuracy (n), 4/I2
achieve (v), 12/D1
acquisition (n), 6/I1
activate (v), 2/I1
adapt (v), 5/D1
add (v), 3/I1, 8/I1
address details (n), 11/I2
adequate (adj), 8/I1
adjust (v), 4/I1, 4/D1
adjustment (n), 8/I2
advantage (n), 12/I1, 12/D1
advertise (v), 6/I2
advertisement (n), 6/I2
advice (n), 3/I1, 8/I1, 11/I1
affect (v), 5/D1, 12/I2, 12/D1
agency (n), 12/D1
agenda (n), 12/D1
agree (v) a standard, 5/I1
agree (v), 5/I1, 8/I1, 9/I2
airport (n), 7/D1
align (v), 11/I2
allocation (n), 4/I2

allow (v), 2/I1, 4/I2, 5/I2, 5/D1, 8/I2, 12/I1
alphabetic (adj), 11/D1
alphabetical (n), 2/I2
alphabetical order (n), 2/I2
alter (v), 8/I2, 11/I2, 12/D1
alteration (n), 12/I1
alternative (n), 4/I1, 10/I2
amend (v), 3/I1, 4/I1
amount (n), 11/I1, 12/I1
ampersand (n), 11/I2
analyst (n), 5/D1
annual (adj), 10/I1, 11/I1
annual summary (n), 10/I1
appear (v) on the screen, 2/D1
appear (v), 2/D1
applicant (n), 6/I2, 8/D1
application (n), 2/I1, 5/I1, 5/D1
application form (n), 6/I2
applications programming (n), 6/I2
applications software (n), 1/I2, 10/D1
appoint (v), 5/I2
approach (n), 5/D1
appropriate (adj), 12/I2
approval (n), 4/I1
approve (v), 4/I1
approximately (adv), 10/I2
architecture (n), 12/I2
archiving (n), 4/D1
argument (n), 9/I2
arise, arose, arisen (n), 8/I1
arrangement (n), 1/D1
arrival (n), 7/D1
ascending order (n), 2/I2
ascertain (v), 11/I1

ask (v) whether [X is true], 8/I1
ask (v), 8/I1
assemble (v), 3/I1
assembly language (n), 5/D1
assess (v), 5/I1
assistant (n), 1/I1
Assistant Manager (n), 1/I1
asterisk (n), 11/I2
asynchronous (adj), 10/I2
asynchronous printer (n), 10/I2
at a time (adv), 2/I2
at different rates (adv), 12/I2
at frequent intervals (adv), 3/I1
at least (adv), 7/I2
at low cost (adv), 10/I2
at present (adv), 9/I1
at regular intervals (adv), 3/I1
at the beginning (adv), 10/D1
at the end (adv), 10/D1
at the outset (adv), 10/I2
at the same rate (adv), 12/I2
at the same time (adv), 10/I1
attach (v), 9/D1
attachment (n), 10/I2
attempt (n), 2/D1
author (n), 1/I1
authoring packages (n), 5/D1
authorship (n), 6/I2
automatic feed (n), 4/D1
automatic loading (n), 2/D1
automatic loading facility (n), 2/D1
availability (n), 4/I1
available (adj), 1/I2, 6/I1, 6/I2

backslash (n), 11/I2
bank (n), 6/D1
bank sort code (n), 3/I1
bar code (n), 3/I2
bar code reader (n), 3/I2
based in (p, 5/I2
based: to be based [at/in], 1/D1
batch (n), 3/I1, 4/D1, 10/I
batch control (n), 3/I1
batch number (n), 3/I1
batch system (n), 12/I1
batch type (n), 3/I1
batched (adj), 3/I1
beneficial (adj), 9/I1
bid (n), 5/I1
bidder (n), 5/I1
bits and pieces (n), 10/D1
black box (n), 9/I1
blank (adj), 11/I1, 11/D1

book (v), 7/D1
bookings (n), 8/D1
bottom line (n), 11/I2
break down (v), 6/D1
break, broke, broken (v), 1/D1
broken: to be broken down into (v), 1/D1
building (n), 12/I2
bulk (n), 9/I1
business awareness (n), 5/D1
business relationship (n), 7/I2
busy (adj), 8/D1
button (n), 2/I1
buy (v) [something] in, 6/I1
buy, bought, bought (v), 6/I1
by-product (n), 4/I2

C.V. (curriculum vitae) (n), 6/I2
cable (n), 9/I1, 10/I2, 12/I2
cable (v), 10/I2
cable installation (n), 9/I1
cable installation costs (n), 9/I1
cabling (n), 8/D1, 9/I1, 10/I2, 10/D1, 12/I2
cabling interface (n), 12/I2
cabling requirements (n), 10/D1
cabling system (n), 10/I2, 12/I2
cancellation (n), 4/I1, 12/I1
capabilities (n), 5/I1
capability (n), 4/I2
capable (adj), 7/I1
capacity (n), 1/D1, 4/D1, 8/I1, 9/I1
capacity planning (n), 1/D1
capital (n), 11/I2
capture (n), 12/D1
capture (v) data (v), 7/I2
capture (v), 7/I2
career (n), 6/I2
carry out (v), 3/I1, 12/D1
cash (n), 11/I1, 12/I1
cassette (n), 4/D1
catch (v), 8/I2
cater for (v), 12/I2
central processor (n), 3/I2
centre (n), 11/I2
centred (adj), 11/I2
change (n), 1/D1, 8/I2, 10/I1
change (v), 3/I1
change the order (n), 2/I2
channel controller (n), 3/I2
character (n), 2/I2, 11/I2, 11/D1
charge: in charge of (p), 1/D1
chat (n), 8/D1
check (v) [my/your] diary, 8/D1
check (v), 3/I1, 4/I1, 8/D1, 11/D1, 10/D1

check-out (n), 4/I2
check-stands (n), 4/I2
cheque (n), 4/D1
choose, chose, chosen (v), 2/I1, 9/I2
clerical (adj), 3/D1
clerical error (n), 3/D1
clerk (n), 3/I1
click (v), 2/I1
client (n), 1/I2
client site (n), 1/I2
closed system (n), 9/I1
cluster (n), 5/I2
co-ordinate (v), 1/D1
co-ordinator (n), 1/I1
coaxial cable (n), 10/I2
coaxial cabling (n), 10/I2
coaxial connection (n), 10/I2
coaxial system (n), 10/I2
code (n), 3/I1, 4/I2, 5/D1, 11/I1, 12/D1
code (v), 5/D1
code list (n), 11/D1
coding (n), 5/D1, 10/I
collect (v), 3/I1
column (n), 11/I2
come (v) into force, 8/I2
command (n), 9/D1
comments (n), 12/I2
commercial data processing (n), 5/D1
commercial requirements (n), 5/D1
commitment (n), 7/I1, 7/I2
communicate (v), 1/I2, 9/I1
communication requirements (n), 9/I1, 12/I2
communicative ability (n), 5/D1
company (n), 4/D1
compatibility (n) between sites, 1/D1
compatibility (n), 1/D1
compatible (adj), 10/I2
competition (n), 10/I2
complete (v) a questionnaire (v), 7/I2
complete (v), 6/I2
component (n), 12/I2
comprehensive (n), 12/D1
comprise (v), 4/I1
computer (n), 2/D1
computer language (n), 5/I1
computer processing (n), 1/D1
computer room (n), 3/I2
computer services (n), 7/D1
computer system (n), 11/I1
computer-literate (adj), 5/D1
computerised (adj) 3/I1
computerised system (n), 3/I1
computing (n), 3/I2
computing facilities (n), 3/I2, 10/I2
concern (n) (n), 12/I2

concern (v), 10/D1
conclusion (n), 9/I1
conductivity (n), 12/I2
confident (adj), 8/I1
configuration (n), 8/I1
configuration size (n), 8/I1
confirm (something) in writing (n), 8/I2
confirm (v), 8/I1, 8/I2
confirmation (n), 4/I1
conform (v) [to X], 1/D1, 11/D1
connect (v), 3/I2, 7/D1, 10/I2
connected to (p), 3/I2, 4/I2
connecting point (n), 10/I2
connection (n), 3/I2
connector (n), 12/I2
consequence (n), 5/I1
considerably (n), 4/I2
consignment (n), 4/I1
consist of (v), 3/I1
console (n), 3/I2
console terminal (n), 3/I2
consult (v), 5/I1, 8/I1, 12/I2
consultant (n), 5/I2, 8/I1, 12/I2
contact name (n), 4/I1
contain (v), 3/I2
contents (n), 3/I1
contract (n), 5/I2
contribution (n), 7/I2
contributor (n), 6/D1
control (n), 3/I2, 4/I2
control (v), 3/I2
control document (n), 3/I1
control item (n), 3/I1
CONTROL key (n), 2/I2
control unit (n), 10/I2
convenient (adj), 8/D1
convince (v), 9/I2
convincing (adj), 9/I2
convincing argument (n), 9/I2
copy (n), 2/D1, 12/D1
copy (v), 9/D1
copyright (n), 7/I1, 7/I2
copyright agreement (n), 7/I1
corner (n), 11/I2
corporate headquarters (n), 4/I2
corresponding (adj), 11/I2
cost (n), 9/I2
cost (v), 10/I2
cost beneficial (adj), 9/I1
cost estimates (n), 10/I2, 12/D1
cost reduction (n), 4/I2
costly (adj), 7/I1
costs (n), 5/I1, 10/I2
create (v) a file (n), 9/D1
create (v) problems, 12/I2

create (v), 9/D1
credit card (n), 4/D1
credit limit (n), 4/I1
cross connection cabinets (n), 3/I2
cross-check (v), 3/I1
current (adj), 5/I2
current directory (n), 9/D1
current price (n), 5/I2
current year (n), 11/D1
currently (adv), 8/I1
cursor (n), 2/I2, 11/I2
cursor control (n), 2/I2
cursor control key (n), 2/I2
cursor key (n), 2/I2
cursor left/right/up/down key (n), 2/I2
cursor movement (n), 2/I2
customer (n), 1/I2, 3/D1
customer account (n), 4/I1
customer details (n), 4/I1, 11/I2

daily (adj), 3/D1
damage (v), 12/I2
data (n.pl), 2/I2, 12/D1
data capture (n), 4/I2
data capture subsystem (n), 12/D1
data communication requirements (n), 9/I1
data communications (n), 9/I1
data entry (n), 3/I1, 10/I1
data entry facility (n), 12/I1
data entry screen (n), 10/I1
data handling (n), 9/I1
data item (n), 3/I1
data network (n), 3/I2
data prep(aration) (n), 3/I1
data processing (n), 5/D1
data traffic (n), 9/I1
data transfer rate (n), 9/I1
database/data base (n), 3/I1, 4/I1, 5/I2, 6/I1, 12/D1
database products (n), 5/I2
deal with (v), 1/D1
dealer (n), 6/D1
decide (v), 3/D1, 6/I1
decimal point (n), 11/I2
decision (n), 5/I1, 9/I2
default (n), 9/D1
default directory (n), 9/D1
definition (n), 5/I1
delay (n), 10/I1
delay (v), 7/D1
delete (v), 3/I1, 11/D1
delivery address (n), 11/I2
demand (n), 5/D1

department (n), 1/I1
department (n), 1/I1, 4/D1, 7/D1
descending order (n), 2/I2
description (n), 11/D1
design (n), 5/D1, 6/D1, 12/I2
design (v), 4/I2, 5/I1
design process (n), 5/D1
despatch (n), 4/I1
despatch documents (n), 4/I1
destination (n), 3/I1
detailed enquiry (n), 10/I1
details (n), 10/I1, 11/I1
determine (v), 4/I2
detrimental (adj), 8/I1, 12/I2
develop (v), 1/D1, 5/I1, 5/I2, 5/D1
developing field (n), 9/I1
development (n), 4/I2
development costs (n), 5/I1
development proposal (n), 1/D1
developments (n), 9/I1
dialect (n), 5/I1
diary (n), 8/D1
difference (n), 12/I1
digit (n), 11/I2
diplomacy (n), 5/D1
directory (n), 9/D1
directory path (n), 9/D1
disadvantage (n), 12/D1
disconnect (v), 10/I2
discount (n), 5/I2
discuss (v), 8/I1
discussion (n), 8/I1
disk (n), 2/D1, 3/I1
disk directory (n), 9/D1
diskette (n), 2/D1
display (n), 2/I2, 11/I2, 10/I1
display (v) a menu, 2/D1
display (v), 2/D1, 4/I1, 9/D1
display entries (n), 12/I1
display format (n), 2/I2
display sequence (n), 2/I2
dispute (v), 9/I2
distribute (v), 3/I1, 7/I2
distributed processing (n), 5/D1
distributors (n), 5/I2
diversity (n), 9/I1
divide (v), 1/D1
divided: to be divided [into] (v), 1/D1
division (n), 1/D1, 4/I2
do (v) a search, 3/D1
do (v) a study (n), 5/I1
document (n), 2/I1, 3/I1, 9/D1
document (v) (n), 12/I2
documentation (n), 1/I1, 6/I2
double (adj), 5/I2

double-click (v), 2/I1
double-sided (adj), 4/D1
down cursor key (n), 2/I2
drag (v), 2/I1
draw (v) a conclusion, 5/I1
draw up (v), 7/I1
drawback (n), 5/I1
drill (v) a hole, 12/I2
drill (v), 12/I2
drive (n), 2/D1
due (adj), 10/D1
due to, 10/D1
dumb (adj), 10/I2
dumb terminal (n), 10/I2
dumb VDU (n), 10/I2
dummy screen (n), 10/I1
dump file (n), 3/I1

editing (n), 12/D1
educational discount (n), 5/I2
educational software (n), 6/I2
effect (n), 5/D1
efficient (adj), 1/I2
efficiently (adv), 9/I2
electrician (n), 10/I2
eliminate (v), 4/I2
employee (n), 4/I2
employer (n), 6/I2
enable (n), 5/D1, 9/I1
enclosed (adj), 6/I2
end user (n), 7/I2, 12/I1
end user training (n), 12/I1
engineer (n), 12/I2
enhance (v), 12/I2
enhancement (n), 1/I2
enquiries system (n), 3/D1
enquiry (n), 4/I1, 10/I1
enquiry facility (n), 12/I1
enquiry system (n), 12/I1
entail (v), 9/I1
enter (v), 2/D1, 3/I1, 11/I1, 11/I2
entries (n), 12/I1
entry (n), 12/I1
environment (n), 1/I2, 5/I2
equal (adj) to, 11/D1
equipment (n), 3/I2, 8/D1, 10/I2, 10/D1
equipment installation (n), 10/D1
equipment reconfiguration (n), 10/I2
error (n), 3/D1
error code (n), 11/I1
establish (v), 7/I2, 10/I2
estimate (n), 10/I2, 12/D1
evaluate (v), 5/I1

evaluation (n), 5/I1, 8/I1
exceed (v), 4/I1
existing (adj), 12/I1
existing applications (n), 5/I1
existing commitments (n), 7/I1
existing equipment (n), 9/I1
existing systems (n), 1/D1
expand (v), 9/I1, 12/I2
expansion (n), 12/I2
expansion (n), 9/I2
expect (v), 1/I1
expense (n), 9/I1
experience (n), 6/I2
expert (n), 5/I1
explain (v), 12/I1
express (v) concern, 12/I2
extend (v), 2/I1, 12/I2
extension (n), 7/D1, 8/I2
external consultant (n), 8/I1
extra (adj), 4/D1, 9/I1, 10/I2
extra cost (n), 9/I1, 10/I2
extra expense (n), 9/I1
extra level of indexing (n), 4/D1
extract (v), 3/I1

facilities (n), 3/I2, 12/I1, 12/D1
facility (n), 10/I2
factor (n) (*mathematical*), 8/I2
factor (n), 5/D1, 9/I1
fail-safe (adj), 10/I2
fail-safe facilities (n), 10/I2
fall, fell, fallen (v), 5/I1, 5/D1
family name (n), 6/I2
feature (n), 2/I1, 2/D1
feedback (n), 1/I2, 7/I2, 9/I1
field (n), 2/I2, 11/I2
file (n), 2/I2, 3/I1, 9/D1
file-server (n), 5/I2
filename (n), 9/D1
fill in (v) a form, 3/D1
fill in (v), 3/I1, 3/D1
film (n), 4/D1
film (v), 4/D1
finance department (n), 4/I1
financial applications (n), 1/I2
financial sector (n), 6/D1
financial system (n), 10/D1
findings (n), 5/I1
fine tuning (n), 10/D1
first name (n), 6/I2
fit (v), 4/D1
fit together (v), 12/I1
flexibility (n), 4/D1, 12/I2

flexible (adj), 10/I2
flight (n), 7/D1
flight number (n), 7/D1
floor point (n), 12/I2
floppy disk (n), 2/D1
flush (with) (adj), 12/I2
following (adj), 11/I1
force (n), 8/I2
force (v), 10/I2
force down (v), 10/I2
forefront (n), 6/I1
foreign language (n), 6/I2
foreseeable (adj), 9/I1
foreseeable future (n), 9/I1
form (n), 3/D1
format (n), 2/I2, 9/D1, 11/D1
format file (n), 9/D1
fortnight (n), 8/D1
fourth generation language (n), 1/D1, 5/D
free (= not busy) (adj), 8/D1
freelance (n), 5/I2, 6/I2
freelance basis (n), 5/I2
freelance consultant (n), 5/I2
frequency (n), 11/I1
full stop (n), 11/I2
function (n), 11/I1, 11/D1
fund (v), 6/I1
funding (n), 6/I1
future (n), 8/I1
future phase (n), 8/I1

gap (n), 4/D1
garbage (n), 11/I2
general manager (n), 1/D1
general routine (n), 11/D1
generate (v), 11/D1
get (v) [something] wrong, 3/D1
get (v) a printout, 3/D1
get (v) a record, 2/I2
get back (v), 8/I2
get into (v) [a system], 8/I2
get involved (v), 5/I2
get to (v) [a record], 4/D1
graduate (n), 5/D1
graduate trainee (n), 5/D1
greater than, 11/D1
gross amount (n), 11/I2
group manager (n), 8/I1
guarantee (n), 7/I2
guess (v), 8/I2

half-yearly (adj), 11/I1
hand (v), 3/I1
handle (v), 3/I1, 3/I2, 5/I2, 9/I1, 10/I2, 12/D1
handling (n), 9/I1
handover (n), 1/D1
handover arrangements (n), 1/D1
hands-on (adj), 12/I1
hands-on experience (n), 12/I1
hands-on training (n), 1/I2
hardware (n), 1/D1, 5/I1, 10/I2
hardware costs (n), 5/I1, 5/D1, 9/I1
hardware resources (n), 7/I1
hash (n), 11/I2
head office (n), 1/D1, 9/I1
head office site (n), 9/I1
heading (n), 11/I2
headquarters (n), 1/D1, 4/I2
high capacity (n), 4/D1
high intensity (n), 11/I2
high quality (n), 1/I2
high-level languages (n), 5/D1
high-tech sector (n), 6/D1
highlight (v), 10/I1, 11/I2
highlighting (n), 11/I2
hire car (n), 7/D1
hold (v) a meeting (n), 8/I1
hold (v) the line, 7/D1
hold back (v), 4/I1
hold down (v) [a key], 2/I1
hold, held, held (v), 2/I1, 7/D1
hotline (n), 1/I2
hyphen (n), 11/I2

identify (v), 3/I1, 4/I2, 7/I2, 9/I2
illegal (adj), 11/I1
implement (v), 1/I2, 12/I2
implementation (n), 7/I2
improve (v), 4/I2
improvement (n), 5/I1
in alphabetical order (adv), 2/I2
in ascending order (adv), 2/I2
in charge of (p), 1/D1
in descending order (adv), 2/I2
in detail (adv), 7/I2
in fact (adv), 1/I1
in order of [price/importance] (adv), 2/I2
in place (p), 9/I1
in practice (adv), 1/I1
in production (adv), 8/I1

in sequence (adv), 10/I1
in stages (adv), 10/I1
in stock (adv), 4/I1
in terms of (p), 9/I1
in that case (adv), 9/I2
in the long run (adv), 10/I1
in the long term (adv), 10/I2
in theory (adv), 1/I1
in working order, 10/D1
in writing (adv), 8/I2
in-house (adv), 7/I1
inbuilt (adj), 10/I2
inbuilt facilities (n), 10/I2
inbuilt fail-safe facilities (n), 10/I2
include (v), 3/I1, 9/D1
incorporate (v), 3/I2
increase (n), 5/I1
increase (v), 4/I2, 10/I2
increased (adj), 5/D1
incur (v) [costs] (v), 19/I2
indent (v), 11/I2
indentation (n), 11/I2
indexing (n), 4/D1
indicate (v), 9/I1, 10/I2
indicator (n), 11/I1
industry (n), 6/D1
inexpensive (adj), 4/D1
inexperienced (adj), 9/I1
influence (v), 5/D1
information centre (n), 5/D1
influence 5/D1
information kiosk (n), 6/D1
initial (adj), 7/I2
initial (v), 3/I1
initial phase (n), 7/I2
initial saving (n), 10/I2
initial stage (n), 7/I1
initially (adv), 10/I2
input (n), 3/I1, 4/I2
input (v), 2/D1
input advice (n), 3/I1, 3/D1
input data (n), 4/I1
insert (v) a disk into a drive, 2/D1
insert (v), 2/D1
install (v), 1/I2, 3/I2, 9/I1, 10/I2, 10/D1, 12/I2
installation (n), 3/I2, 9/I1, 12/I2
installation costs (n), 9/I1
installation design (n), 12/I2
instructions (n), 2/D1
insurance (n), 6/D1
integer (n), 11/D1
integrated (adj), 1/I2, 5/I2
intelligent microfilmer (n), 4/D1
interact (v), 6/D1
interactive video (n), 6/D1

interchangeable (adj), 10/I2
interface (n), 1/D1, 3/I2, 12/I2
interrupt (v), 12/I1
interview (v), 1/I1, 8/D1
introduce (v), 1/I1
invalid (adj), 11/I1
invalid date (n), 11/I1
inventory (n), 4/I2
investigaton (n), 9/I2
investment (n), 5/I1, 6/D1, 10/I2
invitation (n) to tender, 7/I1
invite (v) [someone] to tender, 7/I1
invite (v) bidders, 5/I1
invoice (n), 4/I1
invoice address (n), 11/I2
involve (n), 1/D1, 5/I1, 10/I1
involved (adj), 5/D1
irrelevant (adj), 6/D1
item (n), 2/I1, 3/I1, 4/D1, 10/I2, 11/I1, 11/I2, 11/D1
item movement (n), 4/I2
item number (n), 4/I2
IV (interactive video) (n), 6/D1

jam (v), 4/D1
job (n), 5/D1
job applicant (n), 8/D1
jump-off point (n), 6/I1
justifiable (adj), 9/I2
justification (n), 10/I2

keep (v) statistics (v), 3/D1
keep track (v) of, 4/I2
keep, kept, kept (v) (v), 3/D1
key (n), 2/I1, 2/I2
key (v) [the details] in, 3/D1
key in (v), 2/D1, 3/I1, 11/I2
key reason (n), 6/D1
keyboard (n), 3/I1, 3/I2, 12/I1
keyboard operators (n), 3/I1
knowledge (n), 12/I2

label (n), 4/I2
label (v), 3/I2, 10/D1
labelling (n), 3/I2, 10/D1
labour (n), 10/I2
labour activity (n), 4/I2
labour scheduling (n), 4/I2
lack (v), 5/D1

LAN (= Local Area Network) (n), 9/I1, 9/I2
language (n), 1/D1, 5/I1, 5/D1
layout (n), 7/I2, 10/I1
leading spaces (n), 11/D1
leading zeroes (n), 11/I2
leave (v), 8/I1
leave for (v), 8/D1
left aligned (adj), 11/I2
left hand corner (n), 11/I2
length (n), 11/D1
less than, 11/D1
let, let, let (v), 2/I1
level (n), 4/D1
level of indexing (n), 4/D1
level of support (n), 8/I1
lever (n), 4/D1
liaise (v), 1/D1
licence (n), 5/I2
life cycle (n), 6/D1
limit (n), 8/I1
limited facilities (n), 12/D1
limiting (adj), 12/I2
line (n), 7/D1, 11/I2
line up (v) [with X] (v), 11/I2
line up (v), 11/I2
link (n), 3/I2, 12/I1
link (v), 3/I2
link together (v), 9/I2
link up (v) [with X], 9/I2
link-up (n), 9/I2
linked to (p), 3/I2
list (n), 3/D1
list (v), 3/D1
list price (n), 5/I2
load (v) a file, 9/D1
load (v) a program, 2/D1
load (v), 2/D1, 9/D1, 12/D1
loading (n), 2/D1
loading facility (n), 2/D1
local (adj), 3/I2, 9/I1
Local Area Network (= LAN) (n), 3/I2, 9/I2, 12/I2
local printer (n), 3/I2
local sales office (n), 3/I2
local sites (n), 9/I2
location (n), 10/I2
lock (v) [someone] out, 2/D1
lock (v), 2/D1
locking (n), 12/I2
locking mechanism (n), 12/I2
log (n), 3/I2
log printer (n), 3/I2
logical (adj), 12/I2
long distance (n), 3/I2
long-term (adj), 1/D1, 7/I2, 8/I1

long-term commitment (n), 7/I2
long-term future (n), 8/I1
long-term needs (n), 9/I2
long-term planning (n), 1/D1
long-term project (n), 7/I2
look after (v), 1/D1
look at (v), 1/D1
look for (v), 6/I1
look into (v), 1/D1
look like (v), 2/I2
look through (v), 4/I1
lookup (n), 4/I2
lookup data (n), 4/I2
loop (n), 10/I2
low intensity (n), 11/I2
low-level languages (n), 5/D1
lower case (n), 11/I2

machine-readable (adj), 7/I2
maiden name (n), 11/D1
main computer (n), 3/I2
main facilities (n), 12/I1
main heading (n), 11/I2
main menu (n), 2/D1
main office (n), 9/I2
main processor (n), 3/I2
main system printer (n), 3/I2
mainframe (n), 1/I2, 10/I2
mainframe computer (n), 10/I2
mainframe control unit (n), 10/I2
maintain (v), 1/I2, 5/I1, 5/D1
maintainability (n), 5/D1
maintenance (n), 5/I2, 10/I2
maintenance contract (n), 5/I2
maintenance costs (n), 10/I2
major contributor (n), 6/D1
management (n), 6/I2
manager (n), 1/D1
managership (n), 8/I1
manpower (n), 7/I1
manpower resources (n), 7/I1
manual (n), 1/I1
manufacturer (n), 2/I2
manufacturing (v), 6/D1
margin (n), 11/I2
mark (n), 4/D1
market (n), 5/I2
market place (n), 5/I2, 10/I2
marketing (n), 6/D1
marketing rights (n.pl), 7/I2
master menu (n), 4/I1
match (v), 3/I1, 3/D1
material (n), 12/I2

Appendix F   225

maximise (n), 5/D1
medium-sized (adj), 4/D1
meet (v) a commitment, 7/I1
meet (v) a need, 9/I1
meet (v) requirements, 5/D1
meet, met, met (v), 1/I1, 7/D1
meeting (n), 1/I1, 7/D1, 8/D1
memo (n), 8/I2
mention (v), 8/I1
menu (n), 2/I1, 10/I1
menu panel (n), 10/I1
merchandise (n), 4/I2
merger (n), 9/I2
message (n), 2/D1, 7/D1, 11/I1
message text (n), 3/I1
method of operation (n), 7/I2
microcomputer-based (adj), 6/I2
microfilmers (n), 4/D1
microstation (n), 3/I2, 10/D1
minicomputer (n), 1/I2
minimise (v), 7/I2
minus (n), 8/I2
missing (adj), 11/I1
mistake (n), 3/D1
modularity (n), 5/D1
module (n), 8/I2
monitor (v), 1/D1, 8/I1, 9/I1
monthly (adj), 10/I1, 11/I1, 12/I1
monthly summary (n), 10/I1
mortgage (n), 6/D1
mouse (n), 2/I1
move (v), 2/I2
move on (v), 12/I1
move through (v), 2/I2
movement (n), 10/I1
multiplexor (n), 3/I2

National Insurance Number (n), 11/D1
natural language (n), 6/I2
natural language interface (n), 6/I2
nature (n), 7/I2
needs (n), 9/I2
net amount (n), 11/I2
network (n), 3/I2, 5/I2, 9/I1
network control (n), 9/I1, 10/I2
networking (n), 9/I2
networking needs (n), 9/I2
new technology (n), 6/I1
next field (n), 2/I2
next line (n), 2/I2
next screenfull (n), 2/I2
next sequential record (n), 2/I2
non-numeric (adj), 11/I1

normal working hours (n), 7/I2
notice (n), 6/I2
notification (n), 8/I2
nought (n), 8/I2
number (n), 7/D1
numeric (adj), 11/D1
numeric integer (n), 11/D1

object-oriented (adj), 5/I2
object-oriented database (n), 5/I2, 6/I1
objective (n), 12/I2
obsolete (adj), 3/I1
obtain (v) feedback, 7/I2
obtain (v), 4/I1, 12/I1
obtain a summary (v), 12/I1
office (n), 6/I1, 7/D1
on a freelance basis (adv), 5/I2, 6/I2
on average (adv), 3/D1
on disk (adv), 3/I1
on hand (adv), 4/I1
on schedule, 12/D1
on screen, 11/I2
on that basis (adv), 10/I2
on-line (adj), 4/I1, 8/D1, 12/I1
on-line system (n), 8/D1, 12/I1
one to one (adj), 10/I2
open (v), 9/D1
open system (n), 9/I1
operating system (n), 9/D1
operating system command (n), 9/D1
operation (n), 12/D1
operational support (n), 1/D1
operations (n), 6/I2
operations staff (n), 5/D1
optimise (v), 1/I2
option (n), 2/D1, 9/I2
option number (n), 2/D1
order (n), 4/I1, 12/I1
order details (n), 11/I2
order entry (n), 4/I1
order processing (n), 4/I1
order: in order (of) (adv), 2/I2
original (adj), 12/I1, 12/D1
original data (n), 12/D1
original plan (n), 12/I1
original target date (n), 12/D1
original timescale (n), 12/D1
otherwise, 11/D1
out of stock (adj), 4/I1
outlet (n), 12/I2
outlet cable (n), 12/I2
outlet point (n), 12/I2
outlet socket (n), 10/I2

output (n), 3/I1, 7/I2
output (v), 3/I1
outset (n), 10/I2
outside supplier (n), 7/I1
outweigh (v), 12/D1
overall (adj), 12/I1
overtime (n), 10/I2
overtime rates (n), 10/I2
overwrite (v), 11/I2
ownership (n), 7/I1, 7/I2
ownership agreement (n), 7/I1

PABX (n), 9/I1, 9/I2
package (n), 1/D1, 6/I2, 9/D1
packaging (n), 3/I2
packet switched data network (n), 3/I2
page (v) backwards, 12/I1
page (v) forward, 12/I1
page (v) through, 2/I2
pallet (n), 10/D1
pallet labelling (n), 10/D1
paragraph (n), 9/D1
parallel (adj), 1/D1
parallel run (n), 1/D1
part number (n), 4/I1
part order (n), 4/I1
partnership (n), 7/I1
pass (v), 3/I1
password (n), 2/D1
path (n), 9/D1
payment (n), 11/I1
payment amount (n), 3/D1, 11/I1
payment date (n), 3/D1, 11/I1
payment transaction (n), 3/D1
pending orders (n), 4/I1
performance (n), 8/I1
period of notice (n), 6/I2
permitted (adj), 11/I1
permitted range (n), 11/I1
personal computer (n), 10/I2
personnel (n), 5/D1, 7/I1
phase (n), 7/I2, 12/I1
physical (adj), 12/I2
physical installation (n), 12/I2
pick (v) someone up, 7/D1
piece of equipment (n), 9/I1
place (v) an order, 4/I1
plan (n), 10/D1
plan (v), 8/D1
plan for (v), 8/I1
plane (n), 7/D1
planned (adj), 8/I1
planned configuration (n), 8/I1

planning (n), 1/D1
plant (n), 10/D1
plug compatible (adj), 10/I2
plug compatible supplier (n), 10/I2
plug in (vs), 10/I2
plus (n), 8/I2
point (n), 8/I1
point of information (n), 6/D1
point of information applications (n), 6/D1
point of sale (n), 4/I2, 6/D1
point of sale applications (n), 6/D1
pointer (n), 2/I1
policy number (n), 3/D1
port (n), 3/I2, 10/I2
position (n), 2/I1
positioning (n), 12/I2
post code (n), 3/I1, 6/I2
potential (n), 6/I1
potentially (adv), 12/I2
power (n), 10/D1
power supply (n), 10/D1
practical exercise (n), 12/I1
preceding (adj), 2/I2
preceding record (n), 2/I2
preformatted (adj), 3/I1
preformatted screen (n), 3/I1
present (adj), 11/D1
press (v) a key, 2/I2, 2/D1, 9/D1
press (v), 2/I1, 2/I2, 9/D1
presuppose (v), 9/I2
previous (adj), 2/I2
previous plan (n), 12/D1
previous record (n), 2/I2
previous screenfull (n), 2/I2
price (n), 4/I2, 5/I2, 11/I2
price list (n), 11/I2
print (v), 3/I1, 3/D1
print record (n), 3/I1
printer (n), 3/I2, 8/D1, 10/I2
printing (n), 3/I1
printout (n), 3/D1
prior to (p), 8/I1
priority (n), 5/D1, 6/I1
procedure (n), 4/I2, 6/D1
procedure manual (n), 1/I1
process (n), 3/I1
process (v), 3/I1, 4/I1
processed (adj), 12/D1
processed text (n), 12/D1
processing (n), 1/D1, 3/I1, 10/I1
processor (n), 3/I2
produce (v), 6/D1, 7/I1, 7/I2
product (n), 5/I2, 12/D1
product development (n), 1/I2
product life (n), 6/D1

product life cycle (n), 6/D1
product line (n), 1/I1
production (n), 1/I1, 3/I2
production costs (n), 5/I1
production plant (n), 3/I2, 10/D1
production system (n), 8/I2
productive (adj), 12/D1
productivity (n), 4/I2, 5/I1
productivity tools (n), 5/I1
profits (n), 4/I2
programmer (n), 5/I1
program (n), 2/D1, 9/D1
program design (n), 5/D1
program disk (n), 2/D1
program specification (n), 5/D1
programmer (n), 5/D1
programming (n), 5/I1
programming language (n), 5/I2
programming methodology (n), 5/I1
progress (v), 8/I1
project (n), 1/D1, 7/I1
project leader (n), 6/I2
project manager (n), 8/I1
project plan (n), 12/D1
project teams (n), 1/D1
promote (v), 5/D1
prompt (n), 2/D1
proposal (n), 1/D1, 7/I1, 7/i2
proposed standard (n), 5/I1
proposed system (n), 7/I2
protected (adj), 11/I2
protected field (n), 11/I2
prototype (n), 5/I1, 10/I1, 12/D1
prototype system (n), 12/D1
prototyping (n), 5/D1
provide (v) support, 8/I1
provide (v), 1/I2, 3/I2, 4/I2, 12/I2
provision (n), 1/D1
publicity (n), 8/I1
purpose (n), 4/D1
put (v) [someone] through, 7/D1
put (v) a meeting off, 7/D1

quality (n), 4/D1
quantities on hand (n), 4/I1
quarterly (adj), 11/I1
questionnaire (n), 7/I2

radiator (n), 12/I2
range (n), 4/D1, 7/I1, 11/I1, 11/D1
range of possibilities (n), 7/I1
rapid (adj), 10/I2

rapidly developing field (n), 9/I1
rate (n), 9/I1, 10/I2, 12/I2
ratio (n) [of X to Y], 10/I2
rationalisation (n), 10/I2
re-code (v), 5/I1
re-invent (v), 6/I1
re-marking (n), 4/I2
readability (n), 5/D1
readable (adj), 5/D1
reaffirm (v), 8/I1
realise (v), 9/I2
reason for error (n), 11/I1
receive (v) an order, 4/I1
receive (v), 4/I1, 6/I2
reception (n), 1/I1
recommendation (n), 9/I1, 9/I2
reconfiguration (n), 10/I2
record (n), 2/I2, 3/I1
redisplay (v), 12/I1
reduction (n), 4/D1
referee (n), 6/I2
reference manual (n), 1/I1
reference number (n), 6/I2, 11/I2
refinement (n), 5/I1
reject (v), 3/D1, 9/I2, 11/I1
rejected (adj), 3/D1
rejected advice (n), 11/I1
rejected transaction (n), 3/D1, 11/I1
relational database (n), 6/I1
relationship (n), 7/I1
relay (v), 3/I2
release (v), 2/I1
reliable (adj), 10/I2
remind (n), 8/I1
removal (n), 10/I2
reorder (v), 4/I1, 4/I2
reorder level (n), 4/I1
reorder quantity (n), 4/I1
reordering (n), 4/I2
replace (v) 11/D1
replacement (n), 10/I2
replay (v), 8/I1
report (n), 8/I1, 9/D1, 12/D1
report (v), 8/I1
report to (v), 1/D1
representatives (n), 5/D1
request (v), 12/I1
request information (v), 12/I1
require (v), 11/I1
required (adj), 5/I1
requirement (n), 1/I2, 1/D1, 5/I1, 5/D1
research (n), 5/I1, 5/I2
Research and Development (n), 1/I2
research establishment (n), 5/I2
research tool (n), 6/I1

reserve (v), 10/I2
reset (v), 2/D1
RESET button (n), 2/D1
resources (n), 7/I1
response (n), 1/I2, 9/I1, 10/I1
response time (n), 9/I1
responsible (adj) [for], 10/D1
restriction (n), 8/I1
result (n), 5/I1
result in (v), 4/I2
retrieval (n), 4/D1
retrieve (v), 4/I1, 4/I2
return (v), 2/D1, 4/I1
RETURN key (n), 2/D1
review (v), 1/D1, 12/I2
revised (adj), 12/D1
revised plan (n), 12/D1
revised project plan (n), 12/D1
right hand corner (n), 11/I2
right-aligned (adj), 11/I2
rights (n.pl), 7/I2
ring, rang, rung (v), 7/D1, 8/I2, 8/D1
rise, rose, risen (v), 5/I1, 5/D1
role (n), 5/D1
roll forwards (v), 2/I2
routine (n), 11/D1
RS232C interface (n), 3/I2
run (v) a program, 2/D1, 3/D1
run, ran, run (v), 2/D1
run-down (n), 12/D1

safety (n), 6/D1
salary (n), 6/I2
sales assistant (n), 4/I1
sales department (n), 4/I1
sales office (n), 3/I2
sales order processing (n), 4/I1, 10/D1
sales order processing system (n), 10/D1
sample (n), 4/D1
satisfactory (adj), 9/I1
satisfied (adj), 12/D1
save (v) a file, 9/D1
save (v), 9/D1
saving (n), 4/I2, 10/I2
scale (n), 7/I1
scanner (n), 4/I2
scanning unit (n), 4/I2
schedule (n), 12/D1
scheduling (n), 4/I2, 10/D1
screen (n), 2/I2, 3/I1, 3/I2, 10/I1, 11/I2
screen display (n), 10/I1, 12/I1
screen layout (n), 10/I1
screenfull (n), 2/I2

scroll (v), 2/I2
scroll downwards (v), 2/I2
scroll upwards (v), 2/I2
search (n), 3/D1
search (v), 3/D1
secondary menu (n), 2/D1
secondary phase (n), 7/I2
secretary (n), 7/D1
section (n), 1/I1, 4/D1, 11/I1
section supervisors (n), 3/I1
sector (n), 6/D1
security (n), 1/D1
security package (n), 1/D1
select (v), 2/I1, 4/I1, 5/I1
selection (n), 2/I1
selling (n), 6/D1
selling rights (n.pl), 7/I2
sensible (adj), 10/I2
sequence (n), 10/I1
sequential record (n), 2/I2
serial number (n), 11/D1
service (n), 9/I1
session (n), 12/I1
set (n), 5/I1
set of requirements (n), 5/I1
set up (v), 4/I2, 10/I2
share (v), 10/I2
shelf label (n), 4/I2
shift (v) left/right, 2/I2
SHIFT key (n), 2/I2
ship (v), 10/D1
shipment (n), 4/I2
shorten (v), 2/I1
side by side (adj), 4/D1
sign on (v), 11/I2
similarities and differences (n), 12/I1
similarity (n), 12/I1
simultaneously (adv), 4/I2
single user (n), 5/I2
site (n), 1/I2, 5/I2, 9/I1, 10/D1
site engineers (n), 10/D1
site licence (n), 5/I2
siting (n), 8/D1
situation (n), 9/I2
size (n), 4/D1
skeleton system (n), 10/I1
skill (n), 6/D1
slash (n), 11/I2
socket (n), 10/I2
software (n), 1/I2, 5/I1, 10/I2
software costs (n), 5/D1
software development (n), 5/I1
software installation (n), 10/D1
software producer (n), 6/I2
software product (n), 5/I2

software production (n), 5/I1
software production costs (n), 5/I1
software support (n), 1/D1
solution (n), 9/I1, 10/I2
sort (v), 3/I1
sort code (n), 3/I1
sound investment (n), 10/I2
source (n), 3/I1
source code (n), 3/I1, 8/I2, 11/I2
spare (v), 9/D1
spec (n), 10/I1
specification (n), 5/D1
specified amount (n), 12/I1
specify (v), 5/I1
speed (n), 4/D1
spend [money] (v), 5/I1
spend, spent, spent (v), 6/I1
split, split, split (v), 1/D1, 6/D1
sponsor (v), 6/D1
spreadsheet (n), 2/I2
staff (n), 7/I1, 9/I1, 12/D1
staffing (n), 1/D1
stage (n), 3/I1, 5/I1, 10/I1, 12/D1
stand-alone (adj), 6/D1
stand-alone terminal (n), 6/D1
standard (n), 5/I1
standard discount (n), 5/I2
standard paragraph (n), 9/D1
standards (n), 1/D1, 9/I1
start date (n), 11/I1
starting point (n), 6/I1
state (v), 7/I2
statement (n), 7/I2
statistics (n.pl), 3/D1
steel trunking (n), 12/I2
stock (n), 4/I1
stock (v), 4/I2
stock availability (n), 4/I1
stocks and shares (n), 6/D1
store (v), 9/D1, 10/I2
study (n), 5/I1, 9/I2
sub-contract (v), 7/I1
sub-contractors (n), 12/I2
sub-heading (n), 11/I2
sub-system (n), 12/D1
submission date (n), 3/I1
submit (v) a proposal, 7/I1, 7/I2
submit (v) an advice, 11/I1
submit (v) an order, 4/I1
submit (v) transactions, 12/I1
submit (v), 11/I1
subsystem (n), 12/D1
subsystem (n), 4/I1
successfully (adv), 12/D1
suffix (n), 9/D1
suitable (adj), 10/I2

summarise (v), 4/I1, 12/D1
summarised data (n), 4/I2
summary (n), 4/I1
supervise (v), 4/I2
supervisor (n), 3/I1
supervisory (adj), 6/I2
supplier (n), 7/I1, 7/I2
supply (v), 4/I1, 4/I2
support (n), 1/I2, 1/D1, 7/I2, 8/I1
support staff (n), 7/I2
suppress (v), 11/I2
surname (n), 1/I1
switch (n), 3/D1
switchboard (n), 7/D1, 10/I2
symbol (n), 4/I2
symbol-marked (adj), 4/I2
system (n), 1/I2, 3/I1
system component (n), 7/I1
system improvement (n), 1/I2
system printer (n), 3/I2
system prompt (n), 2/D1
system software (n), 10/D1
systems analysis (n), 6/I2
systems analyst (n), 5/D1, 12/I1
systems programming (n), 1/D1, 6/I2

take (v), a message (n), 7/D1
take (v) a photograph, 8/I1
take (v) into account, 9/I2
take out a maintenance contract (v), 5/I2
take over (v), 8/I1
tape (n), 12/D1
target date (n), 12/D1
task (n), 5/D1, 6/D1
teaching tool (n), 6/I1
team (n), 1/D1, 5/I1
technical author (n), 1/I1
technical knowledge (n), 5/D1
technical manual (n), 1/I1
technical problems (n), 7/D1
technical support (n), 1/D1
technical training (n), 5/D1
technique (n), 2/I1
telecommunications (n), 6/I2
telephone (n), 1/I2
tender (n), 7/I1
tender (v), 7/I1
terminal (n), 3/I2, 4/D1, 6/D1, 8/I2, 8/D1, 10/I2, 12/I1
terminal user (n), 12/I2
test (n), 4/I2
test (v), 10/I1, 11/I2
testing (n), 5/I1, 5/D1, 10/I1
testing phase (n), 5/I1
text (n), 12/D1

textbook (n), 6/I2
thickness (n), 4/D1
thorough (adj), 6/I1, 9/I2
thorough investigation (n), 9/I2
throughput (n), 4/I2
time of arrival (n), 7/D1
timescale (n), 10/I1, 12/D1
today's date (n), 2/D1
tool (n), 5/I1
tools (n), 5/D1
top left (adj), 11/I2
top line (n), 11/I2
top right (adj), 11/I2
touch screen (n), 6/D1
trade (v), 10/I2
traffic (n), 3/I2, 9/I2
trailing spaces (n), 11/D1
train (n), 8/D1
train (v), 5/D1
trainee (n), 5/D1
training (n), 6/I2, 6/D1
training consultant (n), 6/I2
training costs (n), 9/I1
training manual (n), 6/I2
training materials (n), 1/I1, 6/I2
training package (n), 6/I2
training session (n), 12/I1
transaction (n), 3/I1, 11/I1
transaction data (n), 4/I2
transaction date (n), 3/D1, 11/I1
transaction details (n), 3/I1
transfer (n), 9/I1
transfer (v), 4/I2, 12/I1
transfer rate (n), 9/I1
transmit (v), 4/I2
trial (n), 12/D1
trial (v), 1/D1
trunking (n), 12/I2
twisted pair (n), 10/I2
twisted pair connection (n), 10/I2
type (n), 3/I1, 7/I1, 10/I1
type (v), 2/D1, 9/D1

unit (n), 10/I2
unprotected (adj), 11/I2
unprotected field (n), 11/I2
up-to-date (adj), 1/I2
update (v), 3/I1
upgrade (n), 10/I2
upgrade costs (n), 10/I2
upper case (n), 11/I2
upward cursor key (n), 2/I2
use (v), 3/I1
user (n), 1/I2, 2/I1, 5/I2, 10/I1
user department (n), 5/D1
user representatives (n), 5/D1

user training (n), 10/D1, 12/I1
user trial (n), 12/D1

valid (adj), 3/I1, 8/I2, 11/I2
validate (v), 3/I1, 4/I1, 11/D1, 12/D1
validation (n), 10/I1, 12/D1
validation procedure (n), 10/I1
validation requirements (n), 11/D1
validation subsystem (n), 12/D1
validity (n), 8/I2
value (n), 11/I1
Value Added Tax (VAT) (n), 11/I2
VAT (Value Added Tax) (n), 11/I2
VDU (Visual Display Unit) (n), 3/I2
VDU screen (n), 3/I2
via (p), 3/I2
visitor (n), 8/D1

work (v) on [something], 9/D1
working day (n), 3/I1
working hours (n), 7/I2
worth (adj), 6/I1, 10/I1
worthwhile (adj), 6/I1, 9/I1, 9/I2
write (v) code, 5/D1
written confirmation (n), 8/I2
wrong (adj), 3/D1
wrong amount (n), 3/D1
wrong number (n), 7/D1
warehouse (n), 9/I2
warning (n), 11/D1
waste (v) time, 7/D1
waste (v), 7/D1
weekly (adj), 10/I1, 12/I1
weekly summary (n), 10/I1
widely accepted (adj), 9/I1
widely available (adj), 6/I1
wire (n), 10/I2
wire (v), 10/I2
wiring (v), 12/I2
wonder (v) whether [X is true], 8/I1
wonder (v), 8/I1
word processing (n), 9/D1
word processing package (n), 9/D1

X.25 switch (n), 3/I2

yearly (adj), 12/I1